The Jeune École

History of Warfare

General Editor
Kelly DeVries
Loyola College

Founding editors
Theresa Vann
Paul Chevedden

VOLUME 43

The Jeune École

The Strategy of the Weak

by

Arne Røksund

BRILL

LEIDEN • BOSTON
2007

Cover illustration: French Torpedo Boat No. 63. Probably photographed at Toulon where she served in a coast defense role from 1884 to 1895. The large steam cruiser in the left background is unidentified. (Photograph no. NH 88794: Naval Historical Foundation, Washington DC)

This book is printed on acid-free paper.

ISBN 978 90 04 15723 1
ISSN 1385-7827

© Copyright 2007 by Koninklijke Brill NV, Leiden, The Netherlands.
Koninklijke Brill NV incorporates the imprints Brill, Hotei Publishing, IDC Publishers, Martinus Nijhoff Publishers and VSP.

All rights reserved. No part of this publication may be reproduced, translated, stored in a retrieval system, or transmitted in any form or by any means, electronic, mechanical, photocopying, recording or otherwise, without prior written permission from the publisher.

Authorization to photocopy items for internal or personal use is granted by Koninklijke Brill NV provided that the appropriate fees are paid directly to The Copyright Clearance Center, 222 Rosewood Drive, Suite 910, Danvers, MA 01923, USA.
Fees are subject to change.

PRINTED IN THE NETHERLANDS

CONTENTS

Acknowledgements	vii
Introduction	ix
Chapter One The Theoretical Foundation of the *Jeune École*	1
The Predecessor of the *Jeune École*	1
Strategic Assessment	7
Commercial Warfare	13
Raiding the Enemy's Sea Lines of Communication	13
Bombardment of the Enemy's Coast	21
The *Jeune École* and International Law	24
The Critics of the *Jeune École*	24
International Law Incompatible with War	27
Limited War or Total War—Impacts on Military Thinking	35
From Cabinet War to the Wars of the French Revolution and the Napoleonic Wars	38
The American Civil War and the Franco-Prussian War	45
Summary	50
Chapter Two The *Jeune École* in Office	53
Strategic Assessment	53
Verifying the Excellence of the Torpedo Boats	63
Rapprochement between Aube and the Council of Admiralty	77
Summary	81
Chapter Three The Legacy of the *Jeune École*	85
The Strategic Outlook of the French Navy up to the Fashoda Crisis	86
The Disciples of Aube	97
Total War and International Law	98
The Potential Enemies	100
The Naval Programme of the Heirs	105

The Return of the *Jeune École* to Power 109
    The *Jeune École* and the Staff College 111
    From Lockroy's First Period as Minister of Marine
        to the Fashoda Crisis 130
    Summary 137

Chapter Four   The Fashoda Crisis and the Development
    of a Modern Navy 143
    Confrontation Between France and Great Britain 143
        Italy, the Perfect Enemy 156
    After Fashoda 161
        Lanessan's Analysis 161
        The Reform 165
    Summary 174

Chapter Five   The Revitalisation of the *Jeune École* 177
    Changing Alliances among the European Powers 177
    The Submarine and the *Jeune École* 189
    The Pelletan Regime 213
    Summary 221

Conclusion 225

Appendix: Ministers of Marine 1870–1914 231

Bibliography 233

Index 239

ACKNOWLEDGEMENTS

While working on this study I have incurred a long list of obligations. The Director of the Norwegian Institute for Defence Studies (IFS) in Oslo, Professor Rolf Tamnes, and research associate at the same institute, Rolf Hobson, planted the seeds from which this study grew. Professor Tamnes invited me to undertake the study at IFS, while my employer, the Royal Norwegian Navy, generously allowed me time and financial support to pursue my research.

I owe academic debts to a number of people. First I must thank Professor Helge Pharo, at the Department of History at the University of Oslo, for his attention to analytical detail and the high quality of his comments. Rolf Hobson and Tom Kristiansen at IFS have supported the project from the earliest stages and offered me guidance along the way. They have read the entire manuscript in one version or another and provided me with many useful suggestions.

I am also grateful to Martin Motte, the foremost French specialist on the *jeune école*, and Jean de Préneuf, an expert on the French Navy during the Third Republic, for their valuable comments on the last draft of the study and for interesting discussions on the French Navy and French naval thought in the period covered by this study.

I wish to thank the *Service historique de la Marine* and its director of the Department for historical studies, Philippe Vial, for their hospitality and very efficient support during my research in the archives. I would also like to thank Irene Kulblik, the librarian at IFS, for aiding me in my search in European libraries for relevant literature.

INTRODUCTION

France and Great Britain were involved in an almost continuous naval rivalry and arms race from the 1840s to the mid-1860s. The French Navy came to see itself as having only one real opponent, the Royal Navy. British interests reached further across the globe than French, and the Royal Navy could not limit itself to using the strength of the French Navy as a standard against which to measure itself. Nevertheless, as C.I. Hamilton has underlined, "in the mid-nineteenth century the French Navy was at least the prime factor in naval calculations in Whitehall."[1] During the arms race of the early 1860s, the navies reached a rough parity. Thereafter the increasing financial and industrial resources of Great Britain weakened France's ability to keep up with British naval rearmament. Another factor that played a part in the relative decline of French naval power was the rise of Prussia. Due to its geographical vulnerability France had to maintain a substantial continental army, whereas Britain, thanks to its insular position could concentrate on maritime affairs to a much larger degree.[2]

France's defeat in the war against the North German Confederation in 1871 eventually crushed France's naval ambitions. The country was severely weakened economically and demographically as a consequence of the war. The French became increasingly conscious of Great Britain's enormous lead in industry, trade and colonisation.[3] To continue the naval arms race that had been going on between France and Great Britain from the 1840s to the late 1860s was thus seen as impossible. The most immediate threat against France was in any case perceived to be that of the German army. There was therefore a general understanding that the army should be given priority. In 1872 the Minister of Marine declared that the time had come for the Navy "to sacrifice

---

[1] C.I. Hamilton: *Anglo—French Naval Rivalry 1840–1870* (Oxford, 1993), p. 272.
[2] *Ibid.*, pp. 297–304.
[3] Rolf Hobson writes that "During the second phase [1865–1890] Britain's industrial preeminence was such that the Royal Navy could outbuild any potential rival and bring superior sea power to bear on all the world's oceans." Rolf Hobson, *Imperialism at Sea, Naval Strategic Thought, the Ideology of Sea Power and the Tirpitz Plan, 1875–1914* (Trondheim, 1999) p. 20.

itself on the altar of the nation". The budget was cut by 25 per cent and the total number of vessels was reduced from 439 to 137.[4]

This difficult period called for new ideas on how the Navy should organise itself. French naval thinkers had to consider what they could achieve in a position of inferiority, with the limited resources at hand. The recognition of the fact that France probably would remain inferior to Great Britain was a fundamental starting point for the new, radical ideas that have become known as the *jeune école*.

French traditionalists argued that the Navy should meet the new challenge by sticking to the strategy of the era of sail with its blockades and focus on naval battles between battleships, while gradually adapting new technology to the strategy. This strategy required a fleet consisting of battleships, cruisers and coastal defence units.[5] The proponents of the new naval thinking contested this view and claimed that historical experience of naval warfare had shown that encounters between battle fleets represented a great danger for the inferior power. They argued that even in the era of sail it had been common for the weaker side not to risk destruction of a valuable fleet in battle, but rather to seek refuge in port and maintain its presence as a fleet-in-being. The introduction of steam propulsion had eliminated the element of chance that had been present in the era of sailing ships. Numerical superiority would henceforth almost guarantee victory in an engagement.[6] The *jeune école* was therefore critical of what they saw as the French naval traditionalists' devotion to a battleship navy, and their disregard of the problems raised by challenging the stronger opponent on his own terms. To put most of the French Navy's effort into building a battleship navy contradicted one of the fundamental ideas in the *jeune école*'s naval theory: that the weaker side should resort to alternative strategies and tactics, taking advantage of the possibilities opened up by technological progress.

---

[4] Marie-Raymond Ceillier: "Les idées stratégiques en France de 1870 à 1914: La jeune école" (1928), in Hervé Coutau-Bégarie (ed.): *L'évolution de la pensée navale* (Paris, 1990), p. 197; Philippe Masson: *Histoire de la Marine, Tome II. De la vapeur à l'atome* (Paris, 1992), p. 136.

[5] Volkmar Bueb: *Die "Junge Schule" der französischen Marine. Strategie und Politik 1875–1900* (Boppard am Rhein, 1971), p. 5.

[6] This argument was repeatedly stated by Aube in his writings. See for instance: Th Aube: "L'avenir de la marine française" in *Revue des deux mondes* (Paris, July 1874), p. 188; Th Aube: "Un nouveau droit maritime international" in *Revue maritime et coloniale* (Paris, 1875), p. 23; Th. Aube: "La guerre maritime et les ports militaires de la France" in *Revue des deux mondes* (Paris, 1882), pp. 318–322.

The French Navy devised scenarios in which the potential naval enemies would be Italy, Germany or Great Britain, or combinations of these three powers. Depending on the constellations, the French Navy could be called to fight a superior navy, a navy equal in size or an inferior navy. The *jeune école* viewed Great Britain as the most probable enemy and argued that the French Navy should organise itself accordingly. The assumption that Great Britain was the most probable enemy was based on the traditional rivalry between France and Britain, but equally important for the *jeune école*'s opinion as to which the most likely enemy would be was its understanding of origins of future conflicts. The leaders of the *jeune école* were ardent colonialists, and they were convinced that colonial rivalry would lead to a conflict between Great Britain and France. Their analysis of modern capitalistic Great Britain and the dependence of its national economy on colonies convinced the *jeune école* that it would be very vulnerable to an interruption of trade. A superior but economically vulnerable enemy was thus an assumption underlying the theory of the *jeune école*.

It was initially the introduction of steam and later of the self-propelled torpedo that were regarded as technological leaps opening new opportunities for an inferior navy. Cannons and rams should, however, still play their part in naval warfare. The *jeune école* applied a division of labour to naval warfare and split the capabilities of the battleship among a number of smaller vessels, some with torpedoes, some with guns and the remaining ones with rams. Torpedo boats and gunboats, supplemented by fast rams and a system of telegraphs, semaphores and light scouts to ensure their ability to concentrate against the enemy, would be the principal coastal defences.

The proposal that broke most radically with prevailing naval thought was the idea of the offensive use of these small boats. Most naval thinkers agreed that the advent of steam had made blockades difficult to impose. Furthermore, the introduction of small torpedo boats armed with self-propelled torpedoes was believed to make blockade not only ineffective, but also dangerous. To the men of the *jeune école* this opened up possibilities for offensive and merciless warfare against the enemy's seaborne trade, and for attacking enemy coasts.

In 1886 Admiral Hyacinthe-Laurent-Théophile Aube became Minister of Marine, bringing to office the leader of the new school of naval thought. Aube was a talented writer on naval and colonial issues, and he expressed his opinions on naval strategy in numerous writings. The fundamental ideas of the *jeune école* were outlined as early as the mid-1870s. In two articles, "L'avenir de la marine française" in *Revue des deux mondes* in 1874 and "Un nouveau droit maritime international" in *Revue maritime et coloniale* in 1875, Aube sketched out the strategic challenges France was facing, and what he thought would be the adequate responses to these challenges. In his later writings these ideas were elaborated and often made more explicit.

The journalist and foreign affairs expert in *Journal des débats*, Gabriel Charmes, was an enthusiastic supporter of Aube's ideas, and through numerous articles in the first half of the 1880s he helped to spread the ideas of the *jeune école* to a wider audience. The writings of Aube and Charmes in the 1880s were characterised by the adaptation of new technology and by elaborations of the already existing theoretical framework constructed by Aube in the mid-1870s. The most sensational technological novelty that was to play an important part in the *jeune école*'s naval thought from the 1880s was the introduction of the self-propelled torpedo carried aboard small, so-called autonomous torpedo boats with the alleged capability to cruise on the high seas.

As Minister of Marine, Aube tried out his theories. He ordered extensive sea trials to prove the alleged seakeeping qualities of the small torpedo boats, and he initiated large-scale manoeuvres where formations of torpedo boats fought battleships. Many of the experiments and trials led to adjustments and improvements in tactics and technical solutions. Several of the initiatives and experiments had consequences far beyond Aube's period as Minister of Marine. He ordered the first trial in the French Navy of the melinite shell, which the army had adopted primarily for bombardments. The effect of these shells against practically unarmoured battleships was, as Ropp has put it, "in a way [responsible] for the revival of armor."[7] Aube played a pivotal role in the development of the submarine, ordering the construction of what was to be France's first viable underwater craft, the *Gymnote*. The ideas of the *jeune école* were also mirrored in France's naval construction programme. Aube stopped work on four battleships of the *Hoche* and *Magenta* classes and gave priority to the construction of cruisers, torpedo boats and gunboats.

---

[7] Theodore Ropp: *The development of a Modern Navy. French Naval Policy 1871–1904* (Annapolis, Maryland, 1987), p. 175.

Charmes died at the age of thirty-six at the start of Aube's ministry. After the fall of the Goblet cabinet in May 1887, Aube went into provincial retirement for the last three years of his life and there was no one with Aube's or Charmes' capacity ready to represent or develop the ideas of the *jeune école*. The early 1890s saw, however, a revival of theoretical discussions among naval officers that were clearly inspired by the ideas of Aube and Charmes, and the *jeune école* returned to power in 1895 with the appointment of the civilian politician Édouard Lockroy as Minister of Marine in the government of the radical Léon Bourgeois. A worsening in relations between France and Great Britain, which culminated in the Fashoda Crisis, created favourable conditions for politicians and officers promoting the ideas and solutions of the *jeune école*. The crisis temporarily settled the question of who would be the most likely enemy.

The improved performance of the submarine was another factor contributing to a revitalisation of the *jeune école* at the turn of the century, a revitalisation that has more or less been ignored by historians. The torpedo-carrying submarine represented to the adherents of the *jeune école* a new and revolutionary weapon that they argued would alter the balance of forces between the Royal Navy and the French Navy. The submarine was for the *jeune école* in the first years of the twentieth century what the torpedo boats had been for Aube and Charmes.

While progress in the performance of the submarine led to a revitalisation of the *jeune école*, shifting alliances in European politics undermined much of the relevance of the *jeune école*'s strategy for the French Navy. The conclusion of the Entente Cordiale and a situation in which France and Great Britain from 1905–1906 until the First World War conducted more or less regular military talks on how best to face an ambitious German foreign policy and the rapid expansion of its navy, removed the foreign policy scenario upon which the *jeune école*'s strategic proposals were based.

The radical reforms implemented by Aube in his short period as Minister of Marine have been interpreted as a traumatic and destructive experience for the French Navy. Moreover, French historians and strategists have reduced the theoretical contributions by the proponents of the *jeune école* to no more than a naive belief in the wonders of new technology. The most prominent French naval theoretician in the twentieth century, Admiral Raoul Castex, must bear much of the responsibility for this overly simplified representation of the naval thought of the *jeune école*. In the first volume of his *Théories stratégiques*, Castex sarcastically brushed aside the *jeune école*'s naval theory as:

> representing a phenomenon of spontaneous generation brought about by the appearance of new machines and weapons. Just as Paixhans, in 1821, thought that shells would allow small ships to defeat large ones, the supporters of the "*jeune école*" believed that the torpedo boat and the powerful explosive [the torpedo] of which they ingeniously granted us the monopoly, would revolutionise the principles of war, and give birth to a new strategy.[8]

Castex followed up his negative verdict on the theories of the *jeune école* with some rather disparaging characterisations of the personalities who made up the *jeune école*. Although he admitted that the ideas of the *jeune école* had been advocated by "des esprits sérieux", the ideas had also been promoted by "a certain number of colourful personalities from our profession, military bohemians in search of something original, joined by some well-meaning but incompetent civilians."[9] Castex assured his readers that not everything in the theories of the *jeune école* was bad. He found the *jeune école*'s ideas on the importance of numbers, speed and specialisation to be sensible. Despite these few positive elements which he found in the theory, Castex left the *jeune école* little honour when summing up their over-all contribution. One could not leave the *jeune école* unmentioned in a history book on strategy, he admitted, but "one should quote it as a curious example of the diversions that sometimes can occur under the influence of an exclusively technological preoccupation."[10]

Castex' influence on later French naval historiography and his power to define the posthumous reputation of the *jeune école* is well illustrated in Henri Le Masson's impressive work on the history of French torpedo boats. Although Le Masson gave a rather sober presentation of the ideas of the *jeune école* as they had been formulated by Aube and Charmes, he chose to quote Castex when he claimed that "today with hindsight it is possible to bring an objective judgement of these theories."[11] Le Masson started his "objective" judgement by ascribing to Castex the statement that the French Navy had survived the challenge of the

---

[8] Amiral Raoul Castex: *Théories stratégiques. Tome premier* (Paris, 1929), p. 50.
[9] *Ibid.*, p. 51.
[10] *Ibid.*, p. 52.
[11] Henri Le Masson: *Histoire du torpilleur en France* (Paris, 1968), p. 34.

jeune école, the spreader of "the lethal germs that would have poisoned us had we not eliminated them through judgement, good sense and the historical method."[12]

Hervé Coutau-Bégarie in his study on sea power of 1985 adopted Castex' categorisation and labelled the *jeune école* as a technological theory.[13] A focus on the *jeune école*'s theory as nothing more than certain ideas loosely woven around the possibilities opened up by the introduction of the torpedo, was also prevalent among the presenters at a major seminar held at *École militaire* in Paris in June 1987,[14] although a certain will to give a broader, less prejudiced, presentation of the ideas of the *jeune école* is also evident.[15]

The first presentation in French describing the *jeune école* as a many-faceted, but consistent, theory of naval warfare and organisation was published in 1990. Coutau-Bégarie, in the first edited volume of his series on the evolution of naval thought, published a paper written by Commander Marie-Raymond Ceillier during his course at the "Centres des Hautes Etudes Navales" in 1928. Commander Ceillier treated the *jeune école*'s ideas as more than a theory based merely upon technological innovation. In his brief presentation he sketched the historical, strategic, political and financial reasoning behind the *jeune école*, and thus depicted a theory far more complex and comprehensive than that which emerges from the dominant interpretation of the *jeune école*.[16]

The publishing of Commander Ceillier's paper from 1928 and the seminar at the *École militaire* marked the beginning of a broader discussion in France of the theories of the *jeune école*. This turn in the historical study of the *jeune école* from the late 1980s was, however, coupled with a tendency towards an apologetic historiography in defence of Admiral Aube. There were obvious attempts to rehabilitate Aube because he was a naval officer (he had after all been promoted all the way to vice admiral) by implying that what was perceived as the unsound ideas of the *jeune école* were the product of "incompetent civilians" as Castex

---

[12] *Ibid.*, p. 34; Castex: *Théories stratégiques*, pp. 51–52.
[13] Hervé Coutau-Bégarie: *La puissance maritime. Castex et la stratégie navale* (Paris, 1985): pp. 65–67.
[14] See for example Étienne Taillemite: "L'opinion française et la *jeune école*" in *Marine & Technique au XIXe siècle* (Paris, 1987), p. 481.
[15] This could be seen in Vice Admiral Phillippe Ausseur's paper: "La *jeune école*" in *Marine & Technique au XIXe siècle* (Paris, 1987), pp. 453–476.
[16] Ceillier: "Les idées stratégiques", pp. 195–231.

had put it.[17] This tendency is evident in two articles written by Rear Admiral Rémi Monaque in the series edited by Coutau-Bégarie. He claims that the journalist Gabriel Charmes, incompetent in naval affairs, was responsible for distorting the ideas of the sailor Aube. The same tendency to attribute the most extreme ideas to Gabriel Charmes can also be seen in the works of a leading expert on French naval history, Philippe Masson. In his major work "Histoire de la Marine", Masson claims that Aube's ideas were mostly a reflection of the ideas that were prevalent within the naval establishment. Aube, Masson maintains, advocated a balanced fleet consisting of different types of ships tailored for fleet warfare, coastal defence or commerce raiding. These relatively sound ideas, as viewed by Masson, were however misrepresented:

> But, by an irony of history and through over-zealous propagandists, the theories of Aube would suffer a profound deformation, even a veritable betrayal. With the exploitation of some of his ideas, the admiral had

---

[17] The fact that Aube was promoted all the way to vice admiral implies that he was not viewed by his superiors as an officer with eccentric ideas that were unsound for the French Navy. His ideas were well known within the upper echelons of the French Navy. Aube had published regularly in well-reputed periodicals during the fifteen years preceding his appointment as Minister of Marine. In addition, any article or book by a French naval officer had to be submitted for authorisation by the Minster of Marine. Aube had not followed this procedure when he published an article in 1871. The Minister of Marine criticized Aube strongly for having forgotten to ask for permission to publish the article. He reminded Aube of the regulations of 16th December 1852 and concluded that "I therefore inflict a severe reprimand on Captain Aube [...]." SHM: Ministère de la Marine et des Colonies, Direction du personell: *dossier no 1132, Aube*. To obtain approval was not a mere formality. This was made obvious when Aube asked the Minster of Marine in March 1874 for permission to publish an article in *Revue des deux mondes*. The official person in the Ministry of Marine (it is not clear whether it was the Minister himself) who considered the request wrote that "I fear that M. Aube touches upon political questions that one should be careful about raising." SHM: BB8-2427: *A Monsieur le Ministre de Capitaine de Vaisseaux Aube*, 4 March 1874. The article was then sent over to *La Commission Centrale d'examen des travaux des officiers*, which was headed by a vice admiral, for evaluation. The commission argued that Aube would have to remove the politically sensitive parts of the article and sent it back to Aube. SHM: BB8-2427: *Rapport au Ministre. Etude de M. le Capitaine de vaisseau Aube*, 1 April 1874. Aube made his corrections and sent the article back to the Ministry. SHM: BB8-2427: *A Monsieur le Ministre de Capitaine de Vaisseaux Aube*, 2 May. 1874. The Ministry sent the corrected article to the Commission for evaluation. SHM: BB8-2427: *De Ministère de la Marine, CA, Directeur du Personnel à M. le VA Président de la Commission Centrale d'examen des travaux des officiers*, 7 May 1874. The commission was still not completely satisfied with the article, but recommended that this "remarkably strong work" could be published if the last section was removed. SHM: BB8-2427: *Rapport au Ministre. Etude de M. le Capitaine de Vaisseaux Aube*, 10 June 1874. The Minister of Marine three days later endorsed the Commission's recommendation. SHM: BB8: *Rapport au Ministre*, 13 June 1874.

the sad privilege, in the eyes of posterity, of being accorded paternity of the most questionable and harmful of the ideas that would constitute the *jeune école*.[18]

The American historian Theodore Ropp also put forward the idea that Aube actually wanted a balanced fleet of battleships, coastal defence and cruisers and that it had been first of all Charmes who, in his one-eyed naïveté, proclaimed the end of the era of battleships. Ropp did, however, add that Aube himself had been carried away by an extreme technological optimism, an optimism that led him to decide on a massive construction of torpedo boats at the expense of battleships.[19]

The myth that Charmes should have distorted the thinking of his master has been particularly present in French historical writing. One of the few French historians to have argued against this view is Martin Motte in his doctoral thesis from 2001.[20] Motte's thesis also represents the most comprehensive study of the *jeune école* by a French scholar. Motte analyses French naval thought in this period by establishing a dichotomy between *the jeune école* and what Motte labels the French Mahanian school. He argues that a compromise between the two competing naval schools was found when Castex began to develop a theoretical synthesis in the 1920s.

Generally, French historical writing on the *jeune école* has been characterised by a rather normative approach to the study of the new naval ideas represented by the *jeune école* and the split it created within the French Navy. The prevalent view has been that the *jeune école* had a destructive effect on the French Navy. Most of those who have written on the two competing naval schools of thought have taken a rather clear stand for the naval thought represented by the traditionalists.[21] This

---

[18] P. Masson: *Histoire de la Marine*, p. 160.
[19] Ropp: *The development of a Modern Navy*, pp. 160, 171–173.
[20] Martin Motte: *Une éducation géostratégique. La pensée navale française, de la jeune école à l'Entre-deux guerres*. Thèse d'Histoire pour obtenir le grade de docteur de l'Université Paris IV (Paris, 2001), p. 146.
[21] Most non-French historians have held a more dispassionate view of the *jeune école*. Ropp's doctoral thesis from 1937 on modern French naval history was for many decades the only comprehensive and thorough study of the development of the French Navy in this period. The other non-French study that gives a broader description of the *jeune école* is Volkmar Bueb's study from 1971, *Die "Junge Schule" der französischen Marine, Strategie und Politik 1875–1900*. In almost any general survey of naval strategy there will be references to or short summaries of the *jeune école*. The most recent and a very concise description of the main ideas of the *jeune école* is Geoffrey Till's *Seapower. A Guide for the Twenty-First Century* (London, 2004), pp. 59–62. A first attempt to place the *jeune école* within a context of international law and contemporary military thought is

lack of an analytical approach may explain why the perception of the *jeune école*'s naval theory as no more than some arbitrarily linked ideas superficially centred on the possibilities opened up by the introduction of the torpedo and the autonomous torpedo boat has been prevalent in French historical writing. The descriptions of the *jeune école*'s theory from a solely technological perspective have led to important parts of their theory being ignored or only summarily treated. The importance that the *jeune école* attributed to the strategic context has partially been overlooked. Furthermore, no attempts have been made to try to understand the *jeune école*'s arguments for merciless economic warfare as part of ideas that were present among strategists both in Europe and in America at the time. Much of the historical research also suffers from the fact that researchers either did not have access to the archives of the Ministry of Marine, chose not to consult the archives or limited research to a few categories of the relevant documents available.[22]

---

done in Arne Røksund: "The Jeune École: The Strategy of the Weak" in Rolf Hobson and Tom Kristiansen (eds.): *Navies in Northern Waters 1721–2000* (London, 2004). See also: Hobson, *Imperialism at Sea*; Nicholas A. Lambert: *Sir John Fisher's Naval Revolution* (Columbia, South Carolina, 1999).

[22] This actually also applies to the three most comprehensive studies made of the *jeune école*, those of Ropp, Bueb and Motte. The archives of the Ministry of Marine for the years 1871–1904 were not open for the public at the time when Ropp did his research.

CHAPTER ONE

THE THEORETICAL FOUNDATION OF THE *JEUNE ÉCOLE*

The theoretical foundation of the *jeune école* was mainly formulated by Théophile Aube, the founding father of the *jeune école*, and one of its most prominent advocates, Gabriel Charmes. In 1882, on a voyage to the Levant, Charmes had contracted the malady that led to his death a few years later. He met Aube during the latter's recovery from the illness he had caught in Martinique. Certain historians and officers have wished to attribute some of the more radical aspects of the *jeune école*'s theories to Charmes.[1] There is, however, little reason to make such a distinction. Setting aside the touch of naïveté that characterized some of Charmes arguments, he and Aube developed a unity of views that makes it difficult to distinguish between the ideas of the two men. The arguments put forward by Charmes in the mid-1880s represented a logical development of Aube's earlier writings. As Vice Admiral P.H. Colomb noted concerning the influence of Aube on Charmes's writings: "it is only reasonable to suppose that though the hands are those of Esau, yet the voice is that of Jacob."[2]

THE PREDECESSOR OF THE *JEUNE ÉCOLE*

Some of the basic features of the *jeune école*'s theory had already been expressed in the late 1860s by Captain Richild Grivel. A starting point for Grivel's naval ideas was his assertion that France's historical experience of naval warfare had shown that great encounters between battle fleets represented a severe danger for the inferior power.[3] His analysis of fleet warfare also represented in many ways a theoretical point of

---

[1] See i.e. Remi Monaque: "L'amiral Aube, ses idées, son action" in Couteau-Bégarie (ed.): *L'évolution de la pensée navale*, IV (Paris, 1994); P. Masson: *Histoire de la Marine*, p. 160; Ropp: *The development of a Modern Navy*, pp. 160, 171–173.
[2] P.H. Colomb: "Naval Reform" in *Occasional papers. Journal of Royal United Service Institution* (1887), p. 768.
[3] Richild Grivel: *De la guerre maritime avant et depuis les nouvelles inventions. Attaque et défense des côtes et des ports. Guerre du large. Etude historique et stratégique* (Paris, 1869), p. 253.

departure for what was later to become the *jeune école*, and Grivel is often treated as its precursor.[4] Although Grivel announced a change of direction in French naval thought that was further pursued by the *jeune école*, his reasons for adopting a new strategy designed for an inferior power was based on historical experience. The *jeune école*, for its part, mixed historical experience with an analysis of technological change and a good portion of technological optimism. Grivel's historical analysis convinced him that France had to follow two completely distinct strategies, depending on who the enemy was. The Navy should be designed for use against two different kinds of foe: Against an inferior navy France should stick to *la grande guerre maritime*, a form of warfare Grivel defined as "to blockade the littoral of [the enemy], sweep from the seas its foreign trade, and undertake a major diversion in its rear."[5] Against a superior enemy the French Navy should pursue commercial warfare with cruisers.

Grivel used recent examples such as the Crimean War and the war against Austria in 1859 to highlight the options open to a superior navy. The Crimean War apparently showed that France, then allied with the strongest navy, could conduct extensive combined operations overseas, at the same time blockading Russian ports in the Baltic and the Black Sea and consequently eliminating Russian seaborne trade. French naval superiority in the 1859 war against Austria had again enabled France to choose between the options that Grivel argued constituted *la grand guerre maritime*: In order to be able to conduct such operations one would have to acquire supremacy over the great sea roads by defeating the enemy's battle fleet.

Grivel speculated about a potential war against Prussia and stated that the French Navy would then be master of the sea and able to conduct all the operations of *la grande guerre maritime*:

> As master of the sea, could not France blockade at will the numerous ports of the North German Confederation and actively pursue its seaborne trade on the seas [...]? Could not our navy attack the enemy's shores in the Baltic or the North Sea, creating there diversions large enough to

---

[4] Ropp: *The Development of a Modern Navy*, pp. 19–22; Bueb: *Die "Junge Schule» der französischen Marine*, pp. 7–15; Etienne Taillemite. "Un théoricien méconnue de la guerre maritime: L'amiral Richild Grivel", in Hervé Coutau-Bégarie (ed.): *L'evolution de la pensée navale*, II (Paris, 1992), pp. 99–113; Hobson: *Imperialism at Sea*, pp. 112–117.

[5] Grivel: *De la guerre maritime*, p. 277.

provide powerful support to the operations occurring at the same time on the Rhine?[6]

Fleet warfare was a preliminary to the secondary, but decisive, operations against an enemy's coasts or commerce. Naval battles were, however, a very risky endeavour for the inferior battle fleet. Grivel claimed that the naval battles of Aboukir, Santo-Domingo, Cap Finistère and Trafalgar proved beyond doubt the dangers that a fleet inferior in numbers or quality faces in fleet warfare.[7] To underline the ineffectiveness of a large, but still inferior battle fleet, he quoted Napoleon I complaining to Bernadotte: "I have 100 ships of the line (*vaisseaux*) but no navy!"[8]

Battle fleets were also extremely expensive and Grivel warned that engaging in great naval battles against a superior opponent like the Royal Navy would be to stake all on a single throw. He considered any attempt to outnumber the Royal Navy as futile. Grivel stressed, and this was before the catastrophic defeat against the North German Confederation, that France did not have the necessary preconditions to win a naval arms race. An ambition to fight fleet battles against the Royal Navy should thus be dismissed:

> Should not fleet warfare, or the warfare of big battalions [...] be resolutely avoided as ruinous for the nation that is less rich in sailors and ships as well in the means of renewing them? [...] It is on account of France's failure to understand such a clear situation that she has suffered all the maritime defeats of her history [...] Regardless of the inventions that may appear, in the past or in the future [...] it is not within the power of any human force to displace suddenly [...] a well-established naval preponderance [...] based on the customs, the geographic situation, and the vocation of a people [...] Our navy cannot permit itself any illusions regarding an inequality so clearly revealed by geography, history, and statistics. No more than [inventions like] the steam engine on which we for a long time counted, can the battleship or the ram level out a force ratio that is two-to-one if not three-to-one. One should neither complain too much nor allow oneself to be overly surprised at this, when one considers that with a maritime population at least four times [that of France], with its lead in factories and material resources, England can spend on her navy a budget that is at least *twice* of what is spent on the French fleet.[9]

---

[6] *Ibid.*, pp. 277–278.
[7] *Ibid.*, p. 253.
[8] *Ibid.*, p. 259.
[9] *Ibid.*, pp. 278–279.

Grivel further argued that although naval battles could establish command of the sea,[10] that was not in itself sufficient to end a war. Grivel claimed that contrary to experiences from great battles between armies, no naval battle in French history, however decisive it might have been, had led to the conclusion of an immediate peace. It was the exhaustion of a people due to attacks on its trade that would restore peace on the oceans, and not battles between the "great maritime butchers", Grivel argued.[11] Commercial warfare conducted with cruisers was thus not only a strategy that was *possible* for an inferior navy to carry out, it was also an effective way of fighting maritime war. Grivel followed up the above-mentioned quote from Napoleon by stating that Napoleon I would have got a lot more value for the money if he had spent the same amount on constructing fast and well-armed ships, able to conduct commercial warfare on all oceans, as he actually spent on his battleship program.[12]

Thus, Grivel concluded, instead of attacking Britain's strongest point, the 20,000 cannons of the Royal Navy, France should aim for its weak spot, the 50,000 merchant vessels transporting the riches on which it depended. He argued that this was a form of warfare that France would be able to engage in for an indefinite period of time. However, it was not likely that this cruiser warfare should have to last any longer than a couple of years, since it would most certainly lead to a substantial rise in insurance rates, and after two or three years no one would carry goods on British ships. Britain's principal source of national wealth would consequently dry up.[13]

There were, however, a couple of preconditions that had to be met for this strategy to succeed. First of all, it would require that French diplomacy was able to maintain peace with France's continental neighbours. Grivel argued that the skill of British diplomacy had always ensured she had continental allies. France, on the contrary, had in all its wars against Britain, with the exception of the War of American Independence, seen its maritime war against Britain complicated by the presence of continental adversaries. It had always suffered from her inability to build alliances. "To accept once again war at the same

---

[10] Grivel did not use the term "command of the sea", but he stated its fundamental nature. Ropp: *The Development of a Modern Navy*, p. 19.
[11] Grivel: *De la guerre maritime*, p. 254.
[12] *Ibid.*, p. 259.
[13] *Ibid.*, pp. 260–261.

time against both our sea and land frontiers, would that not represent a serious failure by French diplomacy?", Grivel asked.[14] Alliances or benevolent neutrals were of particular importance in cruiser warfare. Cruisers would often operate far from home waters, and would thus depend on supplies from either colonial, allied or neutral ports.

It was not only diplomatic skills that needed to be improved if Grivel's scheme was to succeed, but also the French Navy's capacity for peacetime strategic planning.[15] He argued that the naval strategy of France had to be worked out in peacetime and that construction programmes should be a consequence of the strategy, and not the other way round. He accused the French construction programmes of being a product of the technological fascinations of engineers rather than the outcome of a carefully prepared strategy. This situation had inevitably led to a fleet that was only suited for fleet warfare and large combined expeditions. Grivel claimed that these big battleships were probably more suited to flattering the pride of the engineers than to serving the actual needs of France.[16]

The *jeune école*'s urge to redefine French naval doctrines was, as had also to a great extent been the case for Grivel, triggered by an understanding that the priority given to fleet warfare, which was a cornerstone in the existing doctrine, would lead to an almost mathematically predictable defeat against an enemy with a battleship fleet superior in numbers. Since both sides in a conflict would know this, Aube argued, the empire of the sea would pass to the stronger side without battle and maritime warfare would cease. Aube had recognized, to a degree not approached by Grivel, that the principles of maritime warfare that could be deduced from a study of history were being significantly qualified by the rapid technological changes of the late nineteenth century.[17]

Aube admitted that in the age of sail one could argue that numerical superiority did not guarantee victory in battle. Speed depended on the details of ship construction, on the quality of the commander and the

---

[14] *Ibid.*, p. 257.
[15] At the time there was no planning staff in the Ministry of Marine, although the Minister of Marine, Admiral Rigault de Genouilly did appoint a chief of staff the very year that Grivel's study was published. He was, however, only given administrative tasks. Taillemite: "Un théoricien méconnu", p. 90.
[16] Grivel: *De la guerre maritime*, p. 262.
[17] Aube's emphasis on the influence of technology also represents a significantly different approach to naval strategy from that of Mahan's influential writings decades later. Hobson: *Imperialism at Sea*, pp. 120–121.

seamanship of the crew, on the spread of sails that allowed numerous combinations etc. This in turn influenced the position one could obtain *vis-à-vis* the enemy, which could be a decisive factor in the battle. Aube claimed, however, as Grivel had done, that even in the age of sail, it had been common for the weaker side not to risk destruction of a valuable fleet in battle, but rather to seek refuge in port and to maintain its presence as a fleet-in-being. The technological developments brought about by the industrial revolution had reinforced this tendency, Aube argued. It was first of all the introduction of steam propulsion that eliminated the element of chance that had been present in the era of sailing ships: "[Speed] is now no more than the maximum effect of a given, blind force."[18] Numerical superiority, given an approximate equality among the individual ships constituting each fleet, would henceforth almost guarantee victory in an engagement. Aube deduced this logic in five points:

1. Given technological equality between the ships that constitute two opposing battleship squadrons, victory is assured the larger of the two squadrons, which does not engage its reserves until after the first phases of combat, shock and the beginning of the melee.
2. Action must be forced by the squadron with the most ships, as the less numerous, all other factors being equal, is sure of being defeated and destroyed.
3. Since the respective size and quality of the two navies will always be known at the outset of hostilities, command of the sea will pass without contest into the possession of the nation with the most numerous battleship fleet (French and German navies, 1870; Russian and Turkish navies, 1877).
4. As the grand naval battles are fought over command of the seas, there will be no more such engagements.
5. Maritime war will cease.

Aube agreed that this was an absurd conclusion, but who could prove that the logic was wrong, he rhetorically asked. It was the premise that the battleship was the foundation of naval power that was false.[19] The French Navy's devotion to a battleship navy thus emerged as

---

[18] Th Aube: "De la guerre maritime" in *Revue maritime et coloniale* (Paris, March 1873), p. 679.
[19] Aube: "La guerre maritime et les ports militaires", pp. 318–324. This argument had repeatedly been stated by Aube in his writings. See for instance: Aube: "De la guerre maritime", pp. 678–682. Aube: "L'avenir de la marine française", p. 188; Aube: "Un noveau droit maritime international", p. 23.

completely meaningless from the *jeune école*'s point of view, given that their strategic analysis identified Great Britain and the Royal Navy as the most likely opponent.

Strategic Assessment

Aube stated that the French Navy could be called on to fight a superior navy, a navy the size of the French or an inferior navy, and in his article *Italie et Levant* he depicted Italy as the most likely and formidable of the inferior navies that France could end up fighting.[20] He did not, however, as Grivel had done, argue in favour of two distinct strategies depending on whether France should fight an inferior or a superior navy, where the strategy against the inferior would be based on fleet warfare with battleships and the one against a superior enemy based on commercial warfare with cruisers. Britain and the Royal Navy was the constitutive enemy; a superior, but economically vulnerable foe was a necessary precondition for important aspects of the theory of the *jeune école*. The assumption that Great Britain was the main enemy was based on the traditional rivalry between France and Britain, but also on a particular understanding of the likely origin of future conflicts: colonial rivalry. Gabriel Charmes claimed that the European countries would continue to turn overseas to secure prosperity for their own nations:

> This drive towards the unoccupied territories, towards the distant shores, towards the vast, uncivilised areas, seems to be the main preoccupation of almost all European nations, who act under the banner of colonial politics.[21]

Charmes agreed that it would be quite rash to assume that the European powers would cease to dispute the hegemony over the continent. Nevertheless, he maintained, what would primarily be disputed was the commercial hegemony of the seas.

Théophile Aube argued along the same lines. He was an ardent supporter of colonialism. In it he saw the solution of many of the social problems of capitalism in Europe:

---

[20] Aube: "De la guerre maritime", p. 685 and Th. Aube: "Italie et Levant" in *A terre et à bord. Notes d'un marin* (Paris, 1884), p. 58.
[21] Gabriel Charmes: "La réforme maritime II. La guerre maritime et l'organisation des forces navales" in *Revues des deux mondes* (Paris, 1 March 1885), p. 139.

on the condition that products of industry find remunerative prices on the world market [...] labour and capital [...] are in accord, in harmony. But [...] by the law today incontestable, which is that of the forward march of humanity, *the struggle for life*, [...] these markets are rapidly glutted. [...] Labour and capital [...] become antagonistic, and the question of labour, exacerbated by misery and hunger, [...] transforms itself into a social question, whose solution appears possible only by the advent of absolute justice in our societies, which are oriented, alas, toward the contingent and the relative. This is essentially the French solution.

Wholly different is the solution sought and found by other nations, more fortunate and of a more practical spirit. [...] One must create and invent new markets, production will revive, and the menace of poverty will be averted. [...] And what are these new markets? They are the colonies with which England covers and transforms the world. [...] Thanks to these colonies [...] the question of labour has not become, will not become for a long time in England, a social question.[22]

Colonialism was however a two-edged sword. It could relieve the social problems of modern capitalism, but the national economy's dependence on colonies made this economy at the same time very vulnerable. The colonial power and its colonies were knitted together by sea lines of communication. It was these sea lines of communication that the *jeune école* defined as the industrialised and trade-dependent Britain's Achilles heel, and they argued that one had to attack private property in order to destroy modern, capitalist economy:

And as public wealth is nothing more than the accumulation of individual wealth, it is clear that in future wars, in order to stop a country's main commercial flow, in order to snatch from it its monopoly, one must hit private property without mercy and seek by a series of individual catastrophes to destroy general prosperity.[23]

The most effective way to make the British economy collapse would therefore be by aggressive and merciless raids against Britain's seaborne trade. The *jeune école* argued that this should be done on all trade routes supplying Great Britain. They maintained that attacks on the trade route from India would pose a serious threat to the British economy, but they underlined that other trade routes were as important as that from India:

---

[22] Th. Aube: "La pénétration dans l'Afrique centrale" in *A terre et à bord. Notes d'un marin* (Paris, 1884), pp. 66–67. Translated in Ropp: *The Development of a Modern Navy*, p. 163.
[23] Charmes: "La réforme maritime II", pp. 139–140.

> Doubtlessly India is one of the most precious elements of [England's] prosperity, but, if cruisers were to interrupt for many months the arrivals of American cotton that flow incessantly into her innumerable factories that produce the textiles that are then spread over all the markets of the universe, could one believe that she would not suffer as much as from the interruption of her relations with India? As soon as her factories stop, thousands of workers will be plunged into misery, and terrible economic crises will break out. Little by little, even famine will make itself felt with all its horrors, for the grain of America is no less necessary than the products of India for feeding England.[24]

The *jeune école*'s assessment of the increased importance of world trade and Britain's pivotal role in it was well founded. Before the 1840s the size and scale of international economic operations were comparatively modest. This was partly due to the absence of adequate surpluses of production for export (except in Britain), and because of the technical or social difficulty of transporting men and goods in sufficient bulk or quantity, and because of the relatively modest balances for investment abroad accumulated up to this point, even in Britain. Between 1800 and 1830 total international trade increased by no more than thirty per cent from about £300 million to about £400 million; but between 1840 and 1870 it multiplied five times over, and by the latter date had passed £2.000 million. From 1875 to 1913 world trade trebled.[25]

American-owned shipping posed a serious challenge to British domination in the 1840s and 1850s. Britain however shook off the American challenge during the transition to the iron and then the steel ship, and American shipping fell seriously behind during the American Civil War in the 1860s. It subsequently never recovered its place in the general expansion of world shipping. By 1890 Britain had more registered tonnage than the rest of the world put together. In 1910 over 40 per cent of tonnage entered and cleared in world trade was still British. British ships were also carriers of the world—not only with her own trade, but also in the tramp markets carrying the trade of third parties not touching at British ports. The shipping sector was one of the only sectors in the economy where Britain kept the world dominance after 1870 that she had enjoyed over a wide industrial field in 1850.[26]

---

[24] Gabriel Charmes: *Les torpilleurs autonomes et l'avenir de la marine* (Paris, 1885), p. 143. Translated in Ropp: *The Development of a Modern Navy*, p. 164.

[25] E.J. Hobsbawm: *Industry and Empire. An Economic History of Britain since 1750* (London, 1968), pp. 114–125.

[26] Peter Mathias: *The First Industrial Nation. An Economic History of Britain, 1700–1914* (London, 1969), p. 314.

Social and political unrest would be the most important strategic consequence of raiding the enormous British seaborne trade, according to the *jeune école*. This effect could be achieved by seriously disturbing the vulnerable financial system linked to shipping and by preventing essential commodities for British industry and the population from reaching the ports of Britain. The *jeune école* was well aware that shipping was very important in relation to the balance of payments position. Where trade was carried on British ships it usually meant that all the financial and commercial services associated with it flowed to Britain. The evolution of London as the world's main centre of international banking, finance and insurance was a function of the dominance of British shipping in world trade. Commerce raiding would consequently severely affect both the shipowners and the financial system linked to shipping. The *jeune école* made references to the Civil War and the consequences of the Confederacy's commerce raiding on insurance rates. They argued that in a future war, as soon as hostilities broke out, insurance rates would rise to a level that would make seaborne trade impossible due to financial constraints. The shipowners would therefore be forced to sell their ships to foreign powers, the *jeune école* argued.[27]

Imported raw materials were crucial for much of British industry, and an interruption in the flow of these materials would surely have a great impact on British industry and consequently on its economy and the welfare of its citizens. Food imports had also increased throughout the nineteenth century, and in contrast with previous decades, the prime imports of the nineteenth century were no longer luxuries, but bread and meat, the necessities of daily existence. The imported luxuries of the past, sugar and tea, tobacco and coffee and cocoa, had now become addictive necessities.[28]

It was very much the international specialization in agriculture that generated these new problems of national strategy. Towards the end of the Napoleonic wars the British parliament had passed the Corn Laws that erected a tariff barrier against foreign grain. The arguments in favour of the law were several: in wartime the nation would have to be fed from domestic resources, and agriculture also had the task of preserving a social balance between the deferential countryside and the

---

[27] Charmes: "La réforme maritime II", p. 142. The interrelations between shipping and London's financial institutions from Mathias: *The First Industrial Nation*, p. 314.

[28] Avner Offer: *The First World War: An Agrarian Interpretation* (Oxford, 1989), p. 81.

restless towns. It should further form a bulwark against foreign dangers and domestic discontent. When the Corn Laws were repealed in 1846, it thus became even more vital for Britain to dominate the seas. Agricultural protection was sacrificed in order to provide cheap food, but this carried an obligation to make the oceans safe. The problem was that not even a large preponderance of warships could guarantee the safe arrival of cargoes in wartime. Gabriel Charmes has evoked this vulnerability with a rhetorical question:

> Last year England imported 75 million hectolitre of grain—requiring about a thousand cargo ships—necessary for her domestic consumption; she imports immense quantities of meat [*bétail*], especially from the United States and Canada, and in addition to alimentary products, cotton, wool, alfalfa, minerals etc., which her industry cannot do without. How many squadrons will she need to escort these immense convoys, in order to protect them against attacks from cruisers? Whether she triples or quadruples her navy, she will not be able to protect these ships [...].[29]

British admirals awoke to this problem in the late 1870s, at about the time when foreign grain began to dominate domestic markets. In order to bring superior firepower and armour to bear, fleets had to be concentrated, but the merchant marine was widely scattered. From the 1870s onwards the Admiralty constructed large numbers of cruisers for trade protection and requested many more. But this was not viewed as a satisfactory solution. At the outbreak of war and possibly for many months afterwards, cargo vessels would be exposed to the menace of enemy cruisers.[30]

On the whole, the *jeune école*'s analysis of some of the preconditions for the British industrial and economical miracle, and what they perceived as the vulnerable parts of this system, was very much in accordance with concerns raised in Britain at the time.[31] Not only were there concurring views regarding the vulnerability of British economy, but, as Avnar Offer's summary of contemporary British worries illustrates, also

---

[29] Gabriel Charmes: "La reforme maritime II", p. 141.
[30] Offer: *The First World War*, pp. 217–223.
[31] One interesting contemporary British comment on the *jeune école*'s theories and their arguments concerning the vulnerability of British seaborne trade and consequently of the British economy, is Vice Admiral P.H. Colomb's review in 1887 of Gabriel Charmes' book *Naval Reform* (it was published in English translation in 1887). Colomb was critical of most of the arguments and reasoning of the *jeune école*, but he shared their view on "how surprisingly open we now are to injury by well-directed efforts against our commerce, and our open towns and harbours." P.H. Colomb: "Naval Reform", p. 784.

concerning the probable social and political implications of a possible disruption of British trade:

> The navy promised that shipping losses would not be large, while shipowners, merchants and underwriters were more pessimistic. Some risk to seaborne trade in wartime was conceded on all sides, while the remedies remained on paper. Even if actual losses at sea were small, underwriters and shipowners were likely to panic and push up insurance and freights. This was certain to jack up food prices and cripple the export industries, where millions would be thrown out of work. Those who kept their jobs could never afford to pay double or triple prices. It was not the hardship itself that gave cause for concern, or not any more than the poverty already existing. What counted was the *political* threat posed by the working classes. If their misery was prolonged, or if resolve and loyalty weakened, they might force governments to make a compromise peace before the danger period was over. Poverty had become a key issue of strategy and of national survival. In the minds of those who feared it, the menace combined the traditional violence of the bread riot with the modern one of political revolution.[32]

The major objective of commercial warfare as propagated by the *jeune école*, was precisely not "to starve out England" or to stop the raw materials and food necessary to carry on a war, but to produce an economic panic that would bring about a social and political collapse. During the American Civil War the French had seen the panic that swept away American shipping, as well as the sufferings of the British cotton workers. The leaders of the *jeune école* had themselves experienced the consequences of the German siege of Paris in 1870–71 and the suppression of the Paris Commune. They had lived through a period of extreme social turmoil, and had been able to study closely some of the preconditions that could ignite a social revolution. At the time Charmes and Aube wrote the articles quoted above, Britain and the world at large were in the depths of a great depression. A social revolution in England did not appear out of the question. In 1885, after a famous bomb plot and explosions in Birmingham, Liverpool, and Glasgow, and in London at the Local Government Board, Victoria Railway Station, the Tower, Westminster Hall, and the House of Commons, the government passed an Explosives Bill.[33] These events probably further convinced the *jeune école* that commercial warfare could destabilize Great Britain, and force it to the negotiating table.

---

[32] Offer: *The First World War*, pp. 221–222.
[33] Ropp: *The Development of a Modern Navy*, p. 163.

Commercial Warfare

Raiding the Enemy's Sea Lines of Communication

Destruction or capture of the enemy's trade was nothing new to maritime warfare. To destroy the enemy's trade has been a key objective for belligerents since at least the fifteenth century. The motives were often to cut off supplies important for the enemy's ability to wage war or to secure them for oneself to improve one's own fighting capability. As European trade became largely seaborne, commercial warfare developed and the theories of siege were adapted to sea warfare.[34]

The strategic objectives of fleet warfare or *guerre d'escadre* differed from *guerre de course*. In fleet warfare the aim was to attack the enemy's fleet in order to win control of the sea or to deny it to the enemy. Once sea control was established it opened up possibilities for secondary operations like landing operations in the enemy's homeland or attacking his colonies, raiding his commerce or blockading his ports. This kind of maritime policy could only be carried out by a large and well-organised fleet that required means that were beyond the resources of private individuals. Building ships and bases, buying stores and recruiting crews for a navy required enormous investments that only a state could provide. An essential distinction between a naval fleet and commerce-raiders was thus that the first was controlled directly by a state, while the second could be contracted out to private ship owners. Commerce raiding could be conducted in two principally different ways. Either the belligerents could organise parts of their navy into squadrons that raided enemy commerce, or this work could be contracted out to private entrepreneurs. Very often commerce raiding was conducted by both naval and private raiders. The activities of privateers were legitimised and sanctioned by the state by a "letter of marque" distinguishing them from pirates. When one discusses *guerre de course* it is often seen as a combination of public and private ships employed to ruin the enemy's trade.[35]

---

[34] Philip C. Jessup and Francis Deák: *Neutrality. Its History, Economics and Law*. Volume I: "The origins" (New York, 1976, first printed in 1935), p. xi.
[35] Geoffrey Symcox: *The Crisis of French Sea Power 1688–1697. From the Guerre d'escadre to the Guerre de course* (The Hague, 1974), pp. 5–7.

Although commerce raiding and fleet warfare could be complementary ways of sea warfare, commerce raiding was often an option that governments fell back on if state finances could not uphold a battle fleet or if major parts of the battle fleet were destroyed or captured and the rest of the fleet was forced to remain in port due to superior opposition. Geoffrey Symcox has shown in his study of the Nine Years War how a combination of financial restraints and superior military opposition changed the French war effort at sea. The transition to *guerre de course* came after the French financial crisis of 1693–94, and after the superior Dutch and English naval forces had succeeded in containing the French main fleet in port. The *guerre d'escadre* and the *guerre de course* had been practised concurrently by France until the main fleet was laid up in 1694. Until then the principal war effort at sea was made by the battle fleet, while commerce raiding played a secondary role. As most of the ships that compromised the main fleet were laid up, the roles changed. Much of the war effort was carried out by privateers. Many of the commerce-raiders were naval ships leased out to private capitalists and operating as business ventures. As Symcox succinctly summarises: "The war at sea had been decentralised; private capital was called in to make good the deficiencies in the state's finances, which were no longer equal to the task of waging war alone and unaided."[36]

The example of the Nine Years War indicates that the relative priorities given to commerce warfare were determined by the extent to which the state was in a position to afford to keep a battle fleet or whether the battle fleet was locked up in port by a stronger enemy. But behind the choice of a particular mode of warfare was also a consideration of where the enemy would be weak and France strong. Both sides in the Nine Years War were locked in a prolonged struggle across western Europe, and victory would go to the one which lasted the longest. France depended upon her large internal resources; the Allies depended, if not exclusively, then to a very considerable extent, upon the riches that accrued from the profits of British and Dutch foreign trade. If the latter were cut off, France's opponents would probably soon sue for peace. As Vauban, the great military expert, put it in 1695 when advocating a naval campaign against Britain and Holland:

> Brest is so placed as though God had made it expressly for the purpose of the destruction of the commerce of these two nations. The most skilful

---

[36] *Ibid.*, pp. 6–8.

policy is the shaking of the buttresses of the League by means of a subtle and widespread form of war [i.e. *guerre de course*].[37]

Great Britain's command of the sea assured her the defence of British soil and of her colonies, and at the same time provided Britain with the opportunity of attacking the French coast and her colonies. Backing away from a head-on collision with the stronger British Navy, the French followed Vauban's advice during the following wars. For a century and a half, from the days of Louis XIV to Napoleon, from the legendary corsair Jean Bart to the equally legendary Robert Surcouf, French frigates and privateers, operating from Brest and Toulon as well from Dunkirk, St Malo, Dieppe and a host of other small ports, raided and harassed British trade.

British losses in each of the great wars against France—the Nine Years War, the War of the Spanish Succession, the War of the Austrian Succession, the Seven Years War and the Wars of the French Revolution and the Napoleonic Wars—amounted to thousands of vessels, with hundred of ships captured every year.[38] French destruction of commerce was particularly effective when French power was at its zenith under Louis XIV and during the Revolution and Empire. The British victory in 1805 in the Battle of Trafalgar over a combined French and Spanish fleet forced Napoleon to restrict French maritime war mainly to *guerre de course*. The reduction of the French fleet and the blockade of French commercial vessels made thousands of French sailors available for privateering. In addition, raiding squadrons of four or six naval vessels were sent out to scour the trade routes. Most of the assaults took place in the Channel, the Bay of Biscay, the North Sea, the Baltic and the Mediterranean, but the larger and more powerful privateers joined the raiding squadrons in commerce-raiding operations all over the globe. For example, the bases at Martinique, Guadeloupe and Mauritius were used to attack the valuable West and East Indies trade.[39]

London, Britain's main trading city, recorded ship entries and departures averaging between 13,000 and 14,000 each year. To protect all these ships in wartime was clearly beyond the bounds of possibility. Paul Kennedy has estimated that 11,000 British merchant vessels were

---

[37] Quoted in Paul Kennedy: *The Rise and Fall of British Naval Mastery* (London, 1983), pp. 78–79.
[38] Azar Gat: *The Development of Military Thought. The Nineteenth Century* (Oxford, 1992), pp. 193, 198.
[39] Kennedy: *The Rise and Fall of British Naval Mastery*, p. 131.

captured by the enemy in the years 1793–1815. In 1810 Britain lost 619 ships, which was the highest number recorded during the Wars of the French Revolution and the Napoleonic Wars. Although this represented a small percentage of the total number of ships and tonnage involved, the French campaign to disrupt British seaborne trade had severe economic consequences and marine insurance rates rose dramatically.[40]

In arguing for *guerre de course* the *jeune école* was very conscious that this fitted into a well-established French tradition. Aube portrayed it as almost a genetic virtue of the French:

> this warfare is the one that is most in accordance with our traditions, it corresponds best with the spirit of our race. What personalities do foreign navies have, even the most proud, of a glorious past that can match those of Jean-Bart, Dugay Trouin, Bouvet, Surcouf, Duperré, whom *la course* has immortalised?[41]

Since the days of these corsairs Great Britain had become increasingly dependent on her seaborne trade. Further, the *jeune école* argued that the command of the seas that had helped protect British trade would be impossible to achieve after the advent of steam and more effective weapons. They claimed that a combination of technological progress and adapted French strategy and tactics would create a new situation that "[would make] command of the sea nothing more than an expression devoid of any meaning."[42]

One of the barriers against French offensive maritime warfare in the days of sail had been the Royal Navy's ability to impose an effective blockade of the French coast. Commerce raiding and privateering had indeed flourished, but as Aube put it: "only when the wind calmed for some moments and forced them [the blockading ships] to turn to the open sea, could our cruisers take advantage of the short, but long awaited moments to escape [...]."[43] The advent of steam made an effective blockade difficult to uphold. Steamships could not keep the sea for weeks at a time in the manner that blockading fleets

---

[40] *Ibid.*
[41] Aube: "L'avenir de la Marine française", p. 191. All of these corsairs are still prominent in the gallery of French naval heroes and all of them have given names to numerous French naval vessels. Surcouf and Jean-Bart are both frigates in active service in the French Navy today.
[42] Gabriel Charmes: "La réforme de la Marine II", p. 136.
[43] Aube: "La guerre maritime et les ports militaires", p. 325.

under sail could and repeatedly had. Owing to the frequent need to coal, the mere maintenance of a close blockade in the days of steam was attended with far greater difficulties than hitherto. While making the vessels independent of the wind, the steam engine tied them to the depot and the collier.[44]

While the steam engine complicated the mission of the blockading forces, the *jeune école* seemed convinced that the steam engine would give French cruisers the upper hand both as blockade-runners and on the high seas:

> That an absolute blockade, effective on all spots of an extensive coast like that of France, will from now on be impossible,—that cruisers with a higher speed, commanded by captains that are real sailors, can always get through the tightest blockade, and on the high seas challenge any pursuit, that is what the incidents of the latest maritime wars have highlighted, [this is obvious] without having to go into the technical considerations.[45]

The assumption that the inferior sea power should have the fastest ships was an expression of the wishful thinking of the *jeune école*. It reflected a prevailing belief in French skill and talent that characterized much of the *jeune école*'s thinking.[46]

Their argument that a number of naval ports, dispersed along the coast, would complicate the mission of the blockading fleet was, however, part of a more coherent reasoning based on two arguments. Firstly, the blockading fleet would have to be divided into several smaller groups in order to blockade each port. This could easily lead to an overstretch of the blockader's resources, and thus make it easier to challenge the enemy. Secondly, it would open up possibilities for what became a

---

[44] John F. Beeler: *British Naval Policy in the Gladstone—Disraeli Era 1866–1880* (Standford, Ca., 1997), p. 212.

[45] Aube: "L'avenir de la marine française", p. 180.

[46] This was one of the arguments that Vice Admiral P.H. Colomb put forward against the theories of the *jeune école*. He reminded his readers rather ironically in a comment on Aube's a priori assumption that the French cruisers would be faster than the pursuers' ships, that it was "not uncommon in speculations as to the future of naval war to see this attitude of mind assumed. One man will have for his plan the heaviest guns, another the thickest plating, another the hardest stem, and M. Aube the fastest ships! It need hardly be said that superiority in any material entity cannot be assumed in naval strategy or tactics. The assumption must always be at least material equality, if it be not better and safer to assume a material inferiority for the study of a tactical or strategic problem. M. Aube cannot obtain the superior speed for his "corsairs", though he may force his enemy to face the same difficulties as he will meet with himself in his efforts." Colomb: "Naval Reform", p. 773.

cornerstone in the *jeune école*'s defensive strategy; the concentration of forces from several centres in order to make a fast and coordinated attack on the enemy with superior forces.[47]

The widespread adoption of the self-propelled torpedo in the early 1870s had made such tactics more credible, and the torpedo was generally perceived to be a direct threat to the blockading ships. No longer could the blockading ships cruise safely off the enemy's ports and coasts. That the Whitehead was, for at least a decade after its commercial introduction in 1870, a primitive and limited weapon, both in terms of range and of speed, was irrelevant; its mere existence created a huge risk that had not previously existed.[48] The more successful trials with torpedoes in the 1880s made these tactics more realistic, and the torpedo and the torpedo boat became central elements in both the defensive and offensive warfare propagated by the *jeune école*. They described enthusiastically how the torpedo boats would break up enemy blockades. The torpedo boats would approach the battleships at the speed of lightning. If the battleships did not detect the torpedo boats at a distance of more than some hundred meters, or even a thousand meters, there would be no hope for the battleship. The battleships would be utterly exposed at night-time, when several torpedo boats in a coordinated attack would easily saturate the battleships' ability to detect the attacking boats and fight back.[49]

The introduction of steamships and self-propelled torpedoes, and the strategic and tactical adaptation to this new technology, had not only made the blockade less feasible and thus facilitated the commerce-raiders putting out to sea. Steam power favoured the commerce-raiders as they operated on the high seas too. The majority of the merchant vessels, transoceanic as well as coastal traders, were still sail-powered in the 1880s. A becalmed merchantman in the days of sail was relatively safe; any pursuing commerce-raider would be becalmed as well. Such was not the case after the advent of steam.

The *jeune école* was eager to underline that the feasibility and the effectiveness of commerce warfare were more than theoretical assumptions. Both Aube and Charmes stressed that this was very well documented, especially by the Confederate commerce-raiders during the American

---

[47] Aube: "La guerre maritime et les ports militaires", pp. 336, 344.
[48] Beeler: *British Naval Policy*, p. 212.
[49] Gabriel Charmes: "La réforme de la Marine I. Torpilleurs et cannonières" in *Revue des deux mondes* (Paris, 15 December 1884), pp. 884–885.

Civil War. The most striking example was the Confederate steam-powered commerce-raider *Alabama*. In twenty months a steam ship—not an especially well-armed or seaworthy one—captured seventy-one Union ships. Although the Confederate commerce-raiders' exploits did not alter the outcome of the war, they diverted numerous Union Navy ships from the blockade, drove insurance rates for American vessels to astronomical heights, forced these vessels to remain in port or convert to foreign registry, and helped topple the American merchant marine from a position where US-owned shipping had seriously contested British domination among the world's merchant marines, a position it never regained.[50] Aube claimed that the Confederate raiders had proved that "the sceptre of the sea had become worm-eaten, more than half broken".[51] He concluded that this had marked the beginning of future maritime warfare where fast cruisers with courageous captains could be everywhere and easily escape any pursuit.

The case of the German naval vessel *Augusta* was another example Aube used to illustrate how a lonely commerce-raider could upset a superior naval power. The Augusta was a fast steam corvette that was originally built for the Confederacy (*CSS Mississippi*) but brought into Prussian service after the end of the American Civil War. Almost at the close of the Franco-Prussian War, at a time when the German ports were closely invested by the French, she suddenly appeared off Rochefort and captured a little Government dispatch boat; a few hours later she was off the mouth of Gironde and captured a couple of merchant ships. Then the *Augusta* disappeared, but was later found in the port of Vigo short of coal. There, French warships blockaded her until the armistice.[52]

The result in numbers of captured ships was rather meagre during the *Augusta*'s brief sortie. The emotions it provoked in France were however enormous. A lot of imaginary warships were reported off the coast of Ireland or at the entrance to the Channel. The chambers of commerce of the Atlantic ports demanded naval protection. The French Navy itself was upset. Five warships were set on high alert to guard

---

[50] Beeler: *British Naval Policy*, p. 213; James M. McPherson: *Battle Cry of Freedom, The Civil War Era* (New York, 1988), pp. 547–548.
[51] Aube: "La guerre maritime et les ports militaires", pp. 325–326. See also Gabriel Charmes: "La réforme de la Marine II", pp. 137–138.
[52] Colomb: "Naval Reform", p. 774; Jack Greene and Alessandro Massignani: *Ironclads at War. The Origin and Development of the Armored Warship, 1854–1891* (Pennsylvania, 1998), pp. 205, 244; Masson: *Histoire de la Marine, Tome II*, pp. 131–132.

the coast from Brest to Bayonne. The Mediterranean Fleet established close surveillance of the strait of Gibraltar, and escorting the seaborne trade almost exhausted the Navy's resources.[53]

Aube stressed that the French Navy had done what it was supposed to do. The French cruisers had been patrolling all the major trade routes, and the blockade of the German coast was as tight as it had been from the moment when the blockade first was imposed. Still the *Augusta* was able to escape the blockade and attack seaborne commerce off the French coast. What had happened explained Aube, was that the caution and lack of confidence among some German naval officers had been replaced by boldness and confidence. Aube viewed the *Augusta*'s endeavours as a convincing example of what skilled, experienced and determined commanding officers could achieve. Luckily, French warships were able to lock the *Augusta* up in a neutral port, but the example had been given, Aube argued. Had the war lasted longer, others would have followed in the wake of the *Augusta*, because from the moment of her escape the incapacity of the French Navy to impose a blockade of the German coast had been revealed.[54]

In the proposals of the *jeune école*, cruisers were soon to be supplemented by small torpedo boats and gunboats as the preferred vessels for commerce warfare. Charmes dated this change to April 1884. While it had been generally accepted that small boats armed with torpedoes could be effective in the littorals where the sea was relatively calm, their capacity on the high seas was very much disputed. Charmes, who was a writer and student of foreign affairs but no sailor, claimed that the torpedo boats *No. 63* and *No. 64* that sailed from Brest to Toulon in April 1884 faced the roughest seas without any problems. These two 33 meter long torpedo boats of 45 tons had also participated in exercises outside the littorals in the Mediterranean. Charmes maintained that while two armoured coastal defence ships were unable to follow the battle fleet's speed of advance due to the weather, the small torpedo boats allegedly faced no difficulties. Charmes concluded that "from now on there is no more doubt that the problem of navigating relatively small boats at high speed is resolved."[55] Aube too, who was a seasoned sailor who in his articles in the 1870s and early 1880s had argued in favour of a fleet of specialised cruisers for commerce raiding, was now

---

[53] Masson: *Histoire de la Marine, Tome II*, p. 132.
[54] Aube: "L'avenir de la marine française", p. 182.
[55] Charmes: "La réforme de la Marine I", pp. 883–884.

obviously convinced that these autonomous torpedo-boats could also be used on the high seas to interrupt British trade routes.[56]

Bombardment of the Enemy's Coast

In his article "La guerre maritime et les ports militaires de la France", published in 1882, Aube described bombardment primarily as a likely threat against French ports and coastal cities. He claimed that this threat had become more acute since command of the seas no longer was sufficient to protect either a nation's coast or its sea trade, and consequently "the masters of the sea will turn their power of attack and destruction [...] against all the cities of the coast, fortified or not, pacific or warlike; burn them, ruin them or at least ransom them mercilessly."[57]

Aube argued that bombardment had also become a more realistic option since technological progress had made modern battleships less exposed when confronted by coastal artillery. Steam propulsion and armour would reduce the effect of coastal batteries. He concluded that battleships attacking at high speed and under cover of smoke, could bombard and set fire to any coastal city within range of its artillery, with little risk of being seriously endangered by the coastal batteries defending the cities.

Aube's agenda when writing this article was very much to forward arguments against plans to close the military port of Rochefort. To have a number of military ports dispersed along the French coastline was part of the *jeune école*'s offensive and defensive strategy. Aube did, however, underline that bombarding coastal cities was not only a venture the enemy would set out upon. It should also be an integral part of French commercial warfare. He underlined that since money was the nerve of war, everything that might deprive the enemy of his wealth would not only be a legitimate target, but it would be an imperative to destroy it. Aube predicted on the basis of this reasoning that one was entering a new system of maritime warfare: that of attacks on the enemy coasts, and consequently the defence of one's own coasts.[58]

---

[56] Th Aube: "Défense nationale—Défense des colonies" in Henri Mager (ed.): *Atlas Colonial* (Paris, 1885), pp. 11–12.

[57] Aube also referred to the deliberate bombardments of the civilian quarters in Strasbourg and Péronne during the Franco-Prussian War as an example of what one should expect in wars to come. Th. Aube: "La guerre maritime et les ports militaires", pp. 331–332.

[58] *Ibid.*, pp. 331–332.

In an article published three years later Charmes was more explicit than Aube in describing naval bombardment of enemy ports as a logical part of the overall idea of commercial warfare:

> And what will happen on the high seas will also happen on the coast, for a logical consequence of commerce warfare is attacks on open harbours, undefended cities, and industrial and commercial warehouses that are not fortified [...]. There will be no more reason to respect an ordinary city, and even less a prosperous city, than to respect a commercial fleet. Whether one sets fire to a nation's products on board a vessel or in its docks or warehouses makes no difference. Or rather the second operation would provide material and moral advantages that would be more decisive than the first operation. It is certain that one will force a people to make peace as effectively by depriving it of one of its commercial ports as by depriving it of one of its military ports. Likewise one will just as surely reach the same result by dispersing its merchant navy as by blowing up its battle fleet.[59]

Charmes's more persistent argumentation in favour of including bombardment as part of the *jeune école*'s offensive strategy was very much due to the euphoria induced by the sea trials of the torpedo boats in 1884. Charmes viewed these small boats as a kind of cheap, universal hull that could be fitted either with torpedoes or guns. If small torpedo boats could cross the high seas, so could small gunboats. Although he primarily argued in favour of attacking open ports and cities, he stressed that small gunboats would also be better suited than battleships for attacking fortified ports and cities. He claimed that not even the heavy artillery of big battleships would be able to break the fortifications protecting the enemy's guns, and he mentioned the bombardment of the forts of Alexandria by the Royal Navy as an example of the limitations of battleships in such a role. But small gunboats with their limited draught and armed with the *mitrailleuse* would be able to close the forts and hit through the crenels. To sail close to the fortresses in order to try to get a lucky shot through the crenels was of course dangerous, but using battleships to subdue a fortress would be more dangerous. They would have to position themselves further out at sea due to their draught, and would thus be exposed to attacks from torpedo boats; a threat that Charmes naturally regarded as far more dangerous than artillery

---

[59] Charmes: "La réforme de la Marine II", p. 149.

fire from the fortresses.[60] Charmes noted that "All nations are indeed preparing to defend their coasts with torpedo boats". He claimed that Germany and Austria were building a substantial number of torpedo boats for this use. So if one planned operations against enemy coasts one should be prepared to meet armadas of these boats. This, according to Charmes' logic, would be a suicidal mission for battleships.[61] Small gunboats would be less vulnerable confronted with enemy torpedo boats. For Charmes this was a matter of calculated risk. The artillery of the fortresses could certainly sink some of the gunboats:

> but what would that matter if some succeeded? One does not fight wars without losing ships and men, and it would certainly be better to lose some small gunboats with their small crews than one third of a battle fleet.[62]

The difference in view between Aube and Charmes should not be overstated. Aube was trying to convince public opinion and the political and military decision-makers that Rochefort should be maintained as a naval base. In order to convince them he had to depict the Royal Navy's main battleships as a threat to French coastal cities. Charmes's article was written three years after that of Aube. In the time span between these two articles, the *jeune école*'s confidence in the excellence of small boats had been strengthened. Charmes's agenda was therefore to convince public opinion and the decision makers of the excellence of small boats. For Charmes, these gunboats, as with the torpedo boats, announced a new era in naval warfare, an era where the poorer could fight the richer on equal terms. Even the poorest country could afford a gunboat with a 14 cm gun, he claimed, and he predicted that: "The time of the big ships hammering on the big fortresses is over, while the time of the small, deadly boats attacking what constitutes the life and wealth of nations will begin."[63]

---

[60] Charmes: "La réforme de la Marine I", pp. 896–898.
[61] Charmes: "La réforme de la Marine II", pp. 160–161.
[62] Charmes: "La réforme de la Marine I", p. 898.
[63] Charmes: "La réforme de la Marine II", p. 149.

The *Jeune École* and International Law[64]

The Critics of the Jeune École

Commerce warfare, as it was advocated by the *jeune école*, raised difficult moral, legal and practical questions that were tightly intertwined. The Declaration of Paris of 1856 had changed profoundly the legal basis for commerce raiding. The signatory states had agreed that blockades had to be effective in order to be binding, neutral ships could carry enemy property as long as it was not contraband, whereas neutral goods, with the exception of contraband of war, were not liable to capture under enemy flag.[65] Privateering, which had been a proud French tradition, was also outlawed. Every major European power save Spain subscribed to the declaration. The United States of America did not sign the declaration because it could not agree to the article outlawing privateering.[66]

---

[64] Several different terms were used to describe international law (which is chosen as a common denominator in this study) by the *jeune école*: *droits des gens, droits de la guerre, droit maritime international, droit de l'humanité* etc. These terms not only covered international law as expressed in such positive enactments as the Declaration of Paris of 1856, the Saint Petersburg Declaration of 1868 and the Geneva Conventions but also constraints which were not codified in formal law. The *jeune école* included in their understanding of international law what Michael Howard has described as "cultural regulations of violence"; what was, in the old fashion phrase, "done" and "not done" in war; constraints of which formal laws were only expressions, or which did not necessarily coincide with formal laws at all." Michael Howard: "Constraints on Warfare" in Howard, Andreopoulos, and Shulman (eds.): *The Laws of War*, p. 1. The *jeune école* explicitly admitted that the way it proposed that commerce warfare should be conducted would be an obvious breach of international law. The adherents of the *jeune école* made no attempts to interpret international law in order to make it agree with the theories of the *jeune école*. The only exceptions may be Commander Chassériaud's effort to describe the merchant marine as a *potential* naval asset and thus a legitimate target (see pp. 31–34), and Commander Degouy's argument that merchant ships had a different legal status sailing independently than when sailing in convoy. Sailing in convoy they would "'ipso facto' [be] subject to all means of warfare." See pp. 126–127.

[65] The Declaration of Paris of 1856 stated that:
 1. Privateering is, and remains, abolished;
 2. The neutral flag covers enemy's goods, with the exception of contraband of war;
 3. Neutral goods, with the exception of contraband of war, are not liable to capture under enemy's flag;
 4. Blockades, in order to be binding, must be effective, that is to say, maintained by a force sufficient really to prevent access to the coast of the enemy.

[66] John B. Hattendorf: "Maritime Conflict" in Michael Howard, George J. Andreopoulos, and Mark R. Shulman (eds.): *The Laws of War. Constraints on Warfare in the Western World* (New Haven, 1994), p. 109.

The critics of the *jeune école* argued that commerce warfare would be almost impossible to carry out within the bounds of the Declaration of Paris. One of the ablest critics of the *jeune école* was Vice Admiral Bourgois. He was one of the greatest French students of international maritime law, and he was also of one of the most pronounced authorities on torpedo work in France. Bourgois designed, along with the naval constructor Charles-Marie Brun, the French Navy's first submarine, the *Plongeur*. Admiral Bourgois was also president of the commission that had recommended the adoption of the Whitehead torpedo, and chairman of the Commission on Submarine Defences for several years after the Franco-Prussian war in 1870–71.[67]

Admiral Bourgois was especially shocked by the *jeune école*'s idea that commerce warfare should be conducted with the use of the torpedo as the primary or only weapon. He claimed that this would inevitably result in violations of international law. Bourgois knew that the torpedo was not a very flexible weapon. It was a weapon that was primarily suited to sink ships, and not for firing warning shots. The tactics advocated by the *jeune école* also confirmed this. Aube depicted a scenario were torpedo boats should follow passenger-liners from afar during daytime, in order to remain invisible, and then close in once night had fallen and attack the liner with torpedoes.[68] The torpedo would most certainly send the liner with cargo, crew and passengers to the bottom of the sea. Bourgois questioned how a torpedo boat, if it kept at a distance during daytime in order to make it impossible to discover her from the liner, could recognize the nationality of the boat she intended to sink. He reminded his readers that in such a situation it would be easy to make a mistake, but impossible to rectify it. The sunken vessel could be the enemy, but it could also be a neutral or French.[69]

Admiral Ernest du Pin de Saint-André, who had produced much of the new defensive system of Toulon against torpedo attacks, argued along the same lines as Bourgois. He warned against the problems distinguishing enemy from neutral and friend, and accused the proponents

---

[67] Ropp: *The Development of a Modern Navy*, pp. 168–169.

[68] This tactical approach was explicitly advocated by Aube in Aube: "Défense nationale", pp. 11–12.

[69] Vice Admiral Bourgois: *Les torpilleurs, la guerre navale et la défense des côtes* (Paris, 1888), pp. 14–17. This book is composed of three studies by Bourgois published in the *Nouvelle Revue* (Paris); the first in April 1886, the second in July and August 1886 and the third in December 1887 and February 1888. The reference above is from the article published in April 1886, i.e. when Aube was Minister of Marine.

of the *jeune école* for not having considered possible counter-measures in commerce warfare. He argued that in times of war the crews of the merchant ships would do their uttermost to remove any overt sign of their nationality, and their first precaution would be to carry the flag of a neutral nation.[70] This was seen in the early stages of the Crimean War when there were some hasty transfers from the Russian to the Danish and Tuscan flags,[71] and during the American Civil War when the Confederacy's commerce-raiders forced American merchant ships to take refuge under foreign flags.[72] Admiral du Pin de Saint-André argued that these countermeasures would force the torpedo boat to approach the merchantman, in order to rule out that the merchant vessel encountered was neutral or friendly. Well aware of the risk of being sunk without warning by a torpedo, merchant ships would be defensively armed to fight torpedo boats. The torpedo boat would thus be confronted with an impossible situation: She could either sink the merchant ships encountered without identifying them, running the risk that that they were neutral or friendly, or she could approach them for identification, and risk being sunk by the merchantmen's guns.[73]

Such a disadvantageous situation, from the commerce-raiders' point of view, could be avoided by using cruisers armed with guns. Bourgois argued, however, that the Declaration of Paris had made commerce raiding with cruisers almost impossible as well. It was the fact that neutral goods, with the exception of contraband of war, were not liable to capture under enemy flag, which also made commerce raiding with cruisers both difficult and dangerous for the cruiser. Bourgois claimed that merchant ships from an enemy state very often carried neutral merchandise. To act in accordance with the Declaration of Paris one would have to sail the prize to a French or allied port. To do this the commerce-raider would have to put a prize crew aboard the captured ship. If the cruiser met an enemy warship, she would have to fight with a reduced crew, i.e. under very disadvantageous circumstances. The other option, in order to avoid such a danger, would be to sink the prize

---

[70] Ernest du Pin de Saint-André: "La question des torpilleurs (II)" in *Revue des deux mondes*, pp. 344–346.

[71] C.I. Hamilton: "Anglo-French sea power and the Declaration of Paris" in *The International History Review*, IV (Victoria, B.C., 2 May 1982), p. 177.

[72] McPherson: *Battle Cry of Freedom*, p. 547. Ropp: *The Development of a Modern Navy*, p. 163.

[73] Ernest du Pin de Saint-André: "La question des torpilleurs (II)", pp. 344–346, 360.

after having taken the crew aboard. This was what the Confederate cruisers did during the American Civil War. To obey the Declaration of Paris, one would, however, be obliged to offer compensation to the owners of the neutral merchandise.[74] Bourgois drew the conclusion that commerce warfare, if one obeyed international law, had lost all its efficiency. For Bourgois there was only one alternative to conducting commerce warfare in compliance with the Declaration of Paris, and that was to abandon *guerre de course* altogether.[75]

Bourgois also criticised the *jeune école* for having ignored obvious strategic consequences of throwing the Declaration of Paris overboard. He pointed to the fact that international maritime law was upheld because it was in the interest of someone, in this case of the neutral powers. Bourgois argued that if the sunken vessel was neutral, or carried passengers from neutral states, one could not count on the patience or tolerance of the powers where the boat or the passengers had their origin. On the contrary, one could expect them to protest energetically and even combine against the offending nation in order to make it comply with international law. Bourgois even claimed that the neutrals would probably define the commerce-raiders as pirates, and treat them accordingly. They would simply be sent to the bottom to join their victims.[76]

To create a situation in which the neutrals rallied against France would be just the opposite of what would seem logical for an inferior navy. It had been a cardinal objective for the French Navy during the Second Empire that even if the French Navy was not equal to the Royal Navy, it could act as a core for an alliance of lesser navies that could, if necessary, overwhelm the Royal Navy.[77] The warfare proposed by the *jeune école* could repulse possible allies, and thus undermine such an approach.

International Law Incompatible with War

It seems that the advocates of the *jeune école* were not very concerned with possible negative consequences of breaking international law. On

---

[74] Bourgois also noted that such a conduct would be in accordance with article 20 in the French instructions for the war of 1870–71. Bourgois: *Les torpilleurs*, pp. 93–94.

[75] Bourgois: *Les torpilleurs*, pp. 14–17, 92–94.

[76] *Ibid.*, pp. 18–19.

[77] Hamilton: "Anglo-French sea power and the Declaration of Paris", p. 170, and same author: *Anglo—French Naval Rivalry*, p. 302.

the contrary, their prime concern was the constraints international maritime law placed on what they defined as their most effective way of fighting Great Britain. Therefore they advocated that in wartime the French Navy should disregard the restraints placed upon commerce warfare by maritime law. This rejection of the Declaration of Paris was founded on two arguments. First, the *jeune école* perceived the Declaration of Paris as an arrangement freezing the imbalance between the strong and the weak, i.e. it favoured Great Britain. Secondly, they disputed the very idea that international law was valid in war.

The *jeune école*'s interpretation of the consequences of the Declaration was quite different from that of British commentators who criticized the signing of the Declaration of Paris. They considered that the Declaration removed the most formidable element of sea power from Britain's arsenal.[78] It was seen as an incredible gesture by the strongest sea power in favour of the continental states' view that the nationality of any merchant vessel should cover its cargo. At one stroke the weapon of the blockade had been neutralized. The British government felt, however, that it would be unwise to defy world opinion on this heated issue, and hoped in any case to have achieved a fair solution by the agreement to abolish privateering. The British acceptance of these clauses also symbolised a high point in the power and influence of the Manchester school, and in the idea of "the freedom of the seas".[79]

Aube, for his part, warned that if war were conducted according to the humanistic ideas advocated by the Declaration of Paris, it would be fatal to France's national security interests.[80] He was convinced that commerce raiding had been, and would be to an even greater extent, the most effective way to fight Britain. Aube was equally convinced that it would be impossible to impose a blockade in the era of steam propulsion and torpedoes. He thus argued that the declaration had deprived France of one of its traditional advantages, the *guerre de course*, whereas Britain by adhering to the same declaration had given up a traditional advantage that had become illusory, the blockade.[81] The Declaration

---

[78] Andrew Lambert: *The Crimean War. British Grand Strategy, 1853–1856* (Manchester, 1990), p. 334.
[79] Kennedy: *The Rise and Fall of British Naval Mastery*, p. 175.
[80] Aube: "Un nouveau droit maritime international", p. 11.
[81] "elle (France) renonçait à la course, le moyen le plus assuré qu'elle eût de combattre l'Angleterre, la France abandonnait un avantage positif, tandis que sa rivale renonçait simplement à des prétentions désormais chimériques, impossibles à maintenir." *Ibid.*, p. 12.

of Paris had thus frozen the imbalance between the stronger and the weaker Navy. To abolish the possibility of waging commerce warfare was for all other navies than the British to abandon the most legitimate and precious right, that of national defence.[82]

Aube's criticism of the Declaration of Paris was also founded on the fundamental view that international law is irreconcilable with war. He admitted the value of international law in peacetime and agreed that it could contribute to avoid or postpone war, but when war had broken out it was in itself contrary to law:

> [Defenders of] Humanity may protest and claim that [*la guerre de course*] represents the return of barbarism; these protests miss the point, and besides it is not the consequences of war one should prevent, but war itself.[83]

> War is the negation of law. It [...] is the recourse to force—the ruler of the world—of an entire people in the incessant and universal struggle for existence. Everything is therefore not only permissible but legitimate against the enemy.[84]

Aube was from his early writings in 1871 and onwards consistent in his view that international law must be subordinated to the demands of war. He argued that war was a necessity imposed on man; it was a last resort for defending a legitimate and ultimate right, that of self-defence. This precious right "takes precedence over the laws of justice."[85] The aim of warfare is thus to weaken the enemy by all available means. The choice between different ways of waging war is not a question of justice or humanity; it depends on considerations of a totally different order. International treaties and conventions cannot be more than a compromise between these demands of a higher order and the sentiments of justice and humanity, according to Aube.[86]

The *jeune école* agreed to the critics' conclusion that commerce warfare would be very difficult to conduct within the limits set by the Declaration of Paris. With the introduction of the torpedo and the torpedo boat as an effective weapon against the enemy's commerce this became even

---

[82] *Ibid.*, p. 23.
[83] Aube: "L'avenir de la Marine française", p. 191.
[84] Aube: "Défense nationale", pp. 11–12. Translated in Ropp: *The Development of a Modern Navy*, p. 165.
[85] Aube: "Un nouveau droit maritime international", p. 15.
[86] Aube: "Les réformes de notre marine militaire", p. 544; Aube: "Un nouveau droit maritime international", pp. 14–23.

clearer. Aube was himself very explicit in describing the incompatibility between international law and commerce warfare with torpedo boats, and he was equally clear in his recommendations:

> In the days when [...] in theory the laws of war were accepted by even the most rebellious spirits [...] how was maritime war practiced? [...] A captured ship was taken to the nearest port if it was worth it, otherwise the captor took aboard its crew and the prize was sunk. Humanity was saved—and also safe were the laws of war. Tomorrow, war breaks out; an autonomous torpedo boat—two officers, a dozen men—meets one of these liners carrying a cargo richer than that of the richest galleons of Spain and a crew and passengers of many hundreds; will the torpedo boat signify to the captain of the liner that it is there, that it is watching him, that it could sink him, and that consequently it makes him prisoner—him, his crew, his passengers—in a word that he has platonically been made a prize and should proceed to the nearest French port? To this declaration [...] the captain of the liner would respond with a well-aimed shell that would send to the bottom the torpedo boat, its crew, and its chivalrous captain, and tranquilly he would continue on his momentarily interrupted voyage. Therefore the torpedo boat will follow from afar, invisible, the liner it has met; and, once night has fallen, perfectly silently and tranquilly it will send into the abyss liner, cargo, crew, passengers; and his soul not only at rest but fully satisfied, the captain of the torpedo boat will continue his cruise.[87]

Charmes wholeheartedly supported Aube's view that commerce warfare had to be conducted without mercy: "Commerce warfare has its rules that one should have the courage to clearly express: attack the weak without mercy and sail away at full speed from the stronger without shame, that is the formula."[88] Like Aube he argued that the overall aim of this warfare was morally good, and that it therefore legitimised the brutality:

> Although the means to achieve this end are brutal and savage, it is certainly not against the progress of civilised societies that this new power in the hands of the weak one day will ensure the total freedom of the seas, and that it will snatch command from some nations more lucky than others, that it will break the sceptre in their helpless hands and distribute the fragments to everyone. It might be necessary to live through this cruel revolution in order to achieve this new arrangement that one really could regard as a triumph for equality.[89]

---

[87] Aube: "Défense nationale", pp. 11–12. Translated in Ropp: *The Development of a Modern Navy*, p. 165.
[88] Charmes: "La réforme maritime II", p. 141.
[89] Charmes: "La réforme maritime II", p. 142.

Admiral Bourgois' criticism of the *jeune école*'s view on naval warfare and international law had been published in the *Nouvelle revue* in April 1886, a few months after Aube had taken office as Minister of Marine. Aube did not himself answer the criticism raised by Admiral Bourgois, but his aide de camp, Commander Chassériaud, replied under the pseudonym *Un ancien officier de marine* in May 1886 in the *Nouvelle Revue*.[90] Chassériaud had distinguished himself as one of the most enthusiastic supporters of the ideas of Aube and the *jeune école* through articles on naval matters before he was appointed aide de camp for the Minister of Marine,[91] and he produced several memoranda on strategic and tactical questions echoing the ideas of the *jeune école* as aide de camp and as officer of the General Staff during the Ministry of Aube.

Chassériaud had Aube's example of the liner, pursued discretely by a torpedo boat during daytime and then sent into the abyss by a well-aimed torpedo fired from the torpedo boat under the cover of darkness of the night, as the starting point for his reasoning. He pretended to arbitrate between Bourgois and Aube's view on the legality and legitimacy of such an act. Chassériaud's conclusion was, however, unambiguous, as one would expect from a supporter of the *jeune école*:

> Between two solutions so opposite, our choice is not characterised by doubt. Without hesitation, without the slightest remorse, with the conviction of fulfilling a duty, we will sink the enemy. [...] First of all there is

---

[90] André-Henri Chassériaud (*Un ancien officier de marine*): "La torpille et le droit des gens. Réponse à M. le vice-amiral Bourgois" in *Nouvelle Revue* (Paris, Vol. 40, 1886), pp. 474–495. Chassériaud was strongly promoting the *jeune école*'s ideas from the early 1880s until the late 1890s, and it seems that he was appointed aide de camp for Aube because of his *jeune école* sympathies. While in service he used the pseudonym *Un ancien officier de marine* (identified as André-Henri Chassériaud by Ropp: *The Development of a Modern Navy*, p. 418) and did not use his own name until after he had retired. The fact that he signed his articles while he still was in service as "A former officer of the Navy" may be due to the fact that all naval officers, in accordance with a departmental ordinance from 16th December 1852, were obliged to apply to the minister for authorization to publish any article. See BB8-2427: *Le Ministre au Préfet Maritime à Toulon*, 7th July 1871. Chassériaud had promoted ideas that were in strong opposition to the prevailing view among French Ministers of Marine until Aube was appointed Minster of Marine. He may therefore have chosen to use a pseudonym indicating that he was not in service, and thus not obliged to apply for authorization.

The arguments that he forwarded in the article in the *Nouvelle Revue* in May 1886 were very much in accordance with the Minister of Marine's views. His position as aide de camp to the Minister, however, most likely made it inappropriate to sign an article with his name when engaged in polemics with an admiral.

[91] See André-Henri Chassériaud: "Torpilleur et Torpilles" in *Nouvelle Revue* (Paris, 1 January 1885); and André-Henri Chassériaud: "La guerre navale par escadres cuirassées" in *Nouvelle Revue* (Paris, Vol. 33, 1885).

no other position to take. He [the captain of the torpedo boat] is facing an absolute necessity.[92]

Fighting according to international law would be to grant Great Britain permanently an upper hand in naval warfare. France would be forced to avoid battles. Chassériaud described Bourgois' attitude as defeatism, and he brushed aside Bourgois' objections as:

> philanthropy that I don't understand either as a sailor or as a patriot, [this philanthropy] will force us to constantly give in to more or less just English demands. To avoid fighting the British [with all means] will thus allow our maritime population to be quietly crushed with the final certitude of having to submit to the will of Britain.[93]

Discussing the example of the torpedo boat sinking the passenger liner, Chassériaud underlined that it was the enemy that was sunk. He made the point that merchant vessels, certainly steam ships, and their crew represented a military potential that the French Navy could not ignore:

> Sailors of the merchant marine are not wimps, they are patriots [...] the merchant vessel, appearing as an innocent victim is not simply private property; it is a war machine manned, not by an inoffensive crew, but by enemies that are or may be organised and militarily led.[94]

Chassériaud built up an argument depicting the merchant vessels as potential naval assets and claiming that the mere fact of this potential legitimised attacks on these civilian vessels. He insisted that all steam ships had the potential of being part of the enemy's military effort, and he stressed that the large passenger liners with their high speed could be transformed into cruisers by arming them with revolving cannon or medium calibre artillery, and equipping them with launching tubes for torpedoes. These ships would be a valuable reinforcement to the naval fleet and he asked rhetorically "if one is hit by a torpedo before it is transformed, will it then be private property that is hit or a naval vessel not yet completed?"[95] Chassériaud also argued that slower merchant vessels could be used for naval purposes. Any steam vessel could be converted to a torpedo boat, he claimed. Chassériaud argued that if preparations were made in advance, it would not require much

---

[92] Chassériaud: "La torpille et le droit des gens", p. 478.
[93] *Ibid.*, p. 482.
[94] *Ibid.*, p. 478.
[95] *Ibid.*, p. 480.

time to arm these vessels and form a naval auxiliary fleet. The British Admiralty did in fact, starting with the 1887–88 estimates, subsidise a large number of fast ocean steamers for use as auxiliary cruisers in wartime. A light armament was to be stored for each of these ships. In addition, armaments should be prepared for a very large number of non-subsidised merchant ships in war.[96]

Chassériaud had with his reasoning erased the distinction between combatants and non-combatants at sea. Torpedo attacks on merchant vessels were not only legitimate as part of an inferior power's strategy to avoid certain defeat in an uneven battle against a superior navy if both stuck to battle fleet warfare. It was measure to prevent a fleet of converted merchant ships from "attacking and burning our ports after our naval fleet has failed", Chassériaud claimed.[97]

Chassériaud's logic on the legitimacy of preventive attacks could of course be extended beyond the question of vessels with the potential to be converted into naval auxiliary ships. A lot of civilian assets, including people, could be converted into a military effort. Chassériaud's logic seems not to have provoked any further discussions in the various French magazines where naval matters tended to be debated. These matters were, however, discussed in lectures in international and maritime law when the staff college was established ten years later.[98]

Chassériaud argued that the brutal truths about modern warfare at sea should be obvious for any one working or travelling by sea. The belligerent parties could thus not be held responsible either for the lives of passengers travelling aboard a liner from one of the belligerent nations or for neutral shipping that did not take adequate precautions. Chassériaud claimed that passengers should choose to travel aboard a neutral liner, and if they "insisted on travelling aboard a ship from their own nation, they would themselves be responsible for their fate."[99] He affirmed that neutral shipping would be respected, but as he had done concerning civilian passengers, he placed the responsibility for avoiding attacks on the neutrals. They should take all necessary precautions and "scrupulously see to that they did not provide any cause for mistake."[100]

---

[96] Arthur J. Marder: *The Anatomy of British Sea Power. A History of British Naval Policy in the Pre-Dreadnought Era, 1880–1905* (New York, 1940), pp. 102–103.
[97] Chassériaud: "La torpille et le droit des gens", p. 480.
[98] See *sous-commissaire* Brière's reasoning on p. 144.
[99] Chassériaud: "La torpille et le droit des gens", p. 479.
[100] *Ibid.*, p. 487.

He suggested that neutral vessels should sail in convoys escorted by neutral warships through the English Channel in an Anglo-French war. Chassériaud detailed a system by means of which neutral merchant ships should be assembled at predetermined ports, and a commission of consuls should inspect and guarantee that the ships did not carry contraband of war.

Chassériaud thus put forward a two-fold argument trying to evade some of the criticism against the *jeune école* for ignoring international law. First, he erased the distinction between combatant and non-combatant maritime activity by belligerent nations. Secondly, he insisted that it was the passengers' and neutral ships' own responsibility to take the necessary measures in order to avoid being sunk. In this way Chassériaud provided a kind of legitimacy to commercial warfare with torpedoes. Any casualties suffered by passenger or neutral shipping could be excused as collateral damage. Despite Chassériaud's effort to construct an elaborate argument in order to fend off the accusations that the *jeune école*'s formula for commercial warfare was a striking breach on international law, he concluded as Aube and Charmes had done:

> In war, there has never been and will never be either international law or conventions, there is nothing but force. [...] War is the opposite of philanthropy and humanity! It is by preparing for and conducting war according to this principle that we will make it quick and less murderous.[101]

Underlying this total rejection of international law in wartime was the assumption that war was an existential fight between the belligerents. Aube and Charmes had both depicted a scenario in which what was perceived as a threat against a nation or a people's existence justified and legitimised indiscriminate and very brutal commerce raiding as a way of waging war. This assumption was strongly criticised by Admiral Bourgois. Not only did he strongly disagree with the moral basis of the reasoning of the *jeune école*, but he also questioned their underlying strategic analysis. He did not question the assumption that Great Britain was a rival of France, but he stressed that a war with Great Britain would be exclusively a maritime war. Consequently, the existence of the nation would not be at stake, Bourgois argued. Nothing would then excuse a war conducted by merciless means. Bourgois claimed that Germany was the only nation that could represent an existential

---

[101] *Ibid.*, pp. 494–495.

threat to France, and he pointed to the fact that the commerce warfare against the North German Federation during the war in 1870–71 had had no impact on the German offensive into the heart of France or the overall war.[102]

Neither Aube nor Charmes explicitly addressed the alleged lack of logic it represented to portray Great Britain as the potential enemy that had to be met with measures which contravened international law whereas it was Germany that was the only obvious possible enemy that could pose an existential threat to France, and thus legitimise the use of such measures. The main reason for this is most certainly that they perceived Great Britain as an existential threat, and this was due to the rather broad definition they gave of the concept of existential threat. It was not restricted to a threat of a possible occupation of France. A threat to the economic wealth of France fell well within their definition of an existential threat. They postulated that economic prosperity was the blood of the nation, and the sea-lanes or trade routes were the veins. Any threat against the sea-lanes would thus be a threat against the nation, and they were convinced that the Royal Navy would be used to interrupt French trade.

Limited War or Total War—Impacts on Military Thinking

One of the fundamental points in the thinking of the *jeune école* was that war was an existential threat that relieved the belligerents from all restraints imposed by international law. The *jeune école*'s arguments in favour of an unrestricted *guerre de course* have led some historians and officers to label Aube and his followers as advocates of total war. Rémi Monaque, for example, summarized as one of the fundamental ideas of Aube that: "Future conflicts will be total wars in which economic factors will play a dominant role."[103] Philip Masson discussed the *jeune école*'s ideas of commercial warfare under the title: *L'idée de la guerre totale*.[104] These authors have, however, limited themselves to stating that Aube's idea of commercial warfare resembles the concept of total war.

---

[102] Bourgois: *Les torpilleurs, la guerre navale et la défense des côtes*, pp. 20–21.

[103] Rémi Monaque: "L'amiral Aube, ses idées, son action", in Hervé Coutau-Bégarie: *L'évolution de la pensée navale IV* (Paris, 1994), p. 140.

[104] Philippe Masson: "La marine française de 1871 à 1914", in André Corvisier *Histoire militiare de la France*, Vol. 3, *De 1871 à 1940*, ed. by Guy Pedroncini (Paris, 1992), pp. 129–30.

Although they have not defined what they mean by total war, using this concept to describe the strategy of the *jeune école* is obviously founded on the *jeune école*'s proposal to wage unlimited economic warfare, without pity, against the enemy, and in a manner where the distinction between combatants and non-combatants is consciously ignored.

Total war is a twentieth century term. Like many parts of everyday vocabulary, total war has been given several more or less precise definitions. It was first coined by French civilian leaders, when, during the late phase of World War I, they used the terms *guerre intégrale* and *guerre totale* in announcing their ambitions to mobilize all the country's resources.[105] The pioneering Italian advocate of air power, Giulio Douhet, further elaborated the term in 1921 when he wrote:

> The prevailing forms of social organization have given war a character of national totality—that is, the entire population and all the resources of a nation are sucked into the maw of war. And, since society is now definitely evolving along this line, it is within the power of human foresight to see now that future wars will be total in character and scope.[106]

Such ideas were common among military thinkers in the 1920s who had witnessed the appalling slaughter on the Western Front in World War I, and who imagined how much better it would be to bypass stalemated trenches and attack the enemy's industries and centres of population remote from their armies.

General Erich Ludendorff, in his book *Der totale Krieg*, published in Munich in 1935, was perhaps among the first to attempt a systematic definition. To him, total war meant total mobilisation of all material resources for the purpose of fighting a war for the survival of a nation. But it also encompassed complete control by a (military) government over every aspect of social, political, and economic life. Such a centralized system was to prepare the nation single-mindedly for the ultimate war well before its outbreak.[107]

---

[105] Roger Chickering: "Are We There Yet? World War II and the Theory of Total War." Paper presented at the International Conference at Hamburg, August 29–September 1, 2001: *A World at Total War. Global Conflict and the Politics of Destruction, 1937–1945*.

[106] Mark E. Neely Jr.: "Was the Civil War a Total War?", in Stig Förster and Jörg Nagler: *On the Road to Total War. The American Civil War and the German Wars of Unification 1861–1871* (Washington, 1997), pp. 33–34.

[107] Förster and Nagler: Editors' introduction to *On the Road to Total War*, p. 10.

Full economic and political mobilization of a society, and waging unlimited war on the economic resources of the enemy rather than on its armed forces alone, are central elements in any definition of total war.[108] Both the total mobilization and economic warfare against the enemy blurs the distinctions between combatants and non-combatant. The *New Oxford Dictionary of English* and Luttwak and Koehl, in their *The Dictionary of Modern War*, stress that total war implies the use of all available resources and weapons in war, and the elimination of all distinction between military and civilian targets.[109] James Turner Johnson in his attempt to define total war claims that:

> there must be disregard of restraints imposed by customs, law and morality on the prosecution of the war. Especially [...] total war bears hardest on non-combatants, whose traditional protection from harm according to the traditions of just and limited warfare appears to evaporate here.[110]

In an article summing up some of the deliberations made at a series of five conferences on the topic of total war at which some of the most prominent scholars in the field were gathered, Robert Chickering mentioned as general ingredients in total war the commitment of massive armed forces to battle, the thoroughgoing mobilisation of industrial economies in the war effort, and hence the disciplined organisation of civilians no less than warriors. He also noted that several of the contributors underlined as one of the most characteristic features of total war the systematic erasure of basic distinctions between soldiers and civilians: "Because civilians, regardless of gender, are no less significant to the war effort than the soldiers, they themselves become legitimate if not preferred targets of military violence."[111]

Total war is one extreme in military thinking and conduct. On the same axis, but at the other extreme, we find cabinet war or limited war. Although the terminology is not clear, the concepts of cabinet war and total war are fruitful in describing the influences on the thinking of the *jeune école* and its contemporary opponents, as well as for understanding

---

[108] See the discussion of the term "Total war" in Neely Jr.: "Was the Civil War a Total War?", p. 35.
[109] *The New Oxford Dictionary of English* (Oxford, 1998), p. 1958; Edward Luttwak and Stuart L. Koehl: *The Dictionary of Modern War* (New York, 1991), p. 625.
[110] James Turner Johnson: *Just War Traditions and the Restraint of War. A Moral and Historical Inquiry* (Princeton, N.J., 1981), p. 229.
[111] Chickering: "Are We There Yet?"

the significance of the theoretical contributions of the *jeune école*. The concepts of cabinet war or total war are what the sociologist Max Weber called an "ideal type"—a theoretical model used to measure a reality that never fully conforms to it but that nevertheless remains a useful tool for analysing reality.

There is an impression that the movement along the axis from cabinet war to total war has occurred in a chronological manner. Cabinet war was typical of the wars of the eighteenth century, whereas the examples closest to the "ideal type" of total war are found in the twentieth century. The transition from cabinet war to total war has, however, neither been sudden nor consistent. While we in the twentieth century have seen the two wars closest to the "ideal type" of total war, i.e. the two world wars, the same century also saw numerous limited wars. Several wars in the nineteenth century contained elements of total war. Historians, who tried to come to terms with the modern aspects of the American Civil War and the German Wars of Unification, two wars that both influenced the thinking of the *jeune école*, have used labels like *people's war, industrialized war, citizen's war, total war,* or simply, *modern war* to describe them.[112]

From Cabinet War to the Wars of the French Revolution and the Napoleonic Wars

Historians who have tried to sum up the characteristics of cabinet war emphasise that the political objectives the war should achieve were limited.[113] War was conducted in order to gain control of a province of a neighbouring state, a colony from a commercial rival or to confirm the rules of succession of a dynasty. Seldom were eighteenth century wars in Europe conducted with the aim of crushing another state or to present it with peace terms that would be totally unacceptable.[114] After the war was lost, a province could be transferred to the conqueror without asking the inhabitants or any other public for their view. Neither parliamentarians (where they existed) nor the press (where it existed) had any strong opinions concerning foreign policy. Later conceptions that states with the same political or social structure, or nations with

---

[112] Förster and Nagler: Editors' introduction to *On the Road to Total War*, p. 8.
[113] I am greatly indebted to Rolf Hobson's exposition of the characteristics of the 18th century cabinet warfare in Rolf Hobson: "Fra kabinettkrigen til den totale krigen"; The same goes for Michael Howard: *War in European History*, pp. 54–116.
[114] The division of Poland was an exception.

related ethnic or cultural backgrounds should be natural allies, were almost totally absent. Alliances were made and dissolved without the subjects being consulted.

The cabinets, which were for the most part constituted by the monarch and his advisors, could govern without taking into consideration other factors than their own self-defined *raison d'état*. Another important factor limiting the war was the fact that the military capacity was not sufficient to subjugate another state to one's will. The armies of the old regime were constituted by officers from the aristocracy and long-serving professional soldiers, of whom a high percentage were foreigners. In the Prussian army, which had a well-organised system for compulsory recruitment of peasants for military service, at least one-third of the force was recruited from abroad. Fredrick the Great argued that the army should ideally be made up of two-thirds foreign professional soldiers. It was only in France and England that there was a mainly nationally based army. The French army recruited mostly volunteers from within its own borders.[115]

The armies of eighteenth century Europe spent most of the time in the profoundest peace. Even during wartime they campaigned for only four or five months of the year. On the Continent commerce, travel, cultural and learned intercourse went on in wartime almost unhindered. The wars were the king's wars. As Michael Howard notes:

> The rôle of the good citizen was to pay his taxes, and sound political economy dictated that he should be left alone to make the money out of which to pay those taxes. He was required neither to participate in making the decisions out of which wars arose nor to take part in them once they broke out. These matters were the concern of the sovereign alone. Their mutual relations were conducted by a precise diplomatic protocol according to clear principles in international law.[116]

In the last decade of the eighteenth century the framework of European society—social, economic, political, and militar—was shaken to its foundations. Twenty-five years of almost uninterrupted warfare, from 1792 until 1815, between revolutionary France and her neighbours contributed to the transformation of European society. The Wars of the French Revolution are generally considered by historians to indicate the end of the limited dynastic wars of the kings and the beginning of

---

[115] Hobson: "Fra kabinettkrigen til den totale krigen", pp. 29–31.
[116] Howard: *War in European History*, p. 75.

the wars of the nations.[117] The introduction of *la levée en masse* in august 1793 removed one of the most important limiting factors of the old regimes warfare. While the monarchies of the old regime depended on professional soldiers who placed a heavy charge on the monarchs' treasuries, the new French regime decided that all Frenchmen could be called out to serve in the military. By 1793, when the supply of volunteers had run out, the Law of August 23rd decreed that "From this day until that when our enemies have been chased off the territories of the Republic, all Frenchmen are on permanent requisition for military service".[118] An almost unlimited numbers of reserves were thus at the French army's disposal. The French revolutionary army succeeded in clearing foreign troops off French territory within twelve months. Conscripts continued to be enlisted with increasing ruthlessness for another twenty years. Lazare Carnot, the organizer of the French revolutionary armies, had by the end of 1794 succeeded in mobilising over a million men under arms. He used this enormous number of soldiers to obtain a crushing numerical superiority on every battlefield. The fierce aggressiveness and violence in war, which had almost been lost sight of in the eighteenth century, now became dominant. "War is a violent condition", wrote Carnot; "one should make it *à outrance* or go home. We must exterminate, exterminate to the bitter end!", he urged.[119]

Although the Wars of the French Revolution are generally viewed as an indication of the end of limited wars, Gunther Rothenberg shows that the behaviour of the revolutionary and Napoleonic troops did not differ very much from that of the old regime's soldiers. He argues that both the rather idyllic picture of the moderate and humane nature of eighteenth century warfare and the views that popular participation in the revolutionary and Napoleonic armies led to unrestrained violence and disregard of international law are both exaggerated. Carnot and the radical regime's call for war *à outrance* did certainly remove restraints on the way war was waged. In September 1793 and May 1794 the Convention prohibited freeing prisoners in return for payment of money and ordered that all émigré prisoners, and later British, Hanoverian and

---

[117] Gunther Rothenberg: "The Age of Napoleon" in Howard, Andreopoulos, and Shulman (eds.): *The Laws of War*, p. 86; Michael Howard: "Constraints on Warfare" in *ibid.*, p. 4; Jean-Yves Guiomar: *L'Invention de la guerre totale* (Paris, 2004), pp. 11–229.
[118] Quoted in Howard: *War in European History*, p. 80.
[119] Quoted in *ibid.*, pp. 80–81.

Spanish captives, should be shot as "an example of the vengeance of an outraged nation."[120] Most commanders and troops, however, evaded the order and by 1795 "regulars, and citizen soldiers turned professional regained control and soon returned to the traditional customs and usages between soldiers. Setting the tone, senior officers began to observe the civilities of the Ancien régime."[121]

The most important strategic consequences of the mobilisation of national resources, was that the French generals could force the enemy to fight battles that impacted on the enemy state's destiny. On the tactical level it was now possible to crush the enemy army's morale on the battlefield and follow up with a pursuit designed to complete the destruction of the enemy and the enemy state; a deep penetration to spread panic among the enemy population and destroy all hope of recovery. Such an annihilating battle could dissolve a coalition or put an end to a major power's independence in a day or two. Wars were no longer to be inconclusive.[122]

The view that the Wars of the French Revolution and the Napoleonic Wars marked the end of the era of limited wars is primarily based on the way in which Revolutionary France and the Empire organised its war effort and on how war was waged on land. At sea the Revolutionary and Napoleonic Wars were a combination of fleet warfare and *guerre de course*. To stop seaborne trade became an increasingly dominant aspect of French and British strategy as the war dragged on.

Naval warfare was conducted within a different political framework than warfare on land. The sea could be as important for the non-belligerents as for the belligerents. In land warfare, politics and strategy were focused on the adversarial relationship between the belligerents. In wars between maritime powers, however, the antagonists also had to take account of a third party, the neutral states. As Carl J. Kulsrud has recognised in his study of maritime neutrality: "When the ensuing wars were extended to the sea, they forthwith involved the interests of nations not otherwise entangled in the combat between the belligerents."[123]

---

[120] Quoted in Rothenberg: "The Age of Napoleon", p. 88.
[121] *Ibid.*, p. 89.
[122] Hobson: "Fra kabinettkrigen til den totale krigen", p. 34; Howard: *War in European History*, p. 84.
[123] Carl J. Kulsrud: *Maritime Neutrality to 1780. A History of the Main Principles Governing Neutrality and Belligerency to 1780* (Boston, 1936) p. 107; see also Hobson: *Imperialism at Sea*, p. 73.

The neutrals' willingness and ability to pursue their rights as neutrals thus influenced the belligerents' ability to exert sea power. Maritime law was for centuries the most sophisticated body of law in Europe, and as Rolf Hobson has underlined, "the laws of war at sea were a *reality* in international politics. They had the ultimate sanction of naval force behind them, and they were an expression of the balance of power that existed between belligerents and neutrals at any given time."[124] Maritime law was, however, not very precise and binding bilateral agreements hardly existed. To secure what the neutrals perceived to be their rights, different neutral maritime states on repeated occasions combined in leagues of armed neutrality.[125]

The British victory in 1805 in the Battle of Trafalgar over a combined French and Spanish fleet secured British sea control for the rest of the war and forced Napoleon to give up the combination of fleet warfare and commerce raiding that France had carried on up till then. Napoleon had to restrict his maritime warfare mainly to *guerre de course*. The use of commerce raiding both on the French and the British side during the Wars of the French Revolution and the Napoleonic Wars did not, as we have seen, in itself represent any significant change in methods of sea warfare. What was new was the scale of economic warfare when other European and North American states were dragged into the Anglo-French conflict.

From the beginning of the Revolutionary Wars the French followed a plan for the economic ruin of Great Britain by closing her markets and chasing her trade from the seas. In her effort to strangle the "nation of shopkeepers" France departed from her traditional policy of encouraging neutral powers to combine against British claims of belligerent rights, and instead arrogated to herself extensive belligerent rights in an extreme economic warfare that culminated in Napoleon's continental system.

In Berlin on the 21st November 1806 Napoleon issued a decree that declared an all-out commercial war against Great Britain and anyone assisting her trade. The Berlin Decree stated (1) that the British Islands were placed in a state of blockade, (2) that communication of any kind with them was forbidden, (3) that every British subject found in

---

[124] Hobson: *Imperialism at Sea*, p. 74.
[125] Kulsrud: *Maritime Neutrality*, pp. 295–337; Ole Feldbæk: "Denmark–Norway 1720–1807: Neutral Principles and Practice" in Rolf Hobson and Tom Kristiansen (eds.): *Navies in Northern Waters 1721–2000* (London, 2004), p. 59.

the territories occupied by the troops of France or her allies was to be made a prisoner of war, (4) that all merchandise belonging to British subjects, or coming from British colonies, was to be lawful prize, (5) that all trade in British goods was to be prohibited, (6) that half the proceeds from the sale of such goods confiscated was to go toward the indemnification of merchants whose vessels had been seized by the British, (7) that no vessel coming from Great Britain and the British colonies, or that had landed at a British port, were to be allowed to enter harbours of the French Empire and (8) that vessels entering by means of false declarations were to be confiscated.[126]

The escalation of measures and countermeasures in the bitter Anglo-French conflict, when both claimed extensive belligerent's rights, created conflicts with the neutrals. The campaigns of the French Army and actions by the Royal Navy ensured, however, that the initiatives of Armed Neutrality failed. No European sea power was capable of insisting on neutral rights, squeezed as they were between the Continental hegemonic power and the master of the seas. The European neutrals were forced into one of the opposing camps in the bitter economic struggle between Great Britain and France. Denmark-Norway's attempts to muddle through as neutrals were stopped by the Royal Navy's attack on Copenhagen in 1801 and the seizure of its fleet in 1807, which eventually pushed it into an alliance with France. The United States was the sea power that best managed to defend its rights as neutral, but conflicts over British rights to search American vessels ended in the War of 1812 between the two countries.[127]

Although commercial raiding and blockades were nothing new in maritime warfare, it was conducted on such a scale and intensity during the Wars of the French Revolution and the Napoleonic Wars that it can be said to be one of the elements of these wars that indicated the end of the era of limited wars. W. Allison Phillips and Arthur H. Reede have gone so far as to characterise Napoleon's Berlin decree as "a declaration of war *à outrance* not only against British commerce, but against that of all those who should dare to trade with her or carry on her trade."[128] The commercial warfare of these wars was, however,

---

[126] The text is quoted from W. Allison Phillips and Arthur H. Reede: *Neutrality, Its History, Economics and Law. Volume II. The Napoleonic Period* (1936, New York, 1976), pp. 132–133.
[127] Hobson: *Imperialism at Sea*, p. 78; Phillips and Reede: *Neutrality*, pp. 170–209.
[128] Phillips and Reede: *Neutrality*, p. 132.

conducted in a much more civilised manner than the kind of warfare the *jeune école* advocated more than seventy years later. One obvious reason for this was the system of privateers that were financed by the prizes they brought in to port. Officers and crews of naval ships were also paid with shares of the value of the prize. Sinking or setting fire to the prizes would hence not be very rewarding.

The Wars of the French Revolution and the Napoleonic Wars had shaken the economic and social balance of eighteenth century Europe. After 1814 the principal concern of the governing classes of Europe was to avoid a repetition of the experience that had almost removed them from power. Their primary aim was to restore the balance that had kept Europe in a stable equilibrium. This was viewed as a far more important task than to study the changes in French society that had released so much military power. If military effectiveness on a scale such as the French armies had demonstrated depended on a revolutionary transformation of society, that was a price the monarchs of the Restoration were unwilling to pay. For another half a century, therefore, the European armies returned so far as they could to an eighteenth-century pattern of aristocratic officers and long-serving professional troops who were kept isolated from the rest of society.[129]

Military leaders, however, could not ignore the experiences of the Wars of the French Revolution and the Napoleonic wars. Officers of every rank wrote of their experiences of the wars and which conclusions were to be drawn from them. As Michael Howard has noted, the most respected strategists were those who emphasized the continuity between the old form of war and the new.[130] Carl von Clausewitz was also searching for fundamental strategic principles. His aim was, however, to analyse what was new about the Wars of the French Revolution and the Napoleonic wars compared to the wars of the old regimes. Clausewitz maintained that moral and political factors were important for how war was waged and that it was the change of these factors brought about by the French Revolution that altered the way war was fought and took the armies of the old regime by surprise. Clausewitz concluded that wars conducted with the full force of national energy in pursuit of total victory would always take a different form from those engaged with limited forces for limited objectives, and he asked rhetori-

---

[129] Howard, *War in European History*, p. 94.
[130] *Ibid.*, p. 96.

cally whether from "now on will every war in Europe be waged with the full resources of the state, and therefore have to be fought over major issues that affect the people? Or shall we again see a gradual separation taking place between government and people?" Clausewitz warned that it would be rash to assert that "absolute wars" would never recur "once barriers—which in a sense consists only in a man's ignorance of what is possible—are torn down, they are not so easily set up again. At least when major interests are at stake, mutual hostility will express itself in the same manner as it has in our own day."[131]

The American Civil War and the Franco-Prussian War

The implications of the military revolution remained unexplored for several decades after Waterloo. The conservative regimes of Europe reintroduced professional armies (with the exception of Prussia) and avoided war altogether. The wars that took place in the 1850s, in the Crimea and in northern Italy, were in many respects reminiscent of cabinet wars.

In the maritime theatre, there was gradual restoration of a new maritime balance that culminated with the Declaration of Paris in 1856.

A turning point came in the 1860s as the American Civil War evolved into a kind of conflict exhibiting several aspects of total war. James McPherson notes that what made the Civil War distinctive in the American experience was the large-scale involvement of the whole population, the shocking loss of life and the wholesale devastation and radical social and political transformation that it wrought. The war accomplished the extinction of a state—the Confederacy. It also extinguished a social system and a distinct set of property relations—slavery. McPherson concludes that few other wars in history have achieved such total results.[132]

---

[131] Michael Howard and Peter Paret (eds.): Clausewitz: *On War* (1976, Princeton, NJ, 1984), (Book 8, ch. 3), p. 593.

[132] James M. McPherson: "From Limited War to Total War in America", in Stig Förster and Jörg Nagler (eds.): *On the Road to Total War*, p. 298. Mark E. Neely has disputed the assumption that the Civil War was a total war. He claims that the essential aspect of any definition of total war asserts that it breaks down the distinction between soldiers and civilians, combatants and non-combatants. Neely claims that the Civil War "knew careful limitations and conscientious scruple." He concludes by stating that "Any assessment of the Civil War's nearness to being a total war can be no more than that: an assertion that it approached total war in some ways", but "By no definition of the term can it be said to *be* a total war". Mark E. Neely Jr.: "Was

In the Franco-Prussian war Bismarck was set against imposing any political or social change on France. German victory did not impose a regime on the French. Here, German aims fell far short of total war.[133] Yet the Germans fought a war exploiting a basic feature of total war, politically motivated attacks on civilians. This was done in three different ways, by executing franc-tireurs, by bombardment and by blockade. The bombardment of Paris was the most spectacular German reprisal against civilian involvement in the war, and as Robert Tombs has noted, the civilians were not targeted because they were franc-tireurs, but because they were citizens demanding *la guerre à outrance*. The operations had no other aim than to intimidate the citizens of Paris into political surrender. But as Tombs observes, although the bombardment was the most spectacular and controversial aspect of the German attack on Paris, it was the blockade that really counted. Food and fuel shortages greatly increased the death rate, especially among the very young and the old. Nearly 42,000 more people died during the siege than in the corresponding months of 1869–70. The message to the Parisians was obvious. Famine would be the consequence of intransigence. The imminent exhaustion of food stocks was what forced Paris to surrender at the end of January.[134]

Stig Förster and Jörg Nagler have summarised some aspects common to both the American Civil War and the Franco-Prussian War that illustrate the evolution of these wars from limited conflicts into wars of a more total character. They argue that both wars started as limited conflicts with limited aims: the prevention or fulfilment of German unification and the break-up or preservation of the United States. As the war progressed, the aims of the stronger sides became more radical: annexation, if not the total subjugation, of France and the destruction as well as the revolutionizing of the South. The citizens participated in both wars, not only as soldiers. They had actively argued for the wars, and as the wars continued they became the backbone of warfare

---

the Civil War a Total War?" in Stig Förster and Jörg Nagler (eds.), *On the Road to Total War*, p. 35. Neely's arguments are valid, but even if the distinction between the combatants and the non-combatants were upheld in the Civil War, it had so many aspects of total war to it, as Neely also implicitly admits in the sentences quoted above, that the term remains useful for understanding the American Civil War, and its influence on the thinking of the *jeune école*.

[133] Robert Tombs: "The Wars against Paris", in Förster and Nagler (eds.), *On the Road to Total War*, p. 563.

[134] *Ibid.*, pp. 546–550.

as both men and women worked to supply the armies and as morale depended on public support. The public were not only crucial for the war effort. They became themselves targets for military aggression as the examples of Sherman's march through Georgia and South Carolina, and the shelling of Strasbourg and Paris demonstrated.[135]

As Clausewitz pointed out; for military thinkers and strategists from the Napoleonic wars and later the possibility that a war could develop into a war with a more total character than previous wars must have been present in their minds. The American Civil War and the Franco-Prussian War were reminders that limited wars could evolve into more total wars. For the strategists of the 1870s and 80s, these two were the most recent wars, and the most prominent representative of the *jeune école*, Aube, had himself actively participated in the Franco-Prussian War. These wars very much constituted a frame of reference for the *jeune école*. Making war on the economic resources of the enemy rather than on its armed forces alone, warfare carried straight to the enemy people so they would loose their zest for war, were the lessons learned from these two wars. In an article written shortly after the end of the Franco-Prussian war, in 1871, Aube discussed the impact this war had on the French perception of laws of war and how war should be waged:

> *the laws of war* [...] as long as war will weigh upon humanity, this phrase will be nothing but vain words, a fraught expression, an ideal that may be impossible to reach. The Germans have shown us the reality of these laws. The mistake made by us, a generous mistake that is, has been to believe in these laws, to obey the obligations they imposed on us, failing to understand what war is, and when faced with war, as a logical consequence all considerations concerning justice, humanity and civilisation fall, since war is, as our enemies have convincingly demonstrated to us, the absolute negation of justice, humanity and civilisation. [...] *Guerre de course*,—is a warfare where the property of the enemy, be it public or private should be annihilated by all possible means, warships or merchant vessels should be set afire and the sailors manning them made prisoners for the rest of the war. This should be done routinely, systematically, with a methodical precision, just like the German generals requisitioned, looted, devastated and exhausted our cities and the countryside. Eight months ago, experience tells us, every Frenchman would have protested against such a way of waging war; but today who would deny the adequacy of this kind of warfare? Moreover, this kind of warfare is the one best adapted to the

---

[135] Förster and Nagler (eds.): *On the Road to Total War*, pp. 2–3.

conditions of modern societies; it attacks the private property, the very foundations of those who wanted or provoked the hostilities. Finally, this warfare is imposed by the logics of history and of reality as well.[136]

Later, Aube stressed that bombarding, burning down and ruining cities had been done and would be done in future wars. Strasbourg and Péronne were the proofs, he wrote.[137] Charmes also referred to the Franco-Prussian War when he argued in favour of bombarding cities:

> one should throw trouble and disarray into the city by bombarding from afar arsenals, warehouses and residential areas, following the example of the Prussians, who fired over the fortifications, and into Strasbourg and Paris, convinced that in a war one should always hit the weak points.[138]

These experiences had formed the thinking of the *jeune école* on what future wars would be like.

Some of the rethinking of what future wars would be like could also be seen within the German officer corps, and the German deliberations were followed with great attention by the *jeune école*. German officers in the aftermath of the Franco-Prussian War started to reconsider the Prussian industrialised cabinet war that had resulted in such shining victories on the battlefield and that had proved sufficient to decide the outcome of wars until the French *levée en masse* in 1871. The experience of the second half of the Franco-Prussian War had demonstrated to German officers that it was no longer sufficient to smash the enemy's field army. In the age of people's war, they would have to deal with whole nations that were ready to fight to the last. In his influential book *Das Volk in Waffen*, Helmuth von Moltke's disciple, Colmar von der Goltz, argued that limited war had become impossible. In the age of a people's war whole nations would fight to the very end, mobilising all their resources. The outcome would be decided by sheer exhaustion.[139]

---

[136] Th Aube (Un officier de marine): "Les réformes de notre marine militaire" in *Revue des deux mondes* (Paris, April 1871), p. 544. The article is signed "Un officier de marine". Aube referred to this article in "De la guerre maritime" (April 1873), although he did not explicitly state that he wrote the article. The article of April 1871 has however a clear touch of Aube in opinions, way of reasoning, and many of the arguments are identical with those put forward in his later writings.

[137] Aube: "La guerre maritime et les ports militaires", pp. 331–332.

[138] Charmes: "La réforme de la Marine II", p. 161.

[139] Stig Förster: "Dreams and Nightmares. German Military Leadership and the Images of Future Warfare, 1871–1914" in Manfred F. Boemeke, Roger Chickering

In his introduction to Aube's book *A terre et à bord—Notes d'un marin*, Charmes chose to quote the following passage from what he referred to as "the admirable book" by Goltz: "The principle according to which one "conducts war these days" ignores if necessary all the ideas of law that prevail in times of peace."[140] Charmes described Aube's book as the counterpart to the work of Goltz. He found that they were both filled with the same uncompromising love of one's country, disdain of popular criticism and audacity in proclaiming the truth.[141] Aube, in an article in 1885, also referred to the "admirable book" by Goltz and boasted that the *jeune école* had pointed out well before Goltz that war was an existential struggle where everything was permitted and legitimate against the enemy.[142]

The perception of the character of future war can to a certain degree explain the different approaches concerning strategy and the composition of the fleet between the traditionalists and the *jeune école*. Admiral Bourgois very clearly advocated the restraints inherent in Cabinet war. He warned that brutal commerce raiding would give an enemy invading French territory a pretext for the abuse of force, and he claimed that the law of reprisals is the only one that subsists when human rights are violated. Bourgois also reminded his readers that in a continental war, the winner of today could be tomorrow's looser, and experience unjust violence on his territory corresponding to the one he carried out on the enemy's territory. He stressed that the warring parties should fight with such moral restraints so that after the fighting was over they could shake hands without any bitterness or hatred.[143] Such an attitude would obviously be more consistent with a traditional navy composed of battleships preparing to fight regular battles between naval units, than with torpedo boats attacking defenceless merchantmen or gunboats bombarding prosperous cities.

---

and Stig Förster, *Anticipating Total War. The German and American Experiences 1871–1914* (Cambridge, 1999), pp. 348–356.

[140] Gabriel Charmes: "Préface" in Aube: "La pénétration dans l'Afrique centrale", p. XIII.

[141] Colmar von der Goltz's book *Das Volk in Waffen* was translated to French and published in 1884 with the title *La nation armée*.

[142] Aube: "Défense nationale—Défense des colonies", p. 11.

[143] Bourgois: *Les torpilleurs, la guerre navale et la défense des côtes*, pp. 20–23.

Summary

In the strategic assessments of the *jeune école*, Great Britain emerged as the main rival. This was due both to the traditional rivalry between the two countries, but also to the colonial ambition that the *jeune école* advocated, an ambition they maintained would further intensify the rivalry between France and Great Britain. The defeat in the Franco-Prussian war had, however, forced France to dramatically reduce its naval ambitions, and to accept that the French Navy would for the foreseeable future remain inferior to the Royal Navy. This situation provoked the *jeune école* to develop a naval theory that was a novel and audacious attempt to solve the historic problem of how best to use a self-evidently inferior navy against a predominant maritime power.

The proposals that broke most radically with the prevailing naval thoughts were the *jeune école*'s ideas of offensive warfare. The *jeune école* proposed an asymmetric approach where one instead of challenging a superior Royal Navy on its own terms, should attack the foundations of British prosperity. They argued that Britain's sea lines of communication were the weak link in an industrialised economy that depended on a well functioning trade with its colonies. Aggressive commercial warfare against British trade routes would therefore be the most effective way to bring about a social collapse in Great Britain.

The *jeune école* saw *guerre de course* as the natural continuation of a proud French traditional way of waging war at sea. While French commerce raiding from the days of Louis XIV to Napoleon had been conducted by a combination of public and private ships employed to ruin the enemy's trade, the *jeune école* argued that commerce raiding should be a corner stone in French naval strategy and thus decide the French Navy's order of battle and how the Navy should be organised. The advent of the self-propelled torpedo and an optimistic view of the seaworthiness of small and cheap torpedo boats and gunboats convinced the proponents of the *jeune école* that commerce raiding would be the most economical form of warfare for the inferior fleet. These low cost boats could be used for defensive purposes and to break possible enemy blockades, but they could also be used to attack enemy trade on the high seas or to bombard open cities and ports.

Unlimited economical warfare, as advocated by the *jeune école*, conducted without pity and in a manner where the distinction between combatants and non-combatants would be consciously ignored, would be a striking breach of international maritime law. The *jeune école*'s view of the character of future wars can probably best explain their rejection of international law in wartime. After the Napoleonic wars there existed two fundamentally different perceptions of what form future wars would take. Whereas earlier wars had been limited wars, the Wars of the French Revolution and the Napoleonic Wars were conducted with the full force of national energy in pursuit of total victory. Limited wars were however still to be the dominant type of war in the nineteenth century, but both the American Civil War and the Franco-Prussian war featured elements of total war. These two wars strongly influenced the thinking of the *jeune école* and functioned very much as a frame of reference when they described the probable nature of future wars. They argued that future wars would be existential wars, where "everything is [...] not only permissible but legitimate against the enemy."[144] The *jeune école*'s rejection of international law in wartime was also influenced by the view that existing international maritime law, represented by the Declaration of Paris of 1856, had frozen the imbalance between the strong and the weak. It had made *guerre de course*, which they saw as France's most effective way to fight Britain, almost impossible to conduct, while the restraints the Declaration of Paris had placed on the blockade, a preferred Royal Navy way of fighting, had no consequences since blockade had anyway become illusory due to the advent of steam and the self-propelled torpedo.

It is often assumed that the *jeune école*'s thinking was primarily a result of or an adaptation to technological inventions. It would seem more correct to state that steam and the self-propelled torpedo fitted into an overall theory on how an inferior navy could fight its enemy and a perception that future wars would be more total in character and scope. The reasoning of the *jeune école* had as its logical consequence what the Council of Admiralty in one of their meetings labelled *guerre de course à outrance*.[145]

---

[144] Aube: "Défense nationale—Défense des colonies", p. 11.
[145] SHM, BB8-914: Conseil d'Amirauté: *Procès-verbal de la séance du 21 Mai 1886*.

CHAPTER TWO

THE *JEUNE ÉCOLE* IN OFFICE

Aube was appointed Minister of Marine in a coalition government of opportunists and radicals, headed by the opportunist Charles Louis de Saulces de Freycinet, which took office on 7 January 1886.[1] The radical René Goblet replaced Freycinet as head of the cabinet on 11 December 1886. Aube stayed in office as Minister of Marine until the Goblet cabinet was replaced on 30 May 1887. Aube's period in office was marked by his determination to impose both the strategic views of the *jeune école* and what he saw as necessary changes in tactics and the composition of the fleet. This effort by Aube, and the reactions from the French naval establishment, can be illustrated by the discussions which took place within and between the Ministry of Marine, the Council of Admiralty and the senior officers in the Mediterranean Fleet, by manoeuvres planned and conducted, and by reforms and construction programmes initiated and adopted.

Predictably Aube stopped the construction of the four battleships of the *Hoche* and *Magenta* class that were begun in 1880. Aube concentrated on cheaper vessels, and forwarded a construction program that included six large and ten small cruisers, twenty large torpedo boats for use against other torpedo boats, fifty gunboats (*bateaux-canons*), one hundred regular torpedo boats, and three armoured coastal defence ships for use as torpedo mother ships. His program went through various "amputations at the hands of the Budget Committee and Aube's successors",[2] but it definitely made its mark on the French order of battle in the years to come.

Strategic Assessment

French foreign policy during Aube's period in office was characterised by a double threat assessment. Germany had been a central problem

---

[1] The 1885 elections had created a Parliament loosely divided into three groupings: conservatives, opportunists (moderate republicans) and radicals.
[2] Ropp: *The Development of a Modern Navy*, p. 172.

of French foreign relations from the late 1860s. It was almost universally accepted that French security required her to fortify the frontier and strengthen the army to try to match the military strength of Germany. Yet the superiority of German military power was more or less accepted, and there was a persistent desire to reduce tension with Germany. Elements of revanchism in French society were present in the decades after France's disastrous defeat in the Franco-Prussian war. This revanchism had its heyday during Aube's period in office, and was vociferously represented by the Minister of War, General Georges Boulanger. He soon became very popular. This was above all due to his defiant attitude towards Germany. Ever since 1871, there had been a distressing fear that Germany might provoke another war before France could regain her military strength. Early in 1887 two crises blew up between Germany and France, and Boulanger played a major role in both. First Bismarck referred to Boulanger's rhetoric and claimed this represented a threat to Germany. Bismarck backed up his statement with an alarmist press campaign. Then in April 1887, a French police officer on frontier duty that included espionage was lured across the border and arrested. Again, Boulanger urged a vigorous response, suggesting a movement of troops and calling up reserves, but he was restrained by his colleagues. When the Germans released the French police officer, the patriotic press lauded Boulanger as the hero who had frightened off Bismarck. Many politicians were, however, scared by the behaviour of the jingoistic general which generated dreadful memories of the *coup d'état* of 1851 and the war of 1870. They forced the government to resign in May 1887.[3]

The tense situation between France and Germany was clearly reflected in the strategic thinking of French naval flag officers and in the General Staff of the Ministry of Marine. In a letter in 1887 to the Minister of Marine, Vice Admiral and later Minister of Marine, Constant-Louis-Jean-Benjamin Jaurés, stated that he saw war against Germany as inevitable, and that the French Navy should be prepared for a two-front war.[4] The assumption of a two-front war, an assumption that was reflected in all strategic thinking in the Ministry of Marine and

---

[3] Pierre Miguel: *La troisième république* (Paris, 1989), pp. 7–12, 320–323; Robert Tombs: *France 1814–1914* (Harlow, England, 1996), pp. 447–449, 473–475. Jean Garrigues: *Le général Boulanger* (Paris, 1999), pp. 75–85.
[4] BB4-1452: Memorandum to the Minister of Marine from Vice Admiral and senator Constant-Louis-Jean-Benjamin Jaurés, 1887.

the Council of Admiralty concerning a war with Germany, was based on the fact that the Triple Alliance, which consisted of Germany, Austria and Italy, had been formed in 1882. For the Navy this meant that in a war against Germany they would most likely have to face the German Navy in the Channel and the Italian Navy in the Mediterranean.

After the Franco-Prussian war, interest in colonial affairs had slowly begun to revive, and a new colonial race among the European powers started after the Congress of Berlin in 1878. French colonial expeditions in the first part of the 1880s once again set Britain and France in competition and conflict with each other. Britain for some years equalled or replaced Germany as France's number one rival. A maritime war against Great Britain was also thought of as a two-front war. The Channel and France's Atlantic coast were considered as being virtually British home waters where the Royal Navy would be able to put considerable pressure on France. The Royal Navy could also pose a substantial challenge to the French in the Mediterranean. This sea was strategically important to Great Britain, and she had naval bases and a considerable naval presence there. But a maritime war against Britain would not be restricted to the Channel and the Mediterranean. It would be a war on all oceans. As we have seen, this would be a consequence of both the strategy that the *jeune école* advocated, and of the Royal Navy's worldwide presence.

A war against either the Triple Alliance or Great Britain opened up different military contingencies and thus demanded different plans and compositions of the fleet. This became evident in the discussions among the leaders of the French Navy. The opinions of leading French naval officers are found in the minutes from the meetings of the Council of Admiralty and the Ministry of Marine's minutes from the discussions concerning exercise planning and debriefing.

The Council of Admiralty was consulted more often on fundamental questions concerning strategy and force structure than had been the case under previous Ministers of Marine. Whereas the Council of Admiralty had only once been conferred with on fundamental issues in the period 1880 to 1885,[5] Aube invited it to discuss matters of profound importance three times during his period in office. The discussions in the Council of Admiralty revealed differences between the admirals and the Ministry

---

[5] Vice Admiral Philippe Ausseur: "La *jeune école*" in *Marine & Technique au XIXe siècle* (Paris, 1987), p. 464.

of Marine with regard to strategic assessment and the composition of the fleet. But what is most striking about the discussions is how the Council of Admiralty had adopted key tenets of Aube's analysis and his visions concerning how warfare against Great Britain should be conducted most effectively. This is evident from reports prepared for the Council of Admiralty by commissions constituted among its members and the subsequent debates held in the Council of Admiralty in May 1886 and in January 1887.

Shortly after Aube had entered office, the Council of Admiralty in a meeting in May 1886 argued for a type of warfare against Great Britain that resembled the reasoning he had followed since the early 1870s:

> If the enemy is England there is no doubt of the objective: Try to ruin her trade, to harass the weak points of her *territoire maritime* and by surprise actions put pressure on some of her important colonies in order to separate them from England. The maritime stake is immensely greater for England than for us. The blows that England can direct at our colonies or our trade are immeasurably less important than the other way round. The role of our cruisers will therefore be: Harass the enemy by all means, hunt *à outrance* her merchant ships, fall upon them like a bird of prey [...][6]

In its meeting in January 1887 the Council of Admiralty elaborated the background to this reasoning. The members agreed that France would have no possibility of equalling British naval forces. Britain was determined to exercise command of the sea at any cost. Whatever effort France made to catch up with the quality and number of vessels of the Royal Navy, Britain would increase her effort and France would consequently lag behind. But in line with Aube's views and its statements from the May 1886 meeting, the Council of Admiralty argued that although France should not pretend that she could gain command of the seas, she could pose a serious threat to Great Britain because "there is a chink in her armour—the immensity of her maritime trade of which the steady flow is of vital importance for Great Britain, and it is against that trade that we should aim our hits."[7] There was, however, no doubt in the minds of the members of the Council of Admiralty that this mission should be carried out by long-range cruisers. They should be deployed on the high seas from the start, or even before hostilities

---

[6] SHM, BB8-914: Conseil d'Amirauté: *Procès-verbal de la séance du 21 Mai 1886*.
[7] SHM, BB8-915: Conseil d'Amirauté: *Procès-verbal de la séance du 7 Janvier 1887*.

broke out, and they would have more or less only one mission: "to search and destroy the merchant ships of the enemy."[8]

Although the Council of Admiralty echoed the *jeune école*'s view on commerce warfare against Great Britain, the Council of Admiralty and the *jeune école* still differed over whether battleships would have any mission in a war against the dominant sea power. Whereas the *jeune école* had written off the option of fleet warfare against the Royal Navy, the Council of Admiralty described a twofold strategy in European waters that required both cruisers and battleships. They argued that the battleships should be concentrated in the Mediterranean and there engage in fleet warfare against the Royal Navy, while *guerre de course* should be conducted from the Atlantic coast. There and in the Channel, France should put up a solid coastal defence with both coastal defence ships and torpedo flotillas.

A certain *rapprochement* of views between the Council of Admiralty and the ideas of the *jeune école* concerning the use of smaller naval vessels for offensive operations was also evident in the strategic scheme outlined by the Council of Admiralty. It proposed that scout vessels and small commerce-raiders (*avisos de course*) could carry out rapid sorties from the Atlantic coast and into the Channel in order to hunt British merchant ships. More interestingly, the Council of Admiralty argued that these vessels could also conduct raids against warships in order to upset the enemy. The idea that these relatively small vessels could conduct this kind of offensive operation very much resembles Aube's view on the inherent capabilities of small, fast vessels, and their ability to challenge major naval units. The opinion of Aube and the Council of Admiralty differed, however, with regard to two aspects. First, Aube thought that torpedo boats would be almost perfect for such missions, while the Council of Admiralty advocated somewhat larger vessels for these operations. The Council of Admiralty's view was thus consistent with the prevalent view among French admirals that torpedo boats had poor seakeeping capabilities. They were too small to operate outside the coastal area, they argued. Secondly, while torpedo boat operations were a cornerstone in Aube's scheme to fight the warships of the Royal Navy, the small scale offensive operations by small boats mentioned by the Council of Admiralty were not thought to have more than a symbolic effect. They should provoke some concern on the British side,

---

[8] *Ibid.*

but they were by no means intended or expected to have a profound impact on the fighting capabilities of the Royal Navy.

While the Council of Admiralty more or less adopted the *jeune école*'s plan for *guerre de course* against Great Britain, the admirals were sceptical as to the efficacy of such warfare should the enemy be Germany or Italy. In such a scenario the French Navy should conduct traditional fleet warfare, they argued. By blockading naval ports and attacking the enemy's warships France should obtain command of the sea. In case of a military conflict with either Italy or Germany, the Council of Admiralty claimed that these two powers probably would combine against France. It maintained that the French Navy would be able to face both even if they were united, and it was precisely for such a contingency that the French fleet should be structured. The Council of Admiralty had analysed the status and the plans of the Italian and German fleets and the most probable operational plans of the two navies if they were to fight the French. The Italian Navy had an offensive character and was probably aspiring to dominate the Mediterranean with its squadrons of big battleships, while the Germans would almost certainly have a more defensive posture based on their coastal defence ships, armoured gunboats and torpedo boats. In addition the German Navy would also employ a small number of cruisers for war on the high seas, the Council of Admiralty concluded.

The French strategy should consequently be designed to meet these naval challenges, and the French fleet should take its positions accordingly from the start of the hostilities. French warships should immediately take measures to contain the German Navy in the Baltic and in Wilhelmshafen. The assumed threat of the German cruisers should be met by both defensive precautions and offensive operations. Coastal defences would be mobilised, while French cruisers were to chase and destroy the German cruisers. The French cruisers should also protect French trade and attack German trade. In the Mediterranean the recommended approach was "to act very vigorously, without hesitation or delay, with the bulk of our battleships supported by our flotillas in order to try to crush the Italian Navy before any attempt could be made to join the German forces."[9]

---

[9] SHM, BB8-915: Conseil d'Amirauté: *Procès-verbal de la séance du 7 Janvier 1887*.

The planning and evaluation of major naval manoeuvres represented a second arena where French strategy was discussed. It was Aube who inaugurated major manoeuvres for the French Navy.[10] This was in itself a major step forward, opening the way for perfecting and integrating into the Navy's organisation the equipment developed during the preceding fifteen years, and supplementing the lessons learned from the Crimean War and the Franco-Prussian War. These manoeuvres were placed in a strategic setting, and the discussions during the exercise planning and the debriefings were characterised by the differences of opinion between the *jeune école* and the traditionalists on strategic, tactical and technical questions.

The manoeuvres focused on methods of traditional naval warfare such as blockading, breaking blockades, attack on and defence of naval ports and open sea encounters between naval formations and units. *Guerre de course* was not tried out in exercises during these manoeuvres. Although these manoeuvres seemingly focused on traditional naval warfare, Aube's idea behind the manoeuvres was to try out some of the theories of the *jeune école*. His ambition was to test, or rather to demonstrate, the utility of the torpedo boats both in coastal defence and on the high seas, and consequently, according to Aube's logic, to prove that the era of battleships was over. Such a conclusion would be a necessary precondition if the French Navy were to be able to conduct *guerre de course* on the scale advocated by the *jeune école*.

In the discussions between Aube and the torpedo boat enthusiasts on the one side, and the supporters of battleships, mainly represented by the staff of the Squadron of Evolutions,[11] on the other, it is difficult to

---

[10] SHM, 1 CC 195 Aa 9: Lecture by Capitain de vaisseau Berryer: *Marine Française: Tactique et Stratégie, Points d'appui* (Ecole Supérieure de Marine, Paris, 1898–1899) p. 351; Ausseur: "La *jeune école*", p. 466.

[11] The Squadron of Evolutions was established in the 1840s as a squadron of seagoing ships of the line maintained in permanent commission in the Mediterranean for training in gunnery, tactics, and squadron navigation. The Squadron should be both classrooms of military instruction and, as noted in the programme of 1872, "a precious instrument of the nation's power, always ready to be thrown into the balance in questions that touch the real and serious interests of France." The Squadron of Evolutions was the nucleus of the French Navy. Its composition and the number of ships did vary somewhat throughout the period covered here, but mostly it consisted of six battleships and a large cruiser and avisos. The backbone of the Squadron was the battleships. The Squadron of Evolutions was stationed in Toulon in the Mediterranean and has often been referred to as the Mediterranean Fleet or the Mediterranean Squadron. Ropp: *The Development of a Modern Navy*, pp. 7, 33, 40, 190, 356.

distinguish between the strategic assessments and the participants' view of the capabilities of the two major naval elements in the exercises: the battleships and the torpedo boats. The discussions during the evaluation of the summer exercise in 1886 revealed that both the Ministry of Marine's and the Squadron of Evolution's perception of the strategic setting of the exercise mirrored their positions as supporters of either torpedo boats or battleships as the mainstay of the French Navy. Even though the summer exercise of 1886 took place in the Mediterranean, it was clear that Aube's point of reference was a superior enemy, the Royal Navy, while the staff of the Squadron of Evolutions focused on an inferior Navy, the Italian.

The Squadron of Evolutions' preference for an Italian scenario was most probably based on the fact that it was a battleship squadron. In a confrontation with the Italian battle fleet the French fleet would be superior, and according to the logic of the *jeune école*, it would be predestined to exercise command of the seas. Such a scenario would thus confirm and legitimise the priority given to the Squadron. The senior officers of the Squadron of Evolutions used the Italian scenario to identify the weak spot of a navy without a battle fleet. They argued that a main mission for the battle fleet would be to take part in attacks against the Italian viaducts and other infrastructure in order to slow down the mobilisation and concentration of the Italian army. How could that be done without the support of battleships, they asked rhetorically. And they answered their own question with the claim that torpedo boats or other small boats (*vedettes*) would not be able to blow up a railway or support a landing. A battle group was necessary in order to carry out such operations.

The main argument forwarded by the Mediterranean Fleet was, however, that as the superior force it would be able to lock up the Italian fleet in port. This assumption was energetically opposed by Aube. He argued that the Italian battleships could operate independently and he followed up his argument by his favourite examples, the cases of the *Alabama* and the *Augusta*. He reminded the French battleship supporters that even though the Union had set out with six ships of equal or better quality than the Alabama, they could not catch up with her. And even though the German battle group remained in port during the Franco-Prussian War, the Germans were able to insult the French coast with one lonely cruiser. The minister concluded the discussion by stating that: "It is sufficient for us to have torpedo boats to protect our coasts, gunboats to attack the battleships, insult the enemy coast and burn her ports, and finally cruisers based in Brest to spot the arrival of merchant vessels and destroy them."[12]

French relations with Germany and the Triple Alliance had dramatically deteriorated from the time of the evaluation of the summer manoeuvre of 1886 to the time of the planning conference for the summer manoeuvre of 1887. When Aube, together with his General Staff and the senior officers of the Mediterranean Fleet, sat down to plan the manoeuvre, France was in the midst of the Boulanger crisis with Germany.[13] The tense situation made it difficult for Aube to sketch a strategic setting that corresponded with the *jeune école*'s traditional assumption of which enemy to plan for. Both in his writings prior to taking office as Minister of Marine and in internal discussions during his period in office, he had focused on Great Britain as the enemy the French Navy should prepare itself to fight.

Aube's critics had often accused him of being obsessed with Great Britain as the probable enemy. They agreed that France would not stand a chance in fleet warfare against the Royal Navy, but they argued that France might very well have to face an inferior navy. In such a situation France could profit from having a superior battleship fleet and might obtain command of the seas just as they thought Great Britain could achieve it in a war against the inferior French fleet.[14] They simply rejected Aube's assertion that fleet warfare was obsolete and that command of the sea had become an illusion after the introduction of the self-propelled torpedo and small torpedo boats. Given the fact that the anti-German mood was very pronounced in France in 1887, not least within the government, and that Germany was allied with Italy, it would have been difficult to argue that the Mediterranean Fleet should not exercise for possible contingencies for a war against Italy in the Mediterranean.

---

[12] SHM, BB4-1452: EMG 1ère section: *Procès verbaux de la Conférence formée pour dégager les conclusions à tirer des grandes manoeuvres de l'été de 1886*, 21–24 July 1886 (filed 4 April 1888).

[13] SHM, BB4-1452: Planning conference for the summer manoeuvre 1887, 3 March 1887.

[14] These ideas were even reflected in some operational contingency plans made by Aube's General Staff, although his staff officers placed greater emphasis on torpedo boat operations than hitherto. See SHM, BB-1452: EMG Ière section: *Note sur les opérations que pourrait avoir à faire l'Escadre d'Evolutions au début d'une guerre avec l'Italie*, September 1886.

Aube, however, did not share in the prevalent hysteria regarding the German and Italian menace, and he stressed that the aim of the manoeuvre was to prepare the foundations of naval strategy and tactics for the future. When he nevertheless chose, as a strategic setting for the summer exercise of 1887, Germany and Italy as enemies, he probably had two motives. First, the tense relations between France and the Triple Alliance constituted a fact that Aube could hardly ignore. To choose Britain as the enemy for the manoeuvre would have seemed somewhat odd and would probably have convinced the sceptics that Aube was obsessed with Britain. Secondly, Aube understood that if he was to convince the sceptics of the torpedo boats' excellence, he had to prove that these boats were a formidable naval weapon even in the battleship supporters' favourite scenario.

Aube's preoccupation with Great Britain as the constituting enemy for the French Navy was nevertheless evident in the way he composed the summer manoeuvre of 1887. The exercise was to be organised in three operations. In the first operation the battle fleet was to convoy the transport of troops from Algeria to France while under attack from the torpedo boats. In the second operation the battle fleet was given the task of defeating the Italian battle fleet in the Mediterranean and joining the forces in the Channel in their fight against the German Navy.[15] Both these operations were plausible given that the enemy was an alliance of Germany and Italy. The first operation was, however, not only relevant in a situation where Italy was the enemy. The General Staff in a memorandum had stressed that convoying troops from Algeria to France would also be necessary in a war with Great Britain.[16]

It was, however, the third operation that revealed Aube's obsession with Great Britain as the most probable enemy. Aube outlined that in this operation the torpedo boats should attack the battle group in the straits of Gibraltar on its return from Brest. Although the whole exercise was placed in a context where France was at war with Italy and Germany, the third operation had no link to such a strategic setting. Aube chose to disconnect this operation from the general strategic setting

---

[15] The problems concerning the fact that most French naval forces were concentrated in the Mediterranean, and that the French naval posture in the Channel was thus weak, had been addressed in a memorandum in the Ministry in 1886. SHM, BB4-1452: The Memorandum had no heading. Author and date are also unknown. Dated by archivist to autumn 1886.

[16] SHM, BB4-1452: Le Capitaine de frégate Chassériaud, aide de camp, 3ème section EMG: *Etude sur la guerre navale dans le bassin occidental de la Méditerranée*, 16 April 1886.

in order to test one of his favourite scenarios in a war against Great Britain. In the debriefing after the 1886 manoeuvre he had described how torpedo boats guarding the strait of Gibraltar could destroy a British battle group entering the Mediterranean:

> If one assumes that the African coast is watched by a hundred torpedo boats and a sufficient number of picket boats [*eclaireurs*] observe the strait of Gibraltar, an English battle group entering the Mediterranean will not be able to sail very far before all this naval dust will stick to it in a pursuit. The battle group will be destroyed before reaching our coast.[17]

Verifying the Excellence of the Torpedo Boats

Despite Aube's difficulties depicting strategic settings for the summer manoeuvres that were consistent with the theories of the *jeune école*, his period in office was marked by a firm will to overrule any objections preventing him from trying out the capabilities of the torpedo boats. He was determined to prove that the torpedo boats represented a deadly threat to the battleships, thus opening up for *guerre de course*. Aube pushed his programme through regardless of the objections raised by the Council of Admiralty or any other forum with pretensions to influence the strategy, tactics or force structure of the French Navy. Shortly after entering office he ordered torpedo boats to undertake extremely demanding transits from Cherbourg, Lorient and Brest to the Mediterranean under rough winter conditions in order to test the boats and their crews. In the summer of 1886, in the first French naval manoeuvres, he set all the torpedo boats against the battleships of the Mediterranean Fleet, and in the planning of the summer manoeuvre for 1887 he decided that the torpedo boats should pursue and attack the battleships across the Mediterranean and all the way up to Brest.

The lessons that could be drawn from the navigational and tactical tests and manoeuvres were disputed during Aube's period in office, and have also been so by officers and historians who have sifted the evidence and drawn conclusions based on the various reports written in the aftermath of the tests and manoeuvres.[18] Theodore Ropp has

---

[17] SHM, BB4-1452: EMG 1ère section: *Procès-verbaux de la Conférence formée pour dégager les conclusions à tirer des grandes manoeuvres de l'été de 1886.*

[18] Captain Berryer, who had studied the manoeuvres in the period 1886–1898, underlined in his lectures at the French Navy's staff college that it was difficult to draw conclusions from the manoeuvres because there were different opinions on how the

concluded, based on a report to the *Préfet maritime* in Toulon from the commanding officer of torpedo boat *No. 61* that was later published in *Revue Maritime*, that "the crews were so worn out from seasickness and the lack of warm food and sleep that there could be no question of their inability to fight at the end of the trip".[19] Although the boats made the journey safely, the *torpilleur autonome* was quietly buried, Ropp concluded. This verdict was further substantiated by the experiences from the summer manoeuvre of 1886, Ropp argued, and he laconically summed up what he saw as the failure of the torpedo boat trials by stating that: "In Aube's budget for 1887, money was again appropriated for the unfinished battleships."[20]

The conclusions drawn by Aube and his General Staff from the independent transits of the torpedo boats and their performance in the summer exercise of 1886 were, however, far more positive than indicated by Ropp. Contrary to Ropp's conclusions, Aube and his men were of the opinion that the way the torpedo boats had tackled the rough challenges they had been exposed to was very promising and supported important parts of the *jeune école*'s theory. They were still convinced that torpedo boats and also the gunboat "Gabriel Charmes" would represent a deadly threat to the battleships as a naval asset. They reduced somewhat the ambitions regarding the autonomous capabilities of the torpedo boats. The scenarios in which torpedo boats cruised the oceans chasing merchant liners were dropped, but they still argued that the torpedo boats could conduct merchant warfare effectively in the Mediterranean.[21]

Aube sent Lieutenant Commander Marsi to Toulon to gain an impression of the experiences of seven crews who had sailed their torpedo boats 1st class independently from the Atlantic ports to Toulon. Marsi wrote enthusiastically of how crews of foreign vessels had saluted the torpedo boats by hurrahs when passing the strait of Gibraltar, and he claimed that:

---

manoeuvres actually had taken place. SHM, 1 CC 195 Aa 9: Lectures by Capitain de vaisseau Berryer: *Marine Française: Tactique et Stratégie, Points d'appui*. Conférences à l'Ecole Supérieure de Marine (Paris, 1898–1899) p. 351.

[19] Ropp: *The Development of a Modern Navy*, p. 176.

[20] Ropp: *The Development of a Modern Navy*, p. 177. Ropp did not have access to the archives of the Ministry, and his conclusions regarding the summer manoeuvre of 1886 was based on a paper delivered at the *Ecole Supérieure de Marine* in 1898.

[21] See i.e. SHM, BB4-1452: Le Capitaine de frégate Chassériaud, aide de camp, 3ème séction EMG: *Etude sur la guerre navale dans le bassin occidental de la Méditerranée*, 16 April 1886, and further discussions and examples in this chapter.

this test of the ability of torpedo boats navigating independently [...] should be considered as a decisive experiment that should give the uttermost confidence regarding the nautical qualities of the torpedo boats. That is the unanimous opinion of the commanding officers [...].[22]

In his rather optimistic conclusion, Lieutenant Commander Marsi somewhat understated the negative experiences that several of the commanding officers reported. A number of the torpedo boats had crews that had no practice sailing torpedo boats. They had suffered from seasickness and the commanding officer of *No. 70* complained that it had been imprudent to go to sea with an untrained crew. The captain of *No. 71* stated that he would not make another such voyage with an untrained crew. He declared that they were lucky to arrive in Toulon and that he would not have been surprised if the boat had been lost. The captain warned that one should not sail on the high seas with a crew picked at random and put into specialised boats like the torpedo boats. These boats needed trained personnel, he concluded.

The commanding officer of *No. 66* had faced both good and bad weather. During bad weather the crew had neither been able to cook nor sleep during transit. Despite this he concluded that: "The nautical qualities are excellent. The crew is ready to go back to sea."[23] The crew of *No. 61*, whom Ropp called on as witness for the alleged weaknesses of the torpedo boats, had some previous experience sailing similar boats. Their morale, according to Lieutenant Commander Marsi, had been very high and the crew had not suffered from fatigue. They had been able to cook every day. The legs had been on average 30 hours with a speed of 12–14 knots. The crew concluded that the torpedo boat had been very seaworthy when confronted with some heavy seas. Marsi's summing-up of the experiences of *No. 61* was in accord with the report the commanding officer, Lieutenant Commander Le Roy presented to the *Préfet maritime* in Toulon about the same time. Lieutenant Commander Le Roy did, however, mention one interesting inconvenience of sailing small boats:

> What is fatiguing on a torpedo boat, and especially hard for men of a nervous disposition, is the continual vibration that constantly shakes you, and with it the throbbing of the engines that produced a kind of

---

[22] SHM, BB4-1452: *Mission du Lieutenant de vaisseau Marsi à Toulon, pour s'enquérir de l'état des torpilleurs arrivés de l'Ocean. Résumé et conclusions*, 28 February 1886.

[23] SHM, BB4-1452: *Mission du Lieutenant de vaisseau Marsi à Toulon, pour s'enquérir de l'état des torpilleurs arrivés de l'Ocean. No. 66*, 28 February 1886.

counterstroke that made the whole stern tremble and gave the impression that the engine itself was likely to become dislocated; this is a fatigue that affects morale rather than the physique, but that in the end inevitably affects the whole organism; I observe nevertheless that one ends up getting used to it.[24]

Ropp quoted a part of this passage from Le Roy's report as one example of why the idea of the autonomous torpedo boat had to be buried.[25] He did not, however, cite the two last sentences that are quoted above: "this is a fatigue that affects morale rather than the physique, but that in the end inevitably affects the whole organism; I observe nevertheless that one ends up getting used to it." Ropp thus omitted one of the main points in the arguments of the proponents of the *jeune école*: that these specialised boats needed well-trained and accustomed crews to function properly.

The main problem raised by the commanding officers was precisely that some of the crew members were inexperienced. There was general agreement among them that these boats were very demanding to operate, and that the crews had to be specially trained for duty aboard torpedo boats. An experienced crew would be better prepared to sustain the strain they would be exposed to serving aboard these small boats. A number of the commanding officers also stressed the need for an additional navigator. Being the only navigator aboard, the commanding officer was forced to spend almost all his time at sea on the bridge. This deprived them of necessary rest.

In his comments made in the margin of Lieutenant Commander Marsi's report, Aube underlined that the boats had proved to have good nautical qualities, and that the main problem was untrained crews. It is fair to say that Lieutenant Commander Marsi's report supported such a conclusion. It can of course not be excluded that a wish to please the Minister of Marine to a certain extent coloured the reports the commanding officers gave to Lieutenant Commander Marsi, and that he in his turn reinforced the positive parts and toned down the negative to please Aube who had sent him to collect information. The central role played by torpedo boats in the Minister of Marine's naval theory was well known within the Navy, and so were his expectations

---

[24] Antoine-Auguste Le Roy: "Rapport de mer du torpilleur 61. Le Lieutenant de vaisseau Le Roy commandant le torpilleur 61 à M. Le Vice-Amiral, Préfet maritime à Toulon", in *Revue maritime et coloniale* (Paris, 1886), pp. 9–10.
[25] Ropp: *The Development of a Modern Navy*, p. 176.

as to the performance of the torpedo boats. Given the minister's ability to influence the career prospects of his naval officers, it might be that his subordinates tended to adapt their reports to what they thought the minister would like to hear. The report does, however, give the impression that Lieutenant Commander Marsi has strived to present a straightforward report from the torpedo boats' transits. Apart from his rather enthusiastic conclusion, Lieutenant Commander Marsi's representation of each of the commanding officers' reports seems credible. They contain some very harsh and seemingly unpolished comments concerning low training standards and minor technical problems. And as we have seen, Lieutenant Commander Marsi's version of the experiences of the crew of torpedo boat *No. 61* concurs very much with Lieutenant Commander Le Roy's report as it was presented to the *Préfet maritime* in Toulon.[26]

That the torpedo boats had good nautical qualities was also supported by a General Staff comment on a report on a torpedo boat 1st class that had sailed later that spring from Brest to Toulon. The General Staff wrote that the commanding officer on torpedo boat *No. 27* described its seagoing capabilities as excellent. He had claimed that the small torpedo boat was indeed habitable, even when it was filled with provisions and spare parts for two weeks.[27]

The good seagoing capabilities of the torpedo boats 1st class were also mentioned repeatedly in the notes made in a technical logbook of the *Division navale d'expérience des Torpilleurs* of 1886.[28] This logbook was most probably written by the young officers manning the torpedo boats of the Division. There they recorded the experiences from different exercises and trials within the Division. The main worry was where to place the torpedo tubes in order to make the launching more reliable. What was symptomatic for the experiences reported in the logbook was, however, the systematic search for improvements on any technical problem that was faced. That the torpedo boats represented an effective naval asset was never questioned.

---

[26] Le Roy: "Rapport de mer du torpilleur 61 Le Lieutenant de vaisseau Le Roy commandant le torpilleur".

[27] SHM, BB4-1452: EMG 1ère section: *Note sur le rapport du torpilleur No. 27 (1ère class) de 44 tonnes*, 20 May 1886.

[28] SHM, BB4-1474: Division navale d'expérience des torpilleurs: *Cahier de Notes*. 1886.

The views of those serving aboard the torpedo boats, both as they were reflected in the reports of Lieutenant Commander Marsi, Lieutenant Commander Le Roy, the comments on the report of the commanding officer on torpedo boat *No. 27*, and in the internal logbook of the *Division navale d'expérience des Torpilleurs*, supported the main argument that Aube repeatedly forwarded in his discussions with the senior officers of the Squadron of Evolutions. In those discussions Aube dismissed objections concerning technical problems, difficulties with regard to launching torpedoes, training standards etc. as problems of secondary importance. They could be solved, he argued. What was important was that small boats actually could operate in rough seas.[29]

The next test of the torpedo boats' capabilities took place during the summer manoeuvre of 1886. In the manoeuvre Aube set all the existing Davids against the Goliaths. Eleven 33-ton (2nd class) and eleven 46 ton (1st class) torpedo boats were pitted against the whole Mediterranean Fleet, representing about twenty times as much money and men.[30] The torpedo boats were given five problems: they should defend Toulon against bombardment, break a blockade of Toulon, close a strait, attack the Squadron of Evolutions at anchor off Ajaccio on Corsica and attack the Squadron transiting to Oran on the Algerian coast. The evaluation of the manoeuvre revealed noticeable disagreements regarding the conclusions to be drawn from the different phases of the manoeuvre.[31]

The bombardment of Toulon was simulated during daytime. Since visibility was good, the torpedo boats defending the port were discovered at a range of 5000 meters when trying to attack the Squadron. The torpedo boats would thus be exposed to enemy fire in their attempt to cross a distance of close to 5000 meters before they could launch their torpedoes. A dispute between the representatives of the Ministry of Marine and the Squadron occurred over whether in a non-simulated situation the big calibre guns of the battleships would produce so much smoke that their visibility, and thus their ability to detect the small

---

[29] SHM, BB4-1452: Planning conference for the summer manoeuvre 1887, 3 March 1887.
[30] Ropp: *The Development of a Modern Navy*, p. 176. The displacement of the torpedo boats varies somewhat within the torpedo boats categories of 1st and 2nd class. The displacement given in the text is therefore an average. *Liste de la Flotte 1885–1889*.
[31] SHM, BB4-1452: EMG 1ère section: *Procès-verbaux de la Conférence formée pour dégager les conclusions à tirer des grandes manoeuvres de l'été de 1886*, 21–24 July 1886 (filed 4 April 1888).

torpedo boats, would be severely reduced. The torpedo boats' alleged ability to benefit from the reduced visibility generated by the smoke from the firing guns and the general confusion of the battle was supposed to be, as the advocates of the *jeune école* repeatedly maintained, one of the advantages small boats would have in a tactical situation. This argument from the Ministry of Marine was dismissed by the Chief of Staff of the Squadron, Captain Humann. He argued that the big calibre guns would have a firing rate during bombardment of one shot every ten minutes, and would thus not produce much smoke.[32]

In the second part of the manoeuvre the aim was to examine a battle fleet's ability to maintain a blockade when confronted with numerous torpedo boats attacking from positions on the coast. The fleet was indeed judged to have sunk a cruiser that tried to break the blockade with the aid of torpedo boats, but on the whole this phase went to the torpedo boats. The Squadron of Evolution reported that: "The torpedo boats made 126 appearances, 48 launchings of torpedoes, got within good range 21 times, and completely surprised the battleships in 8 cases."[33] Even the ardent supporter of fleet warfare, the Commander-in-Chief of the Squadron of Evolutions, Vice Admiral Lafont, praised the potential of the torpedo boats in anti-blockade operations: "The torpedo boat is *par excellence* the weapon of surprise [...] Its intervention makes it impossible to institute a blockade."[34]

In the third phase of the exercise the Squadron was to sail through the straits north of Corsica, which was supposed to be blocked by torpedo boats. Aube had decided that the Squadron should pass no more than 20 nm north off the northern cap of Corsica. This narrowed "strait" was to be guarded by 4 larger ships and 20 torpedo

---

[32] It was the chief of the General Staff of the Ministry of Marine, Rear Admiral Brown de Colston, who argued that the torpedo boats could benefit from cover provided by the smoke of the firing guns aboard the battleships. Brown de Colston supported the Minister of Marine in his discussions with naval officers outside the Ministry of Marine. He did not, however, emerge as an enthusiastic *jeune école* supporter, but rather as a loyal officer of the Ministry of Marine. Later in his career, i.e. as member of the Superior Council, Brown de Colston advocated a rather eclectic strategy with elements both from the traditionalists and the *jeune école*. See the discussions in the Superior Council: SHM, BB8-2424/5: Conseil Supérieur de la Marine. *Séances du 11 Janvier 1899.*

[33] SHM, 1 CC 195 Aa 9: Lecture by Capitain de vaisseau Berryer: *Marine Française: Tactique et Stratégie, Points d'appui* (Ecole Supérieure de Marine, Paris, 1898–1899), p. 352.

[34] SHM, BB4-1452: EMG 1ère section: *Procès-verbaux 21–24 July 1886*. See also SHM, 1 CC 195 Aa 9: Lecture by Capitain de vaisseau Berryer: *Marine Française: Tactique et Stratégie, Points d'appui* (Ecole Supérieure de Marine, Paris, 1898–1899), p. 352.

boats, and passage should be effected within a time span of 72 hours. These restrictions on the Squadron of Evolution's navigational and tactical freedom were imposed to illustrate the kind of threat a battle fleet would be confronted with in the Mediterranean if Aube's visions became reality. In his vision, as presented to the participants in the debrief, in the case of war torpedo boats should block the western part of the Mediterranean basin off from the eastern by stationing 60 torpedo boats in the northern passage, 30–40 in the middle and 60 in the southern passage. This idea had been elaborated in the General Staff of the Ministry of Marine three months earlier by one of Aube's close associates, Commander Chassériaud. In this memorandum, which Aube had studied closely, Chassériaud described how France's geographical location gave it a better position than any other nation to divide the Mediterranean in two. France had a unique possibility of controlling the western basin of the Mediterranean. This control should be imposed from the Mediterranean shores of France via Corsica to the North African shores stretching from Morocco to Tripolitania. The Mediterranean was, according to Chassériaud, perfect for torpedo boat operations. It was narrow enough to give these "new miniscule cruisers" a number of safe havens protecting them against rough weather. A rationally organised French Navy could reduce the Royal Navy's influence in the Mediterranean and severely interrupt the important British trade that passed through the western basin.[35]

The Commander-in-Chief of the Mediterranean Fleet, Vice Admiral Lafont, and his staff were very critical of Aube's decision to carry out controlled exercises to ensure that encounters between the battle group and the flotilla took place. Such a fixed setting imposed restrictions on the Mediterranean Fleet that Lafont found unacceptable. He argued strongly for free-play exercises that would give the battle group a possibility to choose which route to sail and when to pass a strait or bombard a port. Then the battle group could seek open waters or wait for rough seas in order to profit from what they argued was the weak point of the torpedo boats; their assumed poor seagoing capability. Vice Admiral Lafont stated that in a war he would have waited perhaps for as much as eight days in order to profit from rough weather before pass-

---

[35] SHM, BB4-1452. Le Capitaine de frégate Chassériaud, aide de camp, 3ème section EMG: *Etude sur la guerre navale dans le bassin occidental de la Méditerranée*, 16 April 1886.

ing a narrow strait guarded by torpedo boats. He also found it hard to accept as a realistic scenario the fact that the strait had been artificially narrowed to a width of 20 nm and was guarded by 24 naval vessels. According to this logic, there should be at least one boat for every nautical mile across the three straits of the Mediterranean Sea.[36] Such an operation would require an enormous number of torpedo boats, and Vice Admiral Lafont warned that trying to implement such a plan could cause catastrophic chaos. If exposed to bad weather, rough seas and enemy fire, it could cause irreparable damage to the flotillas.

This phase of the exercise seemed to prove Vice Admiral Lafont right, although there was some disagreement over how to interpret the results. The torpedo boats experienced navigational problems. Aube tried to explain away the disappointing results by stating that the torpedo boats that participated were only an embryo of the future flotillas. Eight of the participating torpedo boats were not even so-called autonomous torpedo boats. The others had no navigational problems, Aube explained. His chief of staff, Rear Admiral Brown de Colston, aided his minister by adding that the navigational problems were simply due to trouble with the compasses.

The same differences of opinion concerning the details of what actually happened and what lessons to draw from it were also present in the discussions regarding phase four of the manoeuvres. The Squadron of Evolutions was sent to Ajaccio where it was to improvise its defence. The flotilla was kept in Toulon by a strong westerly wind for two days until its commander decided to leave the smallest torpedo boats behind and set out with twelve 1st and 2nd class torpedo boats, of which seven were autonomous torpedo boats, two cruisers and a coastal-defence ship. Six boats were forced to turn back and another broke down just before the attack. The Commander-in-Chief of the Squadron of Evolutions reported that:

> Five torpedo boats out of twenty-one, harassed by fatigue, waterlogged, and probably incapable of launching their torpedoes, finally attacked the Squadron, [an attack] that simply confirmed that the Squadron had [good] routines for surveillance. This odyssey in summer, on a friendly coast, may demolish the faith of the most dedicated believers in the

---

[36] The three "straits" that Admiral Lafont referred to are the passage between the French Mediterranean coast and Corsica, the Strait of Bonifacio, and the passage between Sardinia and the North African coast.

autonomy, the absolute seaworthiness, the value of these so-called *high seas* torpedo boats, who lost three quarters of their effective strength in twelve hours in the Mediterranean.[37]

Rear Admiral Brown de Colston claimed that many facts had been omitted or distorted in the Squadron's report. He agreed that the 27 meters torpedo boats had had to reduce their speed due to rough seas and had been late for the attack. His mathematical calculations provided a much more positive picture of the torpedo boats' achievement than the report had done. He stressed that five out of six torpedo boats had taken part in the attack on the Squadron of Evolutions and proved that they could operate in rough seas. Brown de Colston's intervention triggered a heated dispute with Vice Admiral Lafont. The Commander-in-Chief of the Squadron of Evolutions even disputed the allegation that the sea had been rough. On the contrary, he claimed, the sea was calm. The important point, according to Lafont, was that the conditions did not affect the crews aboard his ships, whereas the torpedo boats that managed to follow him for three to four hours would not have been able to sustain the stress for more than two days.

It was obvious that this phase of the manoeuvre did not meet the expectations of the representatives of the Ministry of Marine, and they had problems responding to the arguments and the conclusions drawn by Vice Admiral Lafont. Following a discussion about how much rough weather a crew could stand, Brown de Colston had to introduce qualities beyond technical matters and the level of training of the crews to advocate the potential of torpedo boats in naval warfare on the high seas. In closing this part of the discussion he stated that "a sailor with pride and self-respect would be able to stand this exceptionally bad weather."[38]

Phase five, like that of phase three, was based on a scenario that had been elaborated by Commander Chassériaud of the General Staff. He had pointed out that Algeria and Tunisia would be a *place d'armes* in case of a war against Great Britain or Italy. An important mission for the Navy would therefore be to secure the transfer of troops from North Africa to France. This phase, Operation Oran, was thus supposed to

---

[37] SHM, 1 CC 195 Aa 9: Lecture by Capitain de vaisseau Berryer: *Marine Française: Tactique et Stratégie, Points d'appui* (Ecole Supérieure de Marine, Paris, 1898–1899), pp. 354–355.
[38] SHM, BB4-1452: EMG 1ère section: *Procès-verbaux 21–24 July 1886*.

highlight the torpedo boats' ability to detect, follow undiscovered and attack a fleet crossing the Mediterranean.

The report from the Commander-in-Chief of the Squadron of Evolutions pointed to two particular problems faced by torpedo boats in such an operation. First, he pointed to the difficulties torpedo boats faced trying to detect a blacked out fleet at night and if they succeeded, they risked losing sight of it. The second problem was related to the torpedo boats' chances of remaining undetected. To catch up with the fleet, the torpedo boats would have to sail at high speed, with the risk of producing flame-bursts compromising their efforts to remain undetected. Brown de Colston agreed that these objections were relevant. The problem with the occasional flame-bursts was, however, primarily due to the inexperience of the crew, and could consequently be resolved by more training.

The evaluation of the summer manoeuvre was characterised by fundamentally different perceptions of what actually took place and consequently by disagreement over which conclusions to draw from the different phases of the exercise. This was partly due to the character of the exercise. Many of the elements of the exercise were only simulations. No bombardment was conducted during the attack on the harbour of Toulon. Whether an actual bombardment would have produced smoke that would conceal the attacking torpedo boats was thus open to interpretations coloured by the participants' overall view of the ideal strategy and composition of the French Navy. Another, and more important uncertainty, was whether the torpedo boats were able to launch torpedoes in rough seas, and if they were successfully launched, whether they would hit their targets or not. The two opposing groups could not even agree on whether the sea had been rough or not during the manoeuvre.

The two groups did, however, agree on the question of close blockade. Both the Commander-in-Chief of the Squadron of Evolutions and Aube concluded that torpedo boats would make a close blockade very costly, if not impossible to impose. The fact that this phase of the manoeuvre, the blockade of Toulon, went to the torpedo boats was of particular importance, since the *jeune école*'s theory of the nullification of command of the sea was based on the impossibility of close blockade. Whether the torpedo boats could cruise the high seas and thus deserve the label autonomous, was, however, more doubtful. Aube seemed nevertheless convinced that torpedo boats could represent a deadly threat to a battle fleet even on the high seas. This he was determined to have verified during the summer manoeuvre of 1887.[39]

As discussed earlier, the strategic setting for the 1887 summer manoeuvre was a war against Germany and Italy. Instead of exercising the traditional naval contingencies for a war against these two potential foes, i.e. blockades or attacks on the enemy's capital ships and bombardment of infrastructure, Aube designed an exercise composed of three operations in which torpedo boats would play a major part in all three. The leaders of the Squadron of Evolutions agreed with the strategic setting of the manoeuvres, but they were not satisfied with the operational consequences depicted by Aube.

The first operation was to secure the transfer of troops from North Africa to France. This operation was very much the same as the transit to Oran that had been practised during the summer manoeuvre in 1886. Aube stressed the importance of implementing such a scenario, which he argued would be first priority for the French Navy in a war against Italy and Germany. Such a task had not posed any serious problems for the French Navy until quite recently, Aube explained. Not surprisingly, Aube argued that this favourable situation from a French point of view had changed for the worse due to the serious threats Italian torpedo boats would pose. Aube was thus consistent when admitting that the microbes' victory over the giants would be equally true in a war in which France possessed a majority of battleships.

Aube proposed that the ships of the Squadron of Evolutions that were not fully manned should play the role of transport vessels escorted by the fully-manned warships. The convoy should leave Toulon at a predetermined time, but sail freely to Alger and after some days return to Toulon. The torpedo boats, that were to establish a base in Ajaccio on Corsica, should observe the convoy and attack when an opportunity presented itself.

The planning of the first operation triggered off a dispute between the new Commander-in-Chief of the Squadron of Evolutions, Vice Admiral Peyron and Aube. Peyron warned that simulated attacks on troop transports from North Africa to France could give the Italians ideas that were not in the interest of France. Peyron thus unintentionally

---

[39] SHM, BB4-1452: Planning conference for the summer manoeuvre 1887, 3 March 1887.

admitted that torpedo boats could pose a serious threat even to a battle group, a concession that Aube willingly embraced. He did, however, brush aside the objections raised by Peyron that such an operation would reveal a vulnerable point in French plans for reinforcements of the mainland. Aube stated that the Italians were very aware of this Achilles' heel, and that they had moved far beyond theoretical strategies and tactics to exploit this weak point in French war plans. The Italians had already started to put into effect measures that supported such a strategy, Aube claimed. He saw the fortifying of the Italian coast and especially the island of Maddalena on the north-eastern tip of Sardinia as measures pointing in that direction. Aube was not explicit as to how these measures on the part of the Italians could be seen to indicate or prove that they would attack French reinforcements from Algeria in case of a Franco-Italian war. Maddalena would indeed, at least according to *jeune école* reasoning, be a perfect naval base from which torpedo boats could attack the sea lines of communication between Algeria and France, and it was most probably such a scenario Aube had in mind.

The plans for such an operation for the summer manoeuvre inevitably launched a discussion concerning the efficacy of torpedo boats in rough seas. Somewhat surprisingly, Vice Admiral Peyron did not doubt that the torpedo boats would be able to get within range of the battle fleet, but he estimated that they would be unable to launch their torpedoes if there were rough seas. Aube must have been pleased by the fact that Peyron believed the torpedo boats capable of catching up and reaching firing range of the convoy crossing the Mediterranean. The primary motive for Aube was indeed to prove the seagoing capabilities of the torpedo boats, and he overruled Peyron's objections concerning the ability to launch torpedoes as subordinate to the main theme of the exercise, which was to test whether torpedo boats could approach the enemy to within a distance of 3–400 meters, an acceptable firing range. Aube insisted that "whether the torpedo boats would be able to fire the torpedoes or whether the ships hit would be put out of action or not, are subordinate questions that are to be studied later and that will find their solution later."[40] The launching of torpedoes in rough

---

[40] SHM, BB4-1452: Planning conference for the summer manoeuvre 1887, 3 March 1887.

seas was actually a persistent problem that the *Division navale d'expérience des torpilleurs* was trying to resolve.[41]

The question of the torpedo boats' ability to conduct operations in rough seas was also to dominate the discussions concerning the second and third operations. These operations had as their starting point the strategic assumption that the Squadron of Evolutions was first to destroy the Italian battle fleet, and then to join the forces in the Channel in their fight against the German Navy. This gave Aube two more opportunities to test out torpedo boats attacking a battle group on the high seas. In the second operation Aube wanted the battle group to leave Toulon for Brest chased by the torpedo boats during transit. Aube stated that this would be a very realistic situation if war against Italy and Germany should break out. In the third operation the Squadron and the torpedo boats were to return to the Mediterranean and the torpedo boats were to conduct one of the *jeune école*'s favourite operations, closing a strait. In this case they were to attack the Squadron while it was sailing through the Straits of Gibraltar on its return to Toulon.

Several members of the planning board were sceptical about the feasibility of an operation where the torpedo boats were to pursue and attack the Squadron on its transit to Brest. That the representatives from the Squadron of Evolutions were sceptical was hardly a surprise for Aube. They were more or less obliged to advocate the battle fleet's merits compared to torpedo boats on the high seas. What must have been surprising and thought-provoking for Aube, was the fact that even his usually very loyal Chief of the General Staff of the Ministry of Marine, Rear Admiral Brown de Colston, warned that the crews of the torpedo boats would be exposed to extreme fatigue compared to those of the battleships, and that this fact should been taken into account when planning the duration of a transit operation. There seemed to be general agreement among the members of the planning board that Aube was overly optimistic concerning the torpedo boats' potential operational range. Aube insisted that this part of the manoeuvre should be carried out, but he did backtrack somewhat on his initial proposal and accepted that the flotilla should follow the battle group only to the extent the commander of the flotilla judged possible.

---

[41] SHM, BB4-1474: Division navale d'expérience des torpilleurs: *Cahier de Notes*, 1886.

The agreement that apparently was reached during the first day of the planning conference concerning the execution of the manoeuvre had evaporated when the second and last day of the conference began. Vice Admiral Peyron, who had seemed to display a more optimistic attitude regarding the potential of the torpedo boats than his predecessor as Commander-in-Chief of the Squadron of Evolutions, started the second day by stating that he did not approve of the theme of the second operation. He argued that chasing the Squadron all the way to Brest would wear down the material of the torpedo boats. In his usual manner, Aube again rejected these objections as being of secondary importance to the overall aim of the operation, which he claimed was to train the personnel. Aube stressed that he attached great importance to this part of the exercise, and his reference to the importance of training personnel was most probably correct. His most likely motive for pushing through his scheme for the exercise was, however, that a certain measure of success in operations against a battle fleet on the high seas was a prerequisite for winning the necessary support to implement his master plan for restructuring the French Navy. Barbier, who succeeded Aube as minister, stopped the grand manoeuvres that Aube had introduced, and thus there was no summer manoeuvre in 1887 that could either verify or falsify Aube's assumptions.[42]

Rapprochement between Aube and the Council of Admiralty

There are two issues arising from the manoeuvres, the sea trials and the discussions within and between the Ministry of Marine, the Council of Admiralty and the Mediterranean Fleet which deserve to be highlighted. The first is that Aube, although he never expressed it explicitly, had given up the ambition of autonomous torpedo boats cruising the seas of the world chasing enemy merchantmen. The second is the *rapprochement* that could be seen between the Ministry of Marine and the Council of Admiralty concerning *guerre de course à outrance* against Great Britain.

Although there was a certain consensus within the torpedo boat service and in the General Staff of the Ministry of Marine, based on sea trials and on the summer manoeuvre, that torpedo boats could

---
[42] Cellier: "Les idées stratégiques en France", p. 218.

operate in rough seas, there was one lesson learned that Aube seemed to acknowledge, but that he did not admit freely: torpedo boats would not in any foreseeable future be suited for long cruises on the high seas chasing merchant ships. A trained crew was a prerequisite for handling rough seas, but they could not be trained to go without sleep or food for more than a few days. The torpedo boat was not autonomous to the extent that Aube and Charmes had argued in their most optimistic writings. Their vision of torpedo boats cruising the oceans and attacking enemy commerce on "every spot of the ocean" was a pipe dream.[43] Even if the problem of storing or resupplying provisions and coal were solved, the problem of fatigue would still limit the boats' operational radius.

This was first of all obvious from the experiences reported after the winter transits. Three of the seven commanding officers who made the transits from the Atlantic ports to Toulon had stated explicitly that the crew of a torpedo boat could not cope with more than two to three days of bad weather, and three of the other commanding officers also mentioned the need for rest in their reports. The commanding officer aboard *No. 69* expressed the problem quite bluntly: "After 48 hours of bad weather, life aboard a torpedo boat will be unbearable."[44] Lieutenant Commander Le Roy, who presented a comprehensive and detailed report of his transit, warned in his predominantly positive conclusion that: "one can sail and live at sea on a torpedo boat if one does not exaggerate the number of days to be spent on the high seas, can obtain fresh supplies and at same time let the personnel have the rest that they will need after some days cruising [...]."[45]

The lack of autonomy was also clear by the fact that the torpedo boats often had to sail close to the coast in search of calmer waters, and on the transit to Toulon they made frequent port calls so that the crew could rest. If one studies the allegedly successful transit of *No. 61*, one can note that the first attempt to leave the port of Brest took place on the morning of the 30th of January. Due to a strong southwesterly wind the attempt had to be called off, and Lieutenant Commander Le Roy could not leave Brest until the 2nd of February. Well on their way, the *No. 61*'s transit was interrupted by anchoring and port calls

---

[43] Quoted from Th. Aube: "Défense nationale—Défense des colonies", pp. 11–12.
[44] SHM, BB4-1452: *Mission du Lieutenant de vaisseau Marsi à Toulon, pour s'enquérir de l'état des torpilleurs arrivés de l'Ocean. No. 69*, 28 February 1886.
[45] Le Roy: "Rapport de mer du torpilleur 61", p. 21.

in order to resupply and rest. The torpedo boat reached Toulon on the 24th of February. The transits from the Atlantic ports to Toulon proved that these small boats actually could sail under rough wintery conditions. But it also showed that not even a trained crew would be able to make this crossing faster than a poor tramp steamer, as Ropp has pointed out.[46] An additional factor that was not evoked by either Aube or his critics, was that the transit was conducted along a friendly coast. The torpedo boats would have limited opportunities to seek safe haven during offensive operations far from a friendly coast.

Aube seems tacitly to have accepted that torpedo boats were unsuitable for cruising on the high seas. During his period in office he did not advocate torpedo boats as commerce-raiders cruising on the high seas. Neither did the exercises planned or conducted reflect any such use of the torpedo boats. In his writings Aube had, with the exception of one article in *Atlas Colonial* 1885, consistently argued for cruisers as commerce-raiders on the high seas. After the alleged successful transits of the torpedo boats in the spring of 1884, Gabriel Charmes was not the only one who wrote euphorically about torpedo boats cruising the oceans of the world chasing and sinking enemy trade. Even Aube was carried away by the potential advantages such a technological breakthrough could provide an inferior navy, opening up possibilities for inexpensive, deadly boats to hit the vulnerable spots in British society. However, the common sense of the seasoned sailor Aube, combined with the experiments carried out during his period in office, made him give up the idea of small autonomous torpedo boats of 30–50 tons cruising the high seas.

Aube's correspondence with the Council of Admiralty and the questions he asked the admirals give further support to the assumption that he, at least given the state of seaworthiness of the torpedo boats at the time, trusted cruisers as being most suitable for commerce warfare on the high seas. The minutes of the meetings of the Council of Admiralty reveal Aube's preoccupation with cruisers as commerce-raiders, while there is no mention of torpedo boats in such a role. The deliberations also show a *rapprochement* of views between the Council of Admiralty and Aube on the question of commerce warfare. This was clearly seen in the answer they gave Aube in May 1886 to his question of what role

---

[46] *Ibid.*: pp. 5–15; Ropp: *The Development of a Modern Navy*, p. 176.

cruisers should have in future wars.⁴⁷ They supported Aube's visions on commerce warfare that he had forwarded regularly and consistently since the early 1870s. The Council of Admiralty stated that in a war against Great Britain cruisers should patrol the oceans independently, avoid battle with enemy warships, and concentrate on attacking the enemy's trade. They concluded that this warfare should be *"guerre de course* carried out *à outrance*, giving priority to attacks on enemy trade and consequently accepting that our own could not be protected."⁴⁸ There was also a certain *rapprochement* between the Council of Admiralty and Aube on the question of smaller boats conducting commerce warfare. The admirals suggested that commerce warfare in European waters could be conducted by small, high-speed vessels carrying out short and sudden raids out of military ports against enemy commerce. These vessels should be so-called *avisos de course*—smaller than cruisers but larger than torpedo boats.

Suggestions that a concurrence of views had evolved between the Council of Admiralty and Aube regarding *guerre de course* on the high seas was again seen in the meeting of the Council of Admiralty in the beginning of January 1887. Aube had asked the admirals whether cruisers operating south of the equator, far away from French bases of support, should follow the principle that *la guerre nourrit la guerre*—war feeds war. The Council of Admiralty stressed in their answer to the minister that it was important that the cruisers could operate south of the equator. If there were to be a war against Great Britain the mission of the cruisers would be:

> to cut trade routes chasing and destroying without mercy English merchantmen, and the constant threat of their sudden appearance everywhere will no doubt have an even stronger impact than the material losses inflicted on them.—If on the contrary one restrains their area of operations to the coasts of Europe, the naval forces of England will dominate by their superiority in numbers [...].⁴⁹

The admirals agreed that France did not have enough bases around the world to support and resupply cruisers on such missions. They therefore subscribed to the principle that *la guerre nourrit la guerre*, but

---

⁴⁷ SHM, BB8-914: Conseil d'Amirauté: *Procès-verbal de la séance du 21 Mai 1886.*
⁴⁸ *Ibid.*
⁴⁹ SHM, BB8-915: Conseil d'Amirauté: *Procès-verbal de la séance du 7 Janvier 1887.*

urged the Ministry of Marine to plan for supply ships that could support the cruisers.

Although the Council of Admiralty to a large extent supported Aube's vision on commercial warfare against Great Britain, their determination that the Triple Alliance should be met by traditional fleet warfare was always present in their argumentation. They insisted that the cruisers should be built to meet both a scenario for commercial warfare against Great Britain and a scenario for fleet warfare against the Triple Alliance. The Council of Admiralty admitted that light, fast cruisers would have been sufficient for commerce warfare, but against inferior navies like the German and Italian robust cruisers would be necessary to engage the enemy's battle fleet and cruisers. The admirals therefore insisted that the cruisers had to be real warships.[50]

The discussions among the leading flag officers of the French Navy showed that they to a great extent had adopted the strategic view of the *jeune école* concerning how to fight a potential war against Great Britain. But by raising certain reservations concerning how to fight the dominant power (i.e. accepting fleet warfare in the Mediterranean and insisting on robust cruisers) and by stressing that the Triple Alliance should be met by fleet warfare, the Council of Admiralty ended up advocating a rather traditional, balanced fleet of battleships, cruisers and coastal defence vessels. Echoing the *jeune école*'s arguments on commerce warfare against Great Britain thus only to a certain extent threatened the traditional composition of the fleet. The officers of the Council of Admiralty were, however, not traditionalists in the sense that France should concentrate on battle fleet warfare. They rather argued along reformist lines that resemble very much those of the *jeune école*'s predecessor, Admiral Richild Grivel, while rejecting the radical policies of the *jeune école* announcing the end of fleet warfare.

Summary

Théophile Aube entered office as Minister of Marine determined to transform the French Navy according to the ideas of the *jeune école*. The most obvious consequence of the ascendancy of the *jeune école* at the Ministry of Marine was that work on the four battleships of the *Hoche*

---

[50] SHM, BB8-914: Conseil d'Amirauté: *Procès-verbal de la séance du 21 Mai 1886*.

and *Magenta* classes was stopped, and the construction of small gunboats (*bateaux-canons*) and torpedo boats intensified. Aube was not content with using his position just to force through organisational changes and redirect the construction programme. He was bent on convincing his fellow officers that the *jeune école* was right, both concerning his assessment of who the most likely enemy would be and how it should be fought, and on the excellence of torpedo boats and consequently the irrelevance of battle ships.

Aube invited the Council of Admiralty to discuss strategic matters three times, and he also used the planning conferences and the evaluations of the summer manoeuvres to touch upon strategic matters. The years 1886–1887 were, however, not the best time to convince French military leaders that Great Britain was the likely enemy and that the French Navy should plan accordingly. Aube's colleague the Minister of War, General Boulanger, played a pivotal role in a jingoistic campaign against Germany contributing to heated controversies with France's continental rival. The tense situation between France and Germany influenced the strategic outlook of French naval officers. A two-front naval war against the Triple Alliance partners, Germany and Italy, was viewed as the most likely.

Aube did not share the prevalent hysteria with regard to the German and Italian menace, and insisted that French colonial rivalry with Great Britain eventually would lead to a confrontation between the two countries. Although he did not succeed in convincing the admirals that the French Navy should concentrate on preparing itself to fight the Royal Navy, they accepted central elements of the *jeune école*'s guidelines on how the French Navy most effectively should operate if there was to be a war against Great Britain. They agreed that the French Navy would be no match for the Royal Navy in fleet warfare in British home waters, and that it should place its main effort on commerce raiding. While Aube more or less dismissed fleet warfare as an option for the French Navy, the majority of the admirals in the Council of Admiralty argued for a twofold strategy. They maintained that the battleships should be concentrated in the Mediterranean where they could engage in fleet warfare against the Royal Navy, while commerce raiding should be conducted in the Atlantic and on the main trade routes cutting Great Britain off from her colonies. What was fundamentally new in the arguments now put forward by the Council of Admiralty was their insistence that *guerre de course* should be carried out *à outrance*.

Aube and Charmes had argued that small, cheap torpedo boats would be a deadly threat not only to battleships operating close to shore, but also to battleships and enemy trade on the high seas. The Council of Admiralty argued that cruisers should carry out commerce warfare on the high seas, while torpedo boats were suited for coastal warfare. The members opened up for a certain *rapprochement* with the *jeune école*'s advocacy for the efficiency of smaller and cheaper vessels. The Council proposed that small commerce-raiders (*avisos de course*) could be used on the Atlantic coast and in the Channel to chase British merchant ships and even in order to conduct raids against warships. Aube was, however, determined to prove the excellence of the torpedo boats. He ordered a number of torpedo boats to undertake demanding winter transits from Cherbourg, Lorient and Brest to Toulon in order to test the boats and the crew. Aube used the summer manoeuvre of 1886 to test the torpedo boats against the battle fleet. Neither the transits nor the summer manoeuvre seemed conclusive with regard to the qualities of the torpedo boats. Aube noted that the boats had proved to have good nautical qualities, but he seems tacitly to have accepted that they were not autonomous to the extent that he and Charmes had claimed in their most optimistic moments. In the deliberations with the Council of Admiralty he argued for cruisers as commerce-raiders on the high seas, and he did not mention torpedo boats in such a role.

Aube's ministry has been viewed by many naval officers and historians as a traumatic experience splitting the French Navy into two factions. It is no doubt that Aube's tenure as Minister of Marine upset the French naval establishment. He challenged their strategic thinking and disrupted the Navy's building programmes in his effort to build a navy that was consistent with his strategic visions. A certain *rapprochement* between the Minister of Marine and the predominantly traditionalist Council of Admiralty could, however, be seen in some areas. Aube's testing of some of the elements of his theories obviously had a sobering effect on his most optimistic assumptions. Despite the positive reports on the seagoing qualities of the torpedo boats, Aube accepted that they did not have the necessary qualities in order to operate on the high seas chasing British merchantmen. Aube and the Council of Admiralty agreed that commerce warfare on the high seas should be conducted with cruisers. An important concession on behalf of the Council of Admiralty to Aube's radical ideas was the Council's adoption of *guerre de course à outrance* as a legitimate way to fight Great

Britain. The summer manoeuvre of 1886 proved Aube right that the torpedo boats would make a close blockade very costly to impose. Aube did not, however, win through with his view that battle ships and fleet warfare were outdated in naval warfare. The Council of Admiralty still insisted on a balanced fleet.

CHAPTER THREE

THE LEGACY OF THE *JEUNE ÉCOLE*

After the fall of the Goblet cabinet Aube retired to provincial life for the last three years of his life, and there was no one with his capacity ready to represent and develop further the ideas of the *jeune école*. His intellectual predecessor, Grivel, had died at the age of fifty-five of fever in Senegal in 1882, while Aube's most active advocate, Gabriel Charmes, died at the age of thirty-six just at the start of Aube's ministry.

The early 1890s, however, saw a revival of theoretical discussions among naval officers that were strongly inspired by Aube and Charmes. Some of these officers were prolific writers, but they did not hold formal positions in which they could exercise any significant influence on the organisation of the French Navy. These officers were, however, important in that they further developed the theories of the *jeune école* and thereby maintained it as a clear and coherent alternative to the traditionalists who were back in office in the Ministry of Marine.

The first radical ministry to take office during the Third Republic, that of Léon Bourgeois in November 1895, and the appointment of the civilian politician Edouard Lockroy as Minister of Marine, represented the return to power of the *jeune école*. His first period of office lasted six months. He was appointed Minister of Marine a second time in June 1898, and held the office until June the following year. Lockroy's ideas on the challenges facing the French Navy and how it should be organised were in accordance with, and were probably inspired by, the best and most prominent *jeune école* thinker in the post-Aube era, Admiral Fournier. These two men exercised considerable influence over the French Navy because of the prominent positions they held. One of the important decisions made by Lockroy as Minister of Marine was to establish a naval staff college. Lokcroy appointed Admiral Fournier as the first commander of the college. However, the staff college did not turn into an institution preaching the gospel of the *jeune école*. Most of the lecturers in strategy, tactics and international law tried to give a presentation as accurate as possible of the strategic challenges facing the French Navy, although few of them can be said to have had an unbiased view of the different schools within naval thought. The *jeune école*'s prominent position on the curriculum of the college was primarily due to the fact that the *jeune école* represented the only coherent alternative naval theory to that of the traditionalists. The staff college became, along with the Superior Council, newspapers and magazines, and to some extent the Parliament, one of the arenas in which naval strategy was discussed and formulated in the 1890s.

The Strategic Outlook of the French Navy up to the Fashoda Crisis

In a confidential 90-page memorandum on the status of the French Navy written in the aftermath of the Fashoda Crisis, the Minister of Marine, Jean-Louis de Lanessan, sharply criticised French naval strategy as it had been practiced more or less since the establishment of the Triple Alliance. During these years it had been almost an absolute rule that one did not "take any interest in England. One dismissed any idea of war against this power, and consequently, one did not in any manner consider organising our navy with an eye to such a war [...]", Lanessan argued.[1]

Lanessan's allegation that the French naval establishment had been almost single-mindedly occupied with the Triple Alliance as a potential enemy through most of the 1880s and 1890s was not unfounded. We have seen how Aube during his period as Minister of Marine encountered opposition when he attempted to draw up manoeuvres which designated Great Britain the enemy. As we shall see, the strategic considerations and the operational planning of the General Staff of the Ministry of Marine and the commanders in chief in Toulon and Brest also focused on the Triple Alliance well into the second half of the 1890s.

French concerns over the Triple Alliance's naval ambitions in the late 1880s were not unfounded. Italy entered into several diplomatic agreements in the late 1880s to check the ambitions to change the Mediterranean status quo that it believed France to be harbouring.[2] These agreements and naval diplomacy in the form of port calls and

---

[1] SHM, BB4-2437: *Note de M. de Lanessan sur la situation et les besoins de notre marine*, November 1899, p. 3.

[2] Great Britain, Germany and Austria were all involved in different forms of naval diplomacy to convince the French of the strength of the coalition against them. Ropp: *The Development of a Modern Navy*, pp. 192–195.

demonstrations alerted the French Navy to a potential threat from Italy supported by her allies. In November 1888 Germany sent four battleships to Maddalena on Sardinia for a joint visit with the Italian fleet. This made a combined fleet of ten battleships, plus five cruisers, seven torpedo-gunboats, and twenty-four high-seas torpedo boats. The fleet at Toulon at that time comprised five battleships, three older ships with reduced crews, and three cruisers. The French were alarmed by the comparison. Even compared to Italy the French Mediterranean Fleet was inferior in modern ships.[3] In November 1890 the Superior Council, as the Council of Admiralty recently had been renamed, approved the first large naval programme since 1872. The focus of the programme was exclusively on the Triple Alliance, and it was based on the principle that "the fighting units of the French fleet must be equal in number to those of the combined fleets of the Triple Alliance."[4]

Great Britain adopted a massive naval construction programme (the Naval Defence Act of 1889) just before the Superior Council approved the French naval programme. The British government's declared aim was to make the Royal Navy equal to the combined strength of the French Navy and any other naval power. Despite the formidable British building programme, the French felt that the immediate danger in the 1890s came not from the British but from Italy and the Triple Alliance. Whereas the Royal Navy had been strengthened during the 1890s to the extent that it was obvious to any French naval officer during the Fashoda Crisis that the French Navy would be overwhelmed if France chose to fight Great Britain, the Italian Navy experienced a dramatic decline. In 1889 the Italian Navy was, if not equal to the French, at least the third largest in the world; a decade later it had fallen to seventh place. From 158 million lire in 1888, the Italian naval budget dropped to 114 million in 1890 and to 99 in 1893, and it no longer posed any threat to French control of the Mediterranean.[5] Yet the French Navy concentrated its attention on Italy and the Triple Alliance right up to the Fashoda Crisis.

The General Staff of the Ministry of Marine prepared a number of operational plans in the first half of the 1890s for the case of war

---

[3] *Ibid.*: pp. 196–197.
[4] SHM, 1 CC 195 aa 6: Lectures by Capitaine de frégate: *Marine Française. Stratégie, Tactique. 1ère Partie. Stratégie Marine Française* (Ecole des Hautes Etudes de la Marine, Paris, 1897–1898), p. 69.
[5] Ropp: *The Development of a Modern Navy*, pp. 197–199.

88   CHAPTER THREE

against Italy. Despite occasional outcries depicting Italy as a formidable enemy, the plans worked out by the General Staff argued in favour of an offensive approach, which presupposed that the French Navy would have the upper hand both on the high seas and in littoral waters. Smaller units were sent out to do reconnaissance on the Italian coast,[6] and detailed studies of how bombardments should be conducted against several ports, arsenals, railways, factories producing war material etc. were worked out.[7] A bombardment of the strategically important naval base on the Maddelena Island on the northern tip of Sardinia, close to the Strait of Bonifacio, was to be conducted in combination with amphibious attacks. Aube had argued in his writings that any fleet that held the Strait of Bonifacio between Sardinia and Corsica would have a foothold on Corsica. It could not be blockaded since it had two exit routes, and it could defend La Spezia (a port of the same status as Toulon and Malta), cover Genoa, and watch or menace Toulon and all of Provence.[8] The General Staff also worked out plans for a possible amphibious landing and an occupation of parts of Sicily. These plans were, however, discarded in the internal discussions of the General Staff. The possibilities for mooring were not viewed as satisfactory, and the Mediterranean Fleet was not considered to have the necessary resources to carry out such an amphibious landing.[9]

The French Navy's confidence that it would be able to handle the Italian Navy was evident in the reasoning underlying the war plans that were worked out. The plans were characterised by the objective of creating a situation where a conflict between the two navies would be resolved by traditional fleet warfare. Whereas the rationale behind the General Staff's plans for bombarding and potential landings traditionally

---

[6] SHM, BB4-2437: See for example detailed reports from smaller units that undertook reconnaissance on the Italian coast in the autumn of 1891.
[7] SHM, BB4-2437: EMG 3ème section: *Operation de guerre*, April–December 1892. These were different detailed plans worked out for war in the Mediterranean. They all concentrated on Italy as the enemy; EMG 3ème section: (these plans were worked out by a specialist in artillery and sent to the General Staff for further studies): Plans for bombardment of the arsenal of La Spezia, 20 February 1892 and March 1893; EMG 3ème section: Bombardment of San Pied d'Arena, 18 July 1895; Bombardment of Sestri-Fonente, 18 July 1895; Bombardment of Castillamare, 18 July 1895; Bombardment of Tarente, 19 July 1895.
[8] Th. Aube: "Italie et Levant", p. 36.
[9] SHM, BB4-2437: EMG 3ème section: *Occupation éventuelle d'un point de la Sicile*, 19 July 1895; EMG 2ème section: *Occupation éventuelle d'un point de la côte O de la Sicile*, 19 July 1895.

had been to disrupt the mobilisation of the Italian army, the General Staff now argued that it should be carried out in order to provoke encounters between the Italian and French fleets.[10] The French planners were convinced that it would be impossible for the Italian fleet to stay in port while the French fleet was ravaging their coast. The Italian battle fleet would be forced to take up the fight against the French.

The German Navy had not been perceived as a real threat to France before the 1890s. The General Staff and the local commanders in Brest and the Channel ports had kept an eye on it, but the French naval leadership never switched its focus from Italy as the power that could pose a serious naval threat to France. The vast majority of French naval forces were stationed in Toulon in the Mediterranean. In the case of a two-front naval war against the Triple Alliance, the French planned to check the German Navy with the forces at their disposal in Brest and the Channel ports until the Mediterranean Fleet had finished off the Italian Navy. The Mediterranean Fleet would then join the forces in the Channel in what was seen to be an easy match against the Germans.

An increasing concern regarding the capability of the German Navy can, however, be noticed through the 1890s. Late in 1891, the Minister of Marine asked the Commander-in-Chief of the battleship division stationed in Brest, Rear Admiral Gervais, to come up with a contingency plan for a war against the Triple Alliance. Admiral Gervais listed the order of battle of the German fleet and the French Northern Fleet and concluded that the German fleet was at least equal if not superior to the French. The German fleet was superior in cruisers, auxiliary cruisers and definitely in torpedo boats, Gervais maintained. He was, however, well aware that the German Navy faced the same fundamental strategic problem as France did; they both had two coasts separated by narrow straits that were not under the respective states' control. As long as Denmark stayed neutral in a conflict between the Triple Alliance and France, the German Navy could, however, concentrate its force in the North Sea, Gervais maintained.[11]

---

[10] SHM, BB4-2437: EMG 3ème section: *Guerre avec la Tripple-Alliance*, February 1895.

[11] SHM, BB4-2437: *Le Contre-Amiral Gervais, Commandant en Chef de la Division Cuirassée du Nord à Monsieur le Sénateur, Ministre de la Marine*, 19 December 1891. Denmark's position in such a conflict was given some attention by the General Staff, both regarding the Germans' possibilities to freely use the straits and those of France's ally, Russia. See SHM, BB-2437: EMG 3ème section: *Opération de guerre. Cooperation éventuelle du Danemark aux opérations maritimes*, November 1892.

In early 1895, the Commander-in-Chief of the Northern Fleet, Vice Admiral Alquier, in a memorandum to the minister accused French war planning of being based on the illusion that the German Navy was weak and only able to conduct minor, isolated operations that would have no impact on the outcome of the war. Vice Admiral Alquier reminded the minister that the progress of the German Navy over the last 25 years had been considerable, and that this development had accelerated after Wilhelm II acceded to the throne in 1888. Alquier argued that as a consequence the focus of the French Navy should be shifted from the Italian Navy to the German Navy as the most dangerous maritime enemy in case of war against the Triple Alliance. The centre of maritime warfare would thus not be in the Mediterranean as previously envisaged, but in the north. Alquier further claimed that the German Navy would be differently organised and operate much more energetically and offensively than Italy. The German order of battle disclosed that when the German fleet arrived at Pas-de-Calais, it would be with battleships and cruisers far superior to what the French could muster. The Commander-in-Chief of the Northern Fleet's message to the Minister of Marine was thus that the French fleet should be reorganised with a new emphasis on the German naval threat. Alquier demanded that the Northern Fleet should at least be equal to the German fleet in battleships and cruisers.[12]

Vice Admiral Parrayon, who was appointed Commander-in-Chief of the Northern Fleet in November 1896, followed up Alquier's alarmist description of the German threat.[13] He repeated Alquier's argument and claimed that it would be the Northern Fleet that would be in the front line in case of war against the Triple Alliance. Parrayon warned that the German Navy would be able to carry out an attack on Dunkirk, which was geographically as close to Wilhelmshafen as to Brest, with four battleships accompanied by two or three flotillas of the Germans' seaworthy torpedo boats within 24 hours after the outbreak of war. The operational planners in the Ministry of Marine also shared the view that the German Navy probably would try a surprise attack. Such

---

[12] SHM, BB4-2437: *Le VA Alquier, Commandent en Chef l'Escadre du Nord à M. le Ministre de la Marine*, 12 February 1895.

[13] Vice Admiral Régnault de Prémesnil commanded the Northern Fleet in the period (October 1895–November 1896) between the commands of Vice Admiral Alquier and Vice Admiral Parrayon.

an attack would benefit from the fact that the French would need time to mobilise in order to deploy comparable forces against the attacking German fleet. The admiral therefore asked for more permanent crews to enhance the fleet's ability to react quickly. If not, Parrayon complained, he would not be able to deploy more than one or two fast cruisers, a few high-seas torpedo boats and some requisitioned scouting vessels.[14]

By this time the German naval threat had for some years been the overriding question for the commanders of the Northern Fleet, to the extent that when Vice Admiral Barréra took over as Commander-in-Chief in October 1897, he could not find any plans that had been worked out for the case of a war against Great Britain.[15] Despite his surprise at this fact, he followed in the path of his predecessors and continued to modify the plans on how to counter a German attack. In the summer of 1898, paradoxically enough, shortly after the Niger crisis that had embittered the relations between France and Great Britain during the build up to the Fashoda Crisis, Barréra sent the Minister of Marine a detailed plan on how to face a German attack. He envisaged that the German force would sail close to the British coast, where the navigation was easier and where it could avoid being harassed and attacked by French torpedo boats, before it turned towards the French coast. The crucial point, as it had been for his predecessors, was how to gain an early warning of a German attack. To solve this problem he proposed to station a cruiser in the Straits of Dover as a scout, assisted by torpedo boats acting as messengers to the naval authorities on shore.[16]

The rather alarmist campaigns promoted by the commanders of the Northern Fleet exaggerated the alleged German naval build-up. In the 1870s, 1880s, and even in the early 1890s, naval power did not seem very important in Germany. Germany relied primarily on its strong army. After unification in 1870–71, Imperial Germany began to construct a fleet, but it only aspired to second-class strength. The accession of Emperor Wilhelm II to the throne in 1888, marked, however, an end

---

[14] SHM, BB4-2437: *Le VA Parrayon, Commandant en Chef l'Escadre du Nord à M. le Ministre de la Marine* (with comments made in the Ministry of Marine), 19 January 1897.

[15] SHM, BB4-2437: *Le VA Barréra, Commandant en Chef l'Escadre du Nord à M. le Ministre de la Marine*, 1 December 1897.

[16] SHM, BB4-2437: *Le VA Barréra, Commandant en Chef l'Escadre du Nord à M. le Ministre de la Marine*, 26 July 1898.

both of a long era of almost exclusive focus on land power, and of a relative decline for the Navy. The 1890s, up to the Fashoda Crisis, saw the construction of four 10,000 ton *Brandenburg* battleships and the first of the three battleships of the 11,100 ton *Kaiser Friedrich III* class was laid down (1894) and commissioned (1898) in this period. New coastal battleships and armoured cruisers were also part of the modernization of the German Navy. A certain build-up and modernisation of the German Navy did therefore take place during the first part of Wilhelm II's reign, but the Tirpitz Plan and the German Navy Laws were yet to come. On paper, in 1897, France was still the obvious number two, behind Great Britain, in naval strength.[17]

The Northern Fleet commanders' seeming obsession with the German Navy can partly be explained by the fact that their main responsibility was the northern coast, and that they were obliged to keep a close watch on the development of the German Navy and make contingency plans for a possible war against Germany. Yet these admirals went further than just arguing that the German Navy was becoming a serious competitor of the French Navy, at least in the north, given the distribution of the French fleet. They criticised the overall priorities of the French Navy. Their arguments were not restricted to the alleged build-up of the German Navy, but also took account of the decline of the Italian Navy throughout the 1890s. Italy was no longer the principal naval power of the Triple Alliance and the Northern Fleet should hence be given priority at the cost of the Mediterranean Fleet, they concluded.

The shift in attention from the Italian to the German Navy as the most potent naval power within the Triple Alliance did not bring any fundamental change in operational planning. A war against Germany would indeed be more defensive in character, and bombardment of enemy infrastructure with military significance that had been an important part of the naval plans against Italy was not an integral part of the plans against Germany. The challenge would rather be to avoid a surprise attack on French harbours. Such attacks were not estimated to have any significant military consequences, but they could have a

---

[17] Michael Epkenhans: "Technology, Shipbuilding and Future Combat in Germany, 1880–1914" in Phillips Payson O'Brien: *Technology and Naval Combat in the Twentieth Century and Beyond* (London, 2001), pp. 54–55; Kennedy: *The Rise and Fall of British Naval Mastery*, pp. 208–209; Lawrence Sondhaus: *Naval Warfare 1815–1914* (London, 2001), pp. 179–180.

terrible effect on the morale of French public opinion.[18] The objective of the French Navy would thus be to detect the German fleet and concentrate forces to fight traditional fleet warfare assisted by lighter craft that could operate in the Channel. Thus, war planning against Italy and Germany were both based on traditional naval warfare, with the battle fleet playing the pivotal role. Wars against Italy and Germany would be conducted on the premise that the French had the superior navy. Such a precondition did not encourage solutions inspired by the *jeune école*, although the defensive imperatives of a war against Germany called for a good littoral defence based on smaller, fast vessels.

German industrialisation had, however, revealed an Achilles heel that could be targeted by the French Navy, a dependence on seaborne imports that could prove decisive in a protracted war. This insight was clear to Bismarck's successor as Reich Chancellor, Leo Caprivi. Caprivi, who had headed the Admiralty from 1883 to 1888, brought with him an understanding of the role of the Navy in national defence when he took over as Chancellor in 1890. He realized that in a protracted war of attrition with France and Russia the consequences of a naval blockade cutting off German seaborne trade would be much more severe than in earlier wars. Industrialization and economic specialization had made Germany dependent on imports of strategic raw materials, and also on access to overseas export markets.[19]

Protecting German commerce by convoying ships was not practicable, and the other obvious solution, to seek out and destroy the enemy's cruisers with one's own, would be very risky against France with her superior number of cruisers. Germany's geographical position was a further obstacle that would make such an undertaking difficult for the German cruisers. Caprivi pointed out that the exits to the Atlantic passed either through the Channel or north of Scotland. There would be no problem for a superior fleet to close the Channel for German warships, Caprivi warned. An enemy fleet could also without great difficulties observe the passage north of Scotland and make it dangerous for German warships to pass. Germany's geographical position and France's superiority in cruisers would thus make the task of protecting trade in the Atlantic sea-lanes impossible. Caprivi did not, however, think

---

[18] SHM, BB4-2437: *Le VA Parrayon, Commandent en Chef l'Escadre du Nord à M. le Ministre de la Marine*, 19 January 1897.
[19] Hobson: *Imperialism at Sea*, pp. 144–150.

this would stop all trade. He hoped that modern merchant ships had a good chance to escape enemy cruisers, which in turn required that the German Navy could be able to prevent a close blockade. Caprivi trusted the armoured coastal defence ships and torpedo boats to keep the entrances to the harbours open.[20]

The most important factor that would influence the flow of seaborne goods to Germany in a war against France would be the attitude of Britain. Caprivi recognized that if Britain observed the same strict neutrality that it had done in 1870, French operations would to some extent be hampered by the inability to purchase coal in British ports. More important, however, was the question of whether Great Britain and the United States would insist on their rights as neutrals. Then Germany could be supplied with strategic raw materials in neutral holds. German vessels could even transfer to neutral flags to enjoy protection against capture. If Britain were to accept French violations of neutrality or even an extension of the definition of contraband to cover foodstuffs, there was not much Germany could do about it.[21]

Many of the reflections made in Germany concerning her increased dependency on trade and thus her exposure to commercial warfare could also be seen in the French Navy's planning. In the French Northern Fleet detailed instructions were made for how commerce raiding should be conducted in case of war against the Triple Alliance. In the instructions for commerce raiding that the Commander-in-Chief of the French Northern Fleet, Vice Admiral Parrayon, sent to the Minister of Marine for approval, he stressed that the ships dedicated to commerce warfare under his command:

> should seek to hurt enemy commerce as much as possible, while adhering to international law and the laws of humanity. The prizes you have taken shall be destroyed after you have removed all usable goods and you have been able to disembark the crew.[22]

Although the use of commerce warfare against Germany could be seen as an approval of *jeune école* warfare, the restrictions placed on the manner in which this warfare was to be conducted and the minor part in the overall naval war against Germany it was meant to play,

---

[20] *Ibid.*, p. 150.
[21] *Ibid.*, p. 154.
[22] SHM, BB4-2437: *Le VA Parrayon, Commandent en Chef l'Escadre du Nord à M. le Ministre de la Marine*, 10 October 1897.

resembled traditional naval warfare rather than *jeune école* warfare with its emphasis on unrestricted commercial warfare.

The risk of provoking the neutrals to rally against France would have more severe consequences in a war against Germany than against Great Britain. The French considerations concerning the challenge from the neutrals resembled very much the considerations put forward by Caprivi. Commander Houette precisely formulated the problem in his lectures on strategy at the French naval staff college. He predicted that Germany immediately after the first French attack on its commerce would turn to neutral shipping to ensure the necessary flow of goods to and from Germany. To illustrate the strategic consequences for France if the French Navy were still to pursue large-scale commerce warfare he asked his students rhetorically: "How shall we handle this? Inspect all neutral ships on the high seas to ensure that they are not carrying contraband to Hamburg? You know who these neutrals will be and how impossible such actions will be?"[23] Houette's question to his students pointed to the fact that any effective campaign to stop trade to and from Germany would affect the largest merchant marine of the world, and that this merchant marine was protected by the world's most powerful navy. Such warfare could hence risk tipping the balance against France in a way that would be disastrous to the French Navy and the total French war effort. The risk would hence exceed the expected gains.

French diplomats focused much of their attention in the early 1890s on how to counterbalance the Triple Alliance. The sense of insecurity that had been felt by the French towards Germany since the Franco-Prussian War was heightened during the 1890s by a growing awareness of France's inferiority to Germany in material resources.[24] Russia was seen as an ally who could offer some measure of security against Germany. Most Russian statesmen, however, regarded the Third Republic more or less as the headquarters of an international revolutionary movement. The future Tsar Nicholas II declared in 1887: "May God preserve us from an alliance with France [...] It would mean the invasion of Russia by Revolution."[25] But financial reasons and foreign policy interests in the Levant, Central Asia and the Far East contributed to a

---

[23] SHM, 1 CC Aa 6: Lectures by Capitaine de frégate Houette: *Stratégie maritime Française* (Ecole des Hautes Etudes de la Marine, Paris, 1897–1898).

[24] Christopher M. Andrew: *Théophile Delcassé and the Making of the Entente Cordiale* (London, 1968) p. 15.

[25] Quoted in *ibid.*, p. 14.

Russian U-turn.[26] In 1891 France and Russia signed a political entente, which was to be the first stage of the Franco-Russian alliance. A military convention was concluded at the end of 1893.

The Franco-Russian *rapprochement* was made public by the visit of the French fleet to the Russian naval base of Kronstadt in 1891. Two years later a Russian squadron made a return visit to Toulon. Although naval visits played a very visible role in the conclusions of the alliance, the French Navy did not consider the agreement to have much impact on the naval balance between the European powers. A report from the French Navy's General Staff concerning possible assistance from the Russian Navy in the case of a war against the Triple Alliance reveals that the confidence in the Russian Navy's ability to contribute to a joint naval war effort against the Triple Alliance was not very high. The General Staff warned that the French Navy should not count on any substantial assistance from Russia, except for the possibility that the Russian Navy could tie up some German forces in the Baltic.[27] A pessimistic view of the Franco-Russian alliance's significance for the naval balance dominated within the French Navy throughout the 1890s.[28] The Franco-Russian alliance did, however, cause concern in the major European navies and was one of the factors that contributed to the Mediterranean scare of 1893.[29]

The focus on Italy and Germany as the most likely naval opponents during the period between Aube's departure as Minister of Marine and the eve of the Fashoda Crisis was not congenial to *jeune école* strategies. Despite certain attempts to portray both Italy and Germany as redoubtable enemies, French naval planning revealed a persistent belief in French naval superiority. This superiority led to an insistence on the status quo in French naval priorities with a focus on traditional fleet warfare to fight the Triple Alliance. This pause in the rivalry between radically different views on naval strategy seemed to be welcomed and encouraged by a French naval establishment that longed for some stability and predictability.

---

[26] Motte: *Une éducation géostratégique*, p. 245.
[27] SHM, BB4-2437: EMG 3ème section: *Opération de guerre. Concour de la Flotte Russe dans les opérations de guerre contre la Triple Alliance*, June 1892.
[28] See i.e. SHM, 190 GG2 36–37: EMG 1ème Section: *Situation de la flotte russe*, 25 November 1898.
[29] Marder: *The Anatomy of British Sea Power*, pp. 74–187; Ropp: *The Development of a Modern Navy*, pp. 244–246.

Although the *jeune école* no longer held central positions in the Navy, Aube's followers continued to publicise their ideas.

The Disciples of Aube

In the period after the tenure of Aube the successors to the *jeune école* were officers who were productive writers but who did not hold any formal positions where they could exercise any significant influence on the organisation of the French Navy. They did, however, achieve considerable popularity, and contributed to a continued support for the ideas of the *jeune école* among younger officers, the Radicals in Parliament and the press.

The most prolific writers within the *jeune école* tradition were the journalist Paul Fontin (writing under the pseudonym Commandant Z) and Lieutenant Mathieu-Jean-Marie Vignot (writing as H. Montéchant). They had both worked closely with Aube. Commandant Z was the former private secretary of Aube, whereas Montéchant had been Aube's aide de camp. A certain Lieutenant X, who wrote an extensive introduction to Montéchant and Commandant Z's *Essai de Stratégie navale*, complemented their arguments.

Commandant Z, Montéchant and Lieutenant X were known by their contemporaries as disciples of Aube, a label they themselves used to promote their writings.[30] Aube's legacy was evident in most of their writing. Their views on the character of future wars, on the most probable and most dangerous enemy, and on the overall strategy to win a naval war concurred for the most part with those of Aube and Charmes. The most significant difference between the ideas put forward by Aube and Charmes and those of their disciples, had to do with putting the theory into operation. Montéchant, Commandant Z and Lieutenant X argued in favour of what is thought of by some as the naval theory of *jeune école*: small, fast torpedo boats operating in the littorals.[31]

---

[30] Contre-amiral Réveillère: Introduction to Commandant Z and H. Montéchant: *Les guerres navales de demain* (Paris, 1891), p. X.

[31] One recent example is Roald Berg's study of the Norwegian Armed Forces 1814–1905. Here he places the label *jeune école* on Norwegian naval officers who argued that the Navy should give priority to coastal defence, and that it should be based on small, fast gunboats and torpedo boats benefiting from the topography of the Norwegian fiords and littorals. Roald Berg: *Profesjon-union-nasjon, 1814–1905*, Vol. II of *Norsk forsvarshistorie* (Bergen, 2001), pp. 195, 236, 255, 289, 302, 310.

Total War and International Law

The view that future wars would be total in character and scope was fundamental to the *jeune école*. Commandant Z, Montéchant and Lieutenant X paid close attention to two aspects of the total character of future wars. Firstly, they argued, as Aube and Charmes had done, that the character of war had changed. It was a consequence of a combination of social and military change, and experience confirmed that this would enhance the brutality of future wars. Future conflicts would see nations fighting nations in existential wars, they argued, and the interests at stake were such that there would be no limits to the brutality with which they would be waged. Secondly, they argued that it lay in the logic of war that the strongest of the parties had the right to take advantage of his superiority. This was a permanent character of war.

To set the stage, Admiral Réveillère, in his introduction to Commandant Z and Montéchant's *Les guerres navales de demain*, described what future wars would be like:

> What will be really terrifying in the next war is not the bloody drama on the battlefield, it will be the stoppage of society [...] From farmer to banker, everybody will be at the front [...] everybody consumes, nobody produces [...]
> It is [like] the general strike.
> Silence will prevail in the fields, in all the factories, which cannot stop for one day without taking away the bread from thousands of mouths.
> The war will be an economic fight rather than a military struggle.
> Here and there, moreover, one hesitates to stake one's all: the stake is the annihilation of a race.[32]

Commandant Z and Montéchant followed up Réveillère's introductory remarks by quoting Clausewitz and Colmar von der Goltz' reflections on the character of future wars. The quotations served the purpose of underlining that the era of limited wars definitely was over:

> Everyone knows that it [the next war] will be conducted with a destructive violence unknown till this day. It will be the exodus of two peoples and not the fight of two armies. Both sides will mobilise the full extent of their morale in a fight *à outrance* and the total sum of their intelligence in order to annihilate one another.[33]

---

[32] Réveillère: Introduction to Commandant Z and H. Montéchant: *Les guerres navales de demain*, pp. VIII–IX.

[33] Colmar von der Goltz: *La nation armée*, quoted in Commandant Z and H. Montéchant: *Les guerres navales de demain*, p. 3.

The effort put into describing the character of future wars was most probably a result of a genuine interest in the very phenomenon of war and the interaction between the development of military affairs, society and international politics. Their conclusions were obviously also a necessary precondition for another cornerstone in *jeune école*'s theory, that of unrestricted commercial warfare. The important message was that future wars would be existential wars with a brutality that made international law insignificant. Aube and Charmes had both used Colmar von der Goltz as a witness to testify that the French Navy should rid itself of any moral restrictions on warfare. Commandant Z and Montéchant chose to use Colmar von der Goltz for the same purpose. There is, however, no reason to believe that they did not genuinely share the views of Colmar von der Goltz.

The disciples of Aube and Charmes argued that the changes in the nature of wars that had occurred gradually, and that had been clearly seen in both the American Civil War and the Franco-Prussian war, pointed to a strategy that should aim at the very foundations of society and that it should be conducted with few moral restraints. Underlying these changes, there were also some permanent characteristics of war that made international law irrelevant in war, according to Commandant Z, Montéchant and Lieutenant X. It was Lieutenant X, in his introduction to *Essai de stratégie navale*, who developed a reasoning that had as its bottom line that any strategy would have to rest on the assumption of the right of the strongest party. It would always be the strongest side that set the rules, and Lieutenant X had nothing but contempt for what he called generosity in war:

> Generosity can only have its place in treaties. In action, [generosity] is nothing but cowardice, weakness or foolishness. The stronger must exploit to the outmost his terrible superiority in the struggle. There are no limits to pursuing one's interests and the crushing defeat of the enemy.[34]

According to Lieutenant X, the logic of the right of the stronger was also valid in confrontations between warships and merchantmen. He saw in principle no difference between attacking an inferior military unit and attacking a merchant vessel. The fact that a vessel was not able to defend itself was no less an argument against sending her to the bottom than to sink an inferior warship in an engagement. Both

---

[34] Lieutenant X: Introduction to Commandant Z and H. Montéchant: *Essai de stratégie navale* (Paris, 1893), pp. 19–20.

were inferior, and the outcome of the engagement would be the same in both cases. There was therefore no more crime attached to sinking a merchant vessel from the belligerent nation than one of its warships. The purpose of the attack would be the same in both cases, to ruin the enemy.[35] Lieutenant X hence reduced the moral issue to whether the stronger was in his right to destroy the weaker, and not whether the attacked ship was a combatant or a non-combatant.

This approach can only be understood in a context where nations were fighting nations, and where anyone contributing directly or indirectly to the enemy's war effort was a legitimate target. The erasure of the distinction between combatants and non-combatants was also extended to the distinction between belligerents and neutrals. Lieutenant X saw no reason for France to obey the Declaration of Paris of 1856. He claimed that national interests would have to overrule any signed treaty, and he characterised the Declaration of Paris of 1856 as "an imperturbable witness to the concise (*compendieuse*) foolishness of the diplomats."[36]

The Potential Enemies

The heirs of Aube and Charmes predicted an imminent major war. They were not specific about the causes of this war. There was, however, no doubt who the enemies could be. The alternatives were the Triple Alliance or Great Britain. A worst-case scenario where Great Britain joined the Triple Alliance in an effort to crush France was also considered a possibility.[37] Commandant Z and Montéchant argued that the relative importance of the French Navy would be very different in the case of a war against either Great Britain or Germany. War against Italy and Great Britain would be a maritime war, while a war against Germany would mostly be fought with land forces. In the first case the Army would play an auxiliary role, in the second, the Navy would play an auxiliary role.[38]

Commandant Z and Montéchant were convinced that Italy, with only a moderate effort by the French Navy, could be forced to with-

---

[35] *Ibid.*, p. 20.
[36] *Ibid.*, p. 21.
[37] Commandant Z: Avant-propos to Commandant Z and H. Montéchant: *Essai de stratégie navale*, pp. X, XVII.
[38] Commandant Z and H. Montéchant: *Les guerres navales de demain*, p. 4; Rear Admiral Réveillère in the introduction to *ibid.*, p. V.

draw from the Triple Alliance.[39] The reasoning behind this conclusion is a striking example of the *jeune école*'s focus on breaking the morale of the enemy nation, and thus forcing the authorities to the negotiating table. A disregard of international law was a precondition of the plan. Commandant Z and Montéchant argued that the relatively new Italian state lacked national cohesion. "The moral unity of Italy is not yet established", they claimed.[40] It was enough to watch a parading regiment. Although the soldiers wore the same uniform, one could at a glance distinguish the Piedmontese from the Neapolitan, they maintained. They further argued that the North Italians were active and hard working, while the people in the south were lazy and apathetic. The indolence of the South Italians was a result of the climate and the ineffective institutions that governed this part of Italy. The Italian armed forces, like the population from which they were recruited, thus lacked cohesion. Commandant Z and Montéchant also maintained that Italy's situation was further aggravated by the economic and financial situation of the kingdom, which had led to large-scale emigration.[41]

Commandant Z and Montéchant used this analysis as the point of departure for an operational plan that aimed at finding the most effective way of undermining Italian popular support for the war:

> one sees immediately the tactic to use from the start of the war against Italy. One should not carry out any operation but those that are liable to strike at public opinion. When the moral spirit of the nation is broken, material resistance, despite its formidable dimension, will no more be a threat.
>
> Hit fast and hard, submit the Italian coast to repeated strikes, bombard successively all maritime cities, especially Genoa, Leghorn, Naples and Palermo, [...][42]

Commandant Z and Montéchant proposed to start with Leghorn, a city with a defence that did not pose any serious threat to the attacking force. The next city for attack should be Genoa, a better defended city, but as Commandant Z and Montéchant put it:

---

[39] Commandant Z and H. Montéchant: *Les guerres navales de demain*, pp. 108–122; Lieutenant X: Introduction to Commandant Z and H. Montéchant: *Essai de stratégie navale*, pp. 25, 39, 66.
[40] Commandant Z and H. Montéchant: *Les guerres navales de demain*, p. 113.
[41] *Ibid.*, pp. 113–114.
[42] *Ibid.*, p. 114.

one will not be short of targets in a city with 140 000 inhabitants. [...] The Italian west coast has six cities with more than 100 000 inhabitants: Genoa, Leghorn, Naples, Palermo, Messina, Catania. Their destruction will cause an impression on the peninsula of overwhelming danger, which we easily can take advantage of.[43]

Commandant Z and Montéchant did not consider the Italian Navy a formidable enemy. Besides intimidating the Italian population, they thought that the bombardment of Italian coastal cities would force the Italian fleet to leave port and take up the fight against the French Navy. The bombardment of the cities and the defeat of the Italian Navy would force the government to sue for peace. Landing operations on Sicily were considered an additional option to force Italy to surrender. Commerce warfare, except for attacking coastal trade between Italian cities, was not considered effective. In the case of war against Italy, it would rather be French trade that would be exposed, especially the Far East trade that passed through the Suez Canal.[44]

The disciples of Aube admitted that a war against Germany would primarily be decided on the eastern border. They were, however, convinced that the Navy could throw sand in the machinery of German society. They argued that *guerre de course* would have a far greater impact on the outcome of the war than fighting the German Navy. The consequences of sinking cruisers or battleships would be nothing compared to the consequences of sinking a number of transatlantic liners, Lieutenant X argued.[45] As we have seen, the new *jeune école* generation's analysis of what was industrialised Germany's Achilles heel concurred with concerns within the German chancellery. The Reich Chancellor, Leo Caprivi, knew that German industrialisation had led to a dependence on seaborne imports that could prove decisive in a protracted war.[46]

The idea that a war against Germany would be long drawn-out was an important factor in forming the *jeune école*'s view on the optimal French strategy. Commercial warfare and a military alliance with Russia would be the means to wear down German armed forces and

---

[43] *Ibid.*, pp. 118–119.
[44] *Ibid.*, p. 121 (note 1).
[45] Lieutenant X: Introduction to Commandant Z and H. Montéchant: *Essai de stratégie navale*, p. 25.
[46] Hobson: *Imperialism at Sea*, pp. 144–150.

German society. They did not regard the Russian armed forces, and especially the Russian Navy, as a formidable ally in the short term. But they argued that Russia had a geographic, economic and demographic potential it could benefit from in a protracted conflict. According to Admiral Réveillère, Russian generals had maintained that if the initial shock did not crush France, victory would go to the Franco-Russian alliance.[47] The *jeune école* was convinced that if the French Army and Navy's defensive operations succeeded, *guerre de course* and the slow but steady mobilisation of Russian resources would gradually wear down German resistance.

It was, however, as it had been for Aube and Charmes, a war against Great Britain that was the underlying premise for their view on how the French Navy should be organised and fight. Lieutenant X repeated what the *jeune école* saw as the fundamental principle of warfare: "one should seek the sources of welfare of the nation, and then dry up one after the other, beginning with the richest."[48] In the case of Great Britain, her worldwide trade was considered a precondition of and a very important source for the nation's enormous wealth. As his predecessors of the *jeune école* had argued, Lieutenant X insisted that it was the merchant fleet and not the Royal Navy that should be the target of the French Navy:

> To destroy England's fleet, is to aim at her pride rather than her strength. But to sink the ships that bring the English their bread and meat, cotton and wool to the manufactures, gold to the factory owners, wages to the workers, that is what fighting England is all about.[49]

Commandant Z and Montéchant depicted an industrial war against Great Britain that echoed Aube's and Charmes's reasoning behind the strategy of the weak: "*Guerre de course*, industrial warfare, has its formal rules, absolute, tight, from which it is essential never to depart. Fall upon the weak without mercy, run without false shame from the stronger, that is the formula."[50] Commandant Z and Montéchant underlined that the French warships should concentrate their effort on

---

[47] Réveillère: Introduction to Commandant Z and H. Montéchant: *Les guerres navales de demain*, p. VIII.

[48] Lieutenant X: Introduction to Commandant Z and H. Montéchant: *Essai de stratégie navale* (Paris, 1893) p. 25.

[49] *Ibid.*, p. 25.

[50] Commandant Z and H. Montéchant: *Les guerres navales de demain*, p. 59.

hunting merchantmen and flying from the Royal Navy, certainly if the units from the Royal Navy were stronger than the French, but also if they were equal.

The heirs of Aube and Charmes were convinced that France had a geostrategic trump card in commerce warfare, compared to Great Britain, Germany and even Italy. From the shores of France, the Navy could conduct decisive attacks on British, German and Italian trade. Furthermore, France, with a much more self-sufficient economy than the three potential enemies, did not have to fear a corresponding threat.[51] For Commandant Z and Montéchant, it was in the Mediterranean, especially after the French conquest of Algeria and Tunisia, that France had the maximum advantage:

> Politically and commercially, the Mediterranean has become the most important sea on the globe. The power that dominates it will really be number one in Europe. And, the Mediterranean is, of all the seas, the one that is best suited for the tactics and strategy of flotillas. Consequently, France is the only power capable of exercising preponderance there. [...] The situation of France, impregnable on the two shores of the western basin, with the island Corsica as a hyphen, allows her—and only her—to use the flotillas to maximum effect.[52]

The principal theatre of operations would thus be the approaches to France, and not the distant sea routes which Aube and Charmes had identified as the vulnerable parts of the British trade system. As Martin Motte has pointed out in his doctoral thesis on French naval theory, the heirs of Aube and Charmes placed their arguments within a tradition dating back well before the founders of the *jeune école* formulated their theory. Commandant Z and Montéchant's reasoning was very much in accordance with the arguments put forward by Vauban two centuries earlier: "France has advantages in trade warfare that outdo wholly and everywhere those of her neighbours [...], because all the trade of her enemies passes to and fro within range of her coast and her ports" and nobody "can do the same to us because we have little or no foreign trade."[53]

The focus on trade warfare in European waters provided an operational focus on littoral warfare. As Motte has noted, trade warfare

---

[51] Motte: *Une éducation géostratégique*, p. 268.
[52] Commandant Z and H. Montéchant: *Essai de stratégie navale*, pp. 434–435.
[53] Quoted in Martin Motte: *Une éducation géostratégique*, pp. 268–269.

and littoral warfare fused into one operational concept.⁵⁴ It had three complementary elements: the protection of the French coast, offensive commerce raiding close to the French coast and attacks on the enemy's coast.⁵⁵ Although the heirs of Aube and Charmes had a firm belief in the French Navy's potential to bring Great Britain to its knees through offensive warfare, they were well aware of where France was vulnerable. Lieutenant X, Commandant Z and Montéchant underlined that the French coast was extensive and they perceived it to be vulnerable to enemy operations. Therefore Lieutenant X claimed: "The defensive organisation of the French coast is the foundation of her offensive strength."⁵⁶ Commandant Z and Montéchant concurred: "The organisation of the defensive is the first and most essential duty of a navy. It is not until all means of warding off all possible attacks are in place that one can reasonably start to think of the offensive."⁵⁷

The Naval Programme of the Heirs

The defensive and the offensive had several common traits. Like the offensive, the defensive should be active; both required units with a high degree of mobility, Commandant Z and Montéchant argued. An extreme mobility of the naval units would give a certain ubiquity, but speed alone would not be sufficient. Speed could help to track and catch up with the enemy, but whatever speed a naval vessel had, it could not defend two geographically separate positions at the same time. Hence, ubiquity could only be achieved by numbers. Given the economic limits of the French Navy, a numerous fleet could only be obtained by constructing boats with small dimensions.⁵⁸

A modern French Navy should, according to Commandant Z and Montéchant, consist of vessels in which the emphasis was placed on maximum speed and minimum dimensions. Each unit should be autonomous and specialised for one type of armament. This was, they underlined, the programme of the *jeune école* as Gabriel Charmes had detailed in 1885.⁵⁹ Although the programme could be said to be the

---

⁵⁴ *Ibid.*, p. 269.
⁵⁵ Commandant Z and H. Montéchant: *Les guerres navales de demain*, pp. 5, 16.
⁵⁶ Lieutenant X: Introduction to Commandant Z and H. Montéchant: *Essai de stratégie navale*, p. 9.
⁵⁷ Commandant Z and H. Montéchant: *Les guerres navales de demain*, p. 32.
⁵⁸ *Ibid.*, pp. 16–17.
⁵⁹ Commandant Z and H. Montéchant: *Essai de stratégie navale*, p. 88.

same, the conditions for the programme were not identical. Aube's and Charmes's programme rested on the precondition that the small, fast boats that should be the backbone of the new French Navy were seaworthy on the high seas.

This precondition caused the two some worry. They shared much of the technological optimism that had been so pronounced, especially in the works of Charmes. They argued that an increasing number of officers favoured smaller boats due to the "ceaseless progress of naval science." On the other hand, they agreed that the small dimensions of the torpedo and canon boats would reduce their capabilities in bad weather. The question of seaworthiness was, however, not as crucial for the *jeune école* version of Commandant Z and Montéchant as for the original *jeune école* theory of Aube and Charmes. The most significant deviation from the theory of the founder was with regard to the question of where the area of operations should be. While Aube and Charmes had argued for offensive operations on the high seas, their heirs saw European waters as the principal area for both defensive and offensive operations. As naval officers, they were certainly aware that even the Mediterranean, although it can almost be seen as an inland sea, could be rough. Commandant Z and Montéchant knew that the question of seaworthiness was viewed as a weak part of their theory, and consequently they were eager to play down the scale of the problem. They argued that bad weather did not often occur in the Mediterranean and that it was anyway possible to forecast.[60]

The arguments that operations in European waters would make the boats less exposed to bad weather, and that the French Navy thus could construct a fleet almost completely consisting of small boats, were probably not entirely convincing even for Commandant Z and Montéchant. Battleships, or naval monsters as they labelled them, had of course no future in the modern French Navy that they envisaged, but they did propose that vessels up to 8,000 tons should be part of the fleet. An evolution in their thinking can be detected that indicates a greater acceptance of larger ships. In *Les guerres navales de demain*, published in 1891, they insisted that "a displacement of 4,000 to 5,000 tons should never be exceeded."[61] In *Essai de stratégie navale* two years later, they described the ideal composition of the French fleet and detailed

---

[60] Commandant Z and H. Montéchant: *Les guerres navales de demain*, p. 17.
[61] *Ibid.*, p. 219.

each type of naval vessel. There they proposed four lightly armoured (*protégés*) cruisers of 8,000 tons, eight lightly armoured (*protégés*) cruisers between 6,000 to 7,000 tons, 66 cruisers of 2,500 tons, 36 reconnaissance vessels of 1,000 tons, 125 torpedo-gun boats of 360 tons, and 375 torpedo boats of 125 tons.

The programme proposed by Commandant Z and Montéchant was not consistent with the one that Gabriel Charmes had proposed, and which they claimed to represent. On the contrary, their proposal could in many ways be seen as part of an inherent tendency in all navies to increase the size of each new generation of ships. The next generation of the same type of ships would not only have improved technology; it would also be bigger than its predecessors. It was exactly such a development that Charmes had warned against.[62] In his *La réforme de la Marine*, Charmes argued that the torpedo boats *No. 63* and *No. 64* had remarkably good seagoing qualities. These boats displaced only 46 tons. Charmes realized that the accommodation was not too good and that some more space for the torpedoes was to be desired. Charmes accepted an enlarged torpedo boat type of 71 tons that would solve these minor problems, as he viewed them. But he insisted that this size should not be exceeded. The advantages of the torpedo boats lay in their small dimension combined with high speed. A gradual enlargement of torpedo boats would undermine the original *raison d'être* for this type of boat. Charmes argued that French and Western European navies were already experiencing such an unsound development:

> This tendency to increase the dimensions of the torpedo boats [...] can already be seen, it exercises an important influence on our constructions. We already have torpedo boats of 350 tons. We will soon have some with a displacement of 1.200 tons. England is already ahead of us on this road; she has gone, without transition, from the small torpedo boats to *Polyphemus* with a displacement of 2.640 tons and a length of 73 meters. If this tendency towards enlargement continues, if there are reconnaissance torpedo boats, one will have torpedo boats *avisos*, and then torpedo boats with armoured bridges, then armoured torpedo boats, one will finally end up, by a logic evolution, with the monsters of today.[63]

The programme proposed by Commandant Z and Montéchant indicated a certain tendency away from the uncritical belief in the excellence of the small boats towards a more sober recognition of size as a

---

[62] Gabriel Charmes: *La réforme de la Marine* (Paris, 1886), pp. 46–53.
[63] Charmes: *La réforme de la Marine*, pp. 47–48.

factor deciding seaworthiness and the crew's ability to stay at sea for some time. They argued for a number of cruisers suited to operations on the high seas, and torpedo boats that were more than twice the size of those that Charmes had praised for their seagoing qualities. Size had been important for Aube and Charmes for several reasons, most of them shared by Commandant Z and Montéchant. The latter seemed, however, to place less emphasis than Aube and Charmes had done on the fact that the smaller the boat is, the smaller it will be as a target. Their main concern, as it had been for Aube and Charmes, was, however, that speed and number gave strategic and tactical advantages, and that in order to achieve sufficient numbers, the size of each vessel had to be small given the economic restraints of the French Navy. One could get ten torpedo boats for the price of one battleship.[64]

Another inconsistency in Commandant Z and Montéchant's arguments concerned the specialisation of the vessels. One of the fundamental principles of their theory was that each boat should have either guns or torpedoes.[65] In their programme, however, they proposed that the French Navy should have a total of 125 torpedo-gunboats. No explanation was given as to why the principle of specialisation was not valid for these boats.

A very explicit deviation from the programme of Aube and Charmes was Commandant Z and Montéchant's insistence on dropping the ram as a weapon. Aube and Charmes had praised the ram against the background of the experiences gained at the Battle of Lissa in 1866. Commandant Z and Montéchant agreed that the ram could be effective if the attack was carried out with the necessary cold-bloodedness. It was, however, impossible to avoid some damage being suffered by the attacking vessel, and very often it would have to withdraw from battle. It was not a weapon for repeat attacks, they argued. The torpedo, on the other hand, had none of these inconveniences, not because a torpedo could be used twice, but because a torpedo boat could carry several torpedoes.[66]

---

[64] Commandant Z and H. Montéchant: *Les guerres navales de demain*, pp. 218–219.
[65] Commandant Z and H. Montéchant: *Essai de stratégie navale*, p. 88.
[66] Commandant Z and H. Montéchant: *Les guerres navales de demain*, p. 205.

The Return of the *Jeune École* to Power

Naval planning during the period after Aube left his post as Minister of Marine and up to the Fashoda Crisis focused on the Triple Alliance. Initially Italy was regarded as the most potent naval power within the Triple Alliance. Towards the end of the period the German Navy emerged as a considerable challenge. The fact that naval strategic thinking during these years focused on two continental powers with navies inferior to the French one made the ideas of the *jeune école* less relevant. The possibility of a conflict with Great Britain was not ruled out, but a war against the British was considered less likely than one against the Triple Alliance. When plans for war against Great Britain were outlined, commercial warfare was still conceived as the most effective way of fighting the superior power. The General Staff did, as it had during Aube's ministry, emphasise that a war against Britain would be a maritime war, and that the trade routes linking Britain and her empire were the vulnerable spots that the inferior French Navy should aim to hit. The General Staff repeated the *jeune école*'s arguments regarding the consequences of French commerce raiding and predicted that it would provoke a rise in food prices, create unemployment, undermine public welfare and consequently force Britain to sue for peace. The General Staff concluded that commerce raiding was the only way that France could bring a war against Britain to an early end. Consequently, the French Navy should assign its cruisers to commerce raiding.[67]

French naval planners in the early 1890s accepted that the only effective way to fight Great Britain was the one that the *jeune école* had prescribed but underlined that "we only renounce the doctrines of *guerre à outrance* to the extent that they are contrary to international law."[68] They stressed that the commanding officers of the cruisers should send the crews of the captured ships back to their home countries after the necessary agreements for the exchange of prisoners had been signed.

The General Staff admitted that, although *guerre de course* was assumed to be the most effective way of fighting Great Britain, the French Navy was not organised for or prepared to conduct such warfare. This reflected the fact that Britain was not perceived as a likely enemy. The

---

[67] SHM, BB4-2437: EMG 3ème section: *Opèration de guerre. Guerre maritime contre l'Angleterre*, December 1892.
[68] *Ibid.*

fact that the *jeune école* was out of office thus did not remove the confusion among the admirals regarding what strategy the French Navy should plan for. A very loud and active *jeune école* opposition headed by very competent writers like Montéchant, Commandant Z and Lieutenant X further contributed towards the image of a navy that lacked direction. The lack of a clear strategy was reflected in the dialogue between the parliamentary Budget Committee of 1893 and the Navy for a "compromise programme".[69] The Programme of 1894, which replaced the Programme of 1890, remained focused on the Triple Alliance, despite a surge in British naval construction as a result of the 1893 Mediterranean scare. The 1893 scare was based on the fear of possible confrontation with a Franco-Russian coalition.[70]

Theodore Ropp has described the French programme as something that would make everybody happy. The programme included "a few scout cruisers and some battleships for the admirals and a lot of torpedo craft and some special commerce-raiding cruisers for the *jeune école*."[71] Most of these had been provided in the earlier programmes, and the only difference between the Programme of 1894 and that of 1890 was the requirement that all cruisers should be armoured. There was to be no construction of mother ships for torpedo boats, but two special commerce-destroying cruisers were added to the programme. The frequent programmes of the 1890s (there were five programmes from 1890 to 1900 compared to one in the 1880s and two in the 1870s) illustrated that the naval programmes had lost much of their importance and reflected the confusion that reigned in the French Navy regarding which strategy to follow.

The will to formulate a dedicated and coherent strategy was not evident until the aftermath of the Fashoda Crisis. Then a majority of the naval leadership, strongly persuaded by the civilian Minister of Marine, Lanessan, accepted that the French Navy should focus on Great Britain as the probable enemy. The first signs of a shift of attention away from the Triple Alliance to Great Britain could, however, be seen from Edouard Lockroy's first period as Minister of Marine.

The appointment in November 1895 of the civilian politician Edouard Lockroy as Minister of Marine in the Cabinet of the Radical

---

[69] Ropp: *The Development of a Modern Navy*, pp. 282–283.
[70] *Ibid.*, pp. 244–253.
[71] *Ibid.*, p. 283.

Léon Bourgeois marked in many ways a comeback for the *jeune école*. Lockroy's first period in office lasted only half a year, but he was again appointed minister in the summer of 1898. He also exerted an influence on the French Navy through his work as member of parliament. His strategic thoughts concurred with, and were probably inspired by Admiral Fournier who was the best thinker of the *jeune école* in the post-Aube era. Lockroy established the French naval staff college in December 1895 and appointed Admiral Fournier to be the first commander of the college.

The Jeune École *and the Staff College*

Fournier—Renewing the Jeune École

The establishment of the French naval staff college aroused violent opposition at the outset. The traditionalists viewed it as a means of forcing the Parliament's *jeune école* sympathies on the unruly admirals. Admiral Fournier, left in charge of the general organisation of the college, decided that it should be afloat to permit the study of both tactical and theoretical matters. The Ministry of Marine gave him two cruisers with which to go to work. The main course was in four parts: Naval Tactics, Tactics of Scouting and Squadron Cruisers, Battle Tactics, and Naval Strategy. Vice Admiral Besnard returned as Minister of Marine in April 1896, but allowed Fournier's college to complete its term. When the classes were over, the Ministry of Marine sent the traditionalist, Admiral Rieunier, to "inspect" the college. The Superior Council ended up with a recommendation to close the school for two reasons. First, the Superior Council claimed that "[the staff college] appears to wish to direct tactical and strategic studies without submitting them to the test of experience, and to annihilate the Squadron [of Evolution]." Secondly, the admirals on the Council warned that the new staff college "tends to create a special body of a General Staff which will soon be tempted to take over the direction of the Navy."[72] The traditionalists viewed the staff college as a threat to their position. In a situation in which the *jeune école* had sympathisers among influential politicians, it was perceived as unacceptable to encourage opposition circles that propagated ideas contrary to those of the leading admirals.

---

[72] Both quotations from Ropp: *The Development of a Modern Navy*, p. 294.

With Lockroy well established in the Budget Committee, Admiral Besnard could not suppress the school entirely. He chose to reorganise it, deprived it of its commander and its warships, gave it a new name and established it as a kind of adjunct to the Naval General Staff in Paris.[73] In the first years of the school's existence, until the Fashoda Crisis, there seems to have been a certain correlation between the naval faction the minister belonged to, and the strategic ideas taught at the staff college. The ministers of the period, Admiral Besnard and Lockroy, were outspoken advocates of, respectively, the traditionalist camp and the *jeune école*. The lectures were, however, generally characterized by intellectual openness, reflecting the confusion that existed within the naval community on strategic and tactical matters. Two different lecturers teaching strategy-related subjects in the same school year, could advocate totally different views on what should be the preferred French naval strategy.[74]

The quality of the courses depended very much on the competence of the lecturers. They were mostly career officers who served for one or two years at the staff college, and then returned to other posts in the Navy. The strategy classes were taught by commanders, all of them but one were later promoted to admiral.[75] Not all of them were eminent strategists and lecturers. Some of the strategy courses were mainly long accounts of French and foreign naval manoeuvres and listings of the major European navies' order of battle. The majority of the lectures,

---

[73] The school had the following names in the period covered by this thesis: From 1896: *Division Navale constituant l'Ecole supérieure de guerre*; from 1898: *Ecole des Hautes Etudes de la Marine*; from 1899: *Ecole supérieure de Marine*.

[74] See i.e. the classes of Commander Degouy lecturing on foreign navies in the school year 1897–1898. He consistently forwarded *jeune école* arguments. SHM, 1 CC 211 Ac 2: Lectures by Capitaine de frégate Degouy: *Marines étrangères 1ère Partie, Marines Anglaise, Allemande et Italienne* (École des Hautes Études de la Marine, Paris, 1897–1898). His colleague the same year, Commander Houette, teaching French maritime strategy, argued equally consistently along traditionalist lines. SHM, 1 CC Aa 6: Lectures by Capitaine de frégate Houette: *Stratégie maritime Française* (École des Hautes Études de la Marine, Paris, 1897–1898).

[75] Captain Houette was the only one not promoted to admiral among the lecturers in strategy or strategy-related subjects in the period covered. He was promoted to captain in 1898, and died in 1904 at the age of 51. The average age at which the rank of Rear Admiral was obtained in the French Navy was 52. It is impossible to say whether Houette would have been promoted to admiral if he had lived longer. The point is that all lecturers had excellent careers. Thus, the arguments they propagated were most probably representative of the prevailing ideas of the upper echelons of the officer corps. For average age to obtain ranks, see Ray Walser: *France's Search for a Battle Fleet. Naval Policy and Naval Power, 1898–1914* (New York and London, 1992), p. 104.

however, were marked by an effort to analyse France's maritime strategic challenges, and describe options to meet the challenges. They provide a good general view of the ideas present among officers who all were to occupy important posts in the French Navy.[76]

Admiral Fournier differed from other *jeune école* officers in this period because he occupied influential military positions and also had good political connections. His strategic thought and his proposals concerning the composition of the French fleet met with approval in political circles and were an important contribution to naval reforms after Fashoda. Fournier openly claimed the legacy of Aube and underlined his affinity to the radical minister Lockroy.[77] He himself gave the lectures in strategy during the year he commanded the school. The message of his lectures correspond with that of his influential book on naval strategy, *La Flotte nécessaire*, which was published in 1896 while he was still head of the school.[78]

In the introduction to *La Flotte nécessaire* he concluded that his ideas were part of an evolution that had been going on for more than twenty years, and that Aube had been one of the most ardent apostles of these ideas: "He [Aube] did succumb in the fight, but it will for ever be to the credit of this flag officer that he showed the way for our naval reforms."[79]

Fournier's ideas were elaborated in the lectures he gave at the French naval staff college and in *La Flotte nécessaire*, but also in discussions within the Superior Council. In his lectures in strategy to his students at the staff college, he outlined the national strategic ambitions of France. These ambitions very much resembled those that Aube had advocated.

Fournier was a colonialist and an admirer of Great Britain's colonial achievements. He stressed that naval strategy was primarily a peacetime

---

[76] Ropp, in *The Development of a Modern Navy*, pp. 294–295, has a rather critical view of the lectures given at the French staff college in this period. Ropp himself had a highly successful teaching career, and his criticism seems to ignore that those who taught strategy at the staff college were officers, most with a keen interest in strategy, but not trained to present strategic thoughts in a systematic way. Their theories are still interesting as a reflection of ideas present among mid-ranking French naval officers, all on their way up on the career ladder to occupy more influential positions.

[77] F.E. Fournier: *La Flotte nécessaire. Ses avantages stratégiques, tactiques et économiques* (Paris, 1896), pp. XVII, XXIII–XXIV.

[78] The book was authorised by the Ministry of Marine in December 1895. Paul Brière: *Le Vice-Amiral Fournier. Marin, diplomate, savant* (Mayenne, 1931), p. 134.

[79] Fournier: *La Flotte nécessaire*: pp. XXIII–XXIV.

endeavour in that the purpose was to prepare and increase the Navy's area of operation by colonial conquests, establishing protectorates and building alliances. This would be both an end and a means. It would be an end in the sense that the overall ambition should be to secure France's position "at the centre of the concert of Great Powers."[80] It was a means in the sense that the Navy would need bases around the globe in order to encourage French influence. French strategy should thus be implemented in close cooperation with the Ministry of Marine, the Ministry of Colonial Affairs and the Ministry of Foreign Affairs. Such a strategic ambition was likely to run counter to the interests of Great Britain. Fournier was well aware of that possibility and the basis for all his strategic reflections was a possible conflict with Great Britain.

Fournier warned, as Aube had done, that traditional offensive fleet warfare against the Royal Navy would be catastrophic for the French Navy. Both Aube and Fournier argued that certain characteristics of modern war had made it impossible for France to challenge British naval superiority by means of fleet warfare. Fournier's reasoning was, however, somewhat different from that of Aube. Aube focused on the battle and argued that especially the introduction of steam had reduced the influence that chance and human talent had previously had on the outcome of the battle. He believed that the numerically superior fleet would win the battle with an almost mathematical predictability. Fournier added that modern wars would be wars of attrition in which belligerents' demographic, economic and industrial capacity would reduce the significance of each battle provided that no nation engaged its whole battle fleet in one single battle. He referred to the continental wars in which the conscription system had led to an almost inexhaustible reserve of soldiers and in which no single battle would be decisive. Correspondingly, Fournier argued, command of the seas would be won by the power with the best capacity to mobilise reserves, repair ships and launch new ones.

Fournier's reasoning led him to describe a strategy that can be seen as a further development of the theories of the *jeune école* of the 1870s and 1880s. He prescribed a two-pronged strategy consisting of small-scale attacks on parts of the enemy fleet and of commercial warfare. The fact that the Royal Navy's battle fleet was superior to the French

---

[80] SHM, 1 CC Aa 4: Lectures by Rear Admiral Fournier: *Stratégie navale, 4ème Fascicule* (Division Navale constituant l'Ecole supérieure de Marine, 1896), pp. 9–10.

did not mean that it was invulnerable. Fournier argued that French naval forces should seek to establish local superiority. He predicted that the Royal Navy would blockade French ports, an operation that would force it to disperse its forces in order to cover as much of the French coast as possible. French battleships and cruisers supported by torpedo boats could thus under the cover of darkness conduct attacks against isolated and inferior units.[81]

The same logic would be valid for commerce raiding. Fournier argued, just as Aube had done, that commerce-raiders could escape the British blockade and pursue British trade. He also shared Aube's analysis of British exposure to commerce warfare, and he stressed the asymmetric relationship that existed due to the size of the French and British merchant marine and their importance for the two countries. While Britain had the world's largest merchant fleet sailing on all oceans and thus represented a huge naval challenge in terms of need for protection, the French merchant fleet was insignificant in comparison.

Fournier's strategy of small-scale attacks against the Royal Navy and commerce warfare led him to argue for a homogeneous fleet of cruisers. He admitted that for the purpose of pure commerce raiding, special commerce-raiding cruisers would have been sufficient. Fournier warned that France could not afford the luxury of having two distinct classes of cruisers: one dedicated to commerce raiding, the other to fighting enemy naval units. French cruisers should therefore be able to handle both missions. He underlined that numbers were important both in commercial warfare and in traditional naval warfare. To strike a blow at British society, which was the aim of commerce warfare, the French Navy should be able to conduct massive cruiser warfare on all trade routes simultaneously. A numerous cruiser fleet would also be necessary in order to obtain local superiority against Royal Navy units. The size and performance of each cruiser should not be too ambitious in order for the construction programme to include the necessary number of cruisers. Ideally, Fournier argued, the French cruisers should be able to attain speeds of up to 23 knots, just as the fastest British passenger liners did. He reminded his students and readers that the large majority of British merchant ships could not make more than 10–15 knots, and that it was these ships that carried the goods that were important for the industry and population of the British Isles:

---

[81] *Ibid.*, p. 18.

CHAPTER THREE

> One notices that it is not by capturing some English luxury passenger liners that one strikes a sensible blow against England's commercial wealth and vitality, whereas one certainly can obtain such a result by destroying a good part of its cargo boats and the passenger liners of moderate speed that sail the world's oceans. [This can be done] with cruisers that have proved to make 20–21 knots on trials and with a tonnage of at least 6000 tons.[82]

The cruiser that Fournier had in his mind was the *Dupuy de Lôme*. It was ordered by Aube's immediate successor, Senator Edouard Barbey. The *Dupuy de Lôme* was in the vanguard of naval construction. It was the world's first true armoured cruiser, a 6,500 tons ship capable of 20 knots. The *Dupuy de Lôme* was able to do much more than commerce raiding and superior to Italian and British protected cruisers. With great speed and range, carrying almost nothing but large quick-firing guns and using speed to control the range at which engagements were fought, these cruisers could beat British or Italian ships.[83]

Fournier argued that ships built on the *Dupuy de Lôme* concept, increased in size to between 8,000 to 8,500 tons, should constitute a new homogeneous fleet. He maintained that there was no reason to predict any future change in average displacement, shape of the hull, distribution of the main artillery, the calibre of the quick firing guns or in the armour of this class of ships. One should, however, take advantage of technological and industrial progress to improve speed, operational radius, the offensive capacity of the quick firing guns, the quality of the armour etc. for each new batch ordered of this class. The ships should yield the maximum both offensively and defensively, and they should be autonomous.

Fournier stipulated that the French Navy should build 117 cruisers of this class as substitutes for the battleships, armoured coastal defence ships and the numerous ships of different types that existed in the French Navy. This would imply a total renewal of the French fleet over a period of 25 years.[84] Fournier did, however, make an exception for the torpedo boats, of which he suggested that the French Navy should have 300. In defensive operations the squadrons of homogenous cruisers should be supported by numerous flotillas of seagoing torpedo boats.[85]

---

[82] *Ibid.*, p. 22.
[83] Masson: *Histoire de la Marine*, p. 228; O'Brian: *Technology and Naval Combat*, p. 42; Ropp: *The Development of a Modern Navy*, p. 296.
[84] F.E. Fournier: *La Flotte nécessaire*, pp. XII–XXII, 13.
[85] *Ibid.*, pp. 42, 80.

117 cruisers were necessary in order to answer "French strategic needs against England."[86] The cruisers should be divided into squadrons of nine each. Fournier proposed to distribute the squadrons to seven operational areas. Four squadrons should be stationed in the Mediterranean, two for defensive operations on the French and North African coast, while the two others should conduct offensive operations. Three squadrons should operate in the Channel, two offensively and one for coastal defence. The one that should operate in the Bay of Biscay should carry out both offensive and defensive operations. The remaining 45 cruisers should patrol out of French overseas bases.

The distribution of the cruisers and their missions reflected the offensive preferences that characterised the thinking of the *jeune école*. Great Britain could not be forced to the negotiating table by a strategy of pure coastal defence and battleships remaining in port out of fear of losing battles. The success that Aube and Fournier predicted for the daring strategy of commerce raiding and pinprick operations was based on the rather remarkable assumption that the ships meant to constitute the backbone of their recommended fleet structure would be superior in most respects to the equivalents in the navies of their potential enemies. A strategy that differed radically from the traditional strategies of naval powers, combined with a firm belief in French technological genius, thus promised a cheap way to naval great power status.

The *jeune école* under Aube's leadership had argued for a "division of labour" between specialised ships, a concept that apparently was in direct contrast to Fournier's homogeneous fleet of cruisers. Many of the reflections underpinning Aube's and Fournier's conclusions were, however, similar. They were both convinced that numbers would be important in order to stand up to Britain in a war. Aube's specialised ships were built according to the concept of a standard ship armed with either torpedoes or guns. Standardisation was supposed to reduce the construction and operating cost, and the idea behind the standardisation that was common to both Aube and Fournier was that it would enable the French Navy to have a sufficient number of vessels to create local superiority and to be present on the trade routes served by British merchant ships.

Aube's view that future wars would be total in character led him to conclude that international law had to be subordinated to the demands of war. Commerce warfare should be conducted in disregard

---

[86] *Ibid.*, pp. 40–41.

of international law. In his writings and his lectures Fournier was not very explicit as to how commerce warfare should be conducted with regard to international law. This was rather symptomatic for the discussions on commerce warfare among the naval planners and top officers in the period before to the Fashoda Crisis. They were all quite evasive in dealing with the legal and humanitarian consequences of commerce warfare.

There is however no reason to believe that Fournier's views on this differed from Aube's. He did nothing to distance himself from the latter's ideas in his writings or lectures. On the contrary, he stressed his debt to Aube and underlined that the strategy and the composition of the fleet that he proposed would be the logical implementation of Aube's ideas:

> This *homogeneous fleet, with a maximum strategic and tactical output*, and *with autonomous units with a minimum tonnage*, is it not, moreover, the end towards which naval art has evolved in a rational progression over the last twenty years and still does, despite all opposition, with the irresistible force of progress? Admiral Aube was one of the most ardent apostles of these ideas.[87]

Fournier also underlined that modern wars could represent threats to the very existence of nations.[88] With commerce warfare being the major means to fend off a potentially existential threat to France, it is not very likely that he envisaged that this kind of warfare could be conducted according to the Declaration of Paris. After the Fashoda Crisis, as we shall see, he was indeed very blunt in the internal deliberations in the Superior Council as to what he considered the necessary and unavoidable consequences of commerce warfare.

Lecturing in the Crossfire between the Traditionalists and the Jeune École

The schism in the French Navy between the *jeune école* on the one side and the traditionalists on the other side characterised many of the strategy-related lectures held by Fournier's successors at the French naval staff college. The lectures of Commander Houette, who succeeded Fournier as lecturer in strategy, were in many aspects representative of lectures held by traditionally oriented officers. He gave two different courses in strategy, neither characterized by an analytic approach or

---

[87] Italics by Fournier. Fournier: *La Flotte nécessaire*, p. xxiii.
[88] *Ibid.*, p. xviii.

any perspective on future challenges. The lectures consisted of long accounts of French naval construction programmes and the order of battle for potential enemies. The theories of the *jeune école* were also given due attention. The arguments very often had a rather polemical character, but Commander Houette and other traditionalists also raised well-founded questions concerning inconsistencies and weaknesses in the theories of the *jeune école*.

Houette stated that the French fleet should have a traditional composition. The core should be battleship groups supported by armoured cruisers, high-seas torpedo boats, and destroyers.[89] His comparisons between the order of battle of the European powers were alarmist rather than reliable, educational estimates. The order of battle he listed for the Triple Alliance, especially concerning battleships, was greatly exaggerated. In Houette's list the French battleship fleet was only two-thirds the size of the Triple Alliance's, whereas the French Navy's official annual listings, other lecturers' presentation at the staff college and historical research show that the French Navy was vastly superior to the Triple Alliance in battleships in the mid-1890s.[90]

Since the schism within the French Navy was between the *jeune école* and the traditionalists, any lecture supporting traditionalist views would have to demonstrate the weak parts of the reasoning of the *jeune école*. Houette tried to undermine the credibility of some of the most active advocates of the *jeune école* and their supporters. This approach, used by the traditionalists at the time and adopted by many historians as the correct representation of the *jeune école*, was characterized by an attempt to depict the most energetic promoters of the *jeune école* as enthusiastic, carried-away landlubbers. The point of departure for this kind of criticism was the articles of Gabriel Charmes. Houette argued against what he characterized as Charmes's single-minded belief in the torpedo boat as a universal tool in naval warfare. The traditionalists' lack of confidence with regard to Charmes's nautical and military competence was coupled with a corresponding lack of trust in public opinion's

---

[89] SHM, 1 CC 195 aa 6: Lectures by Capitaine de frégate Houette: *Marine Française. Stratégie, Tactique. 1ère Partie. Stratégie Marine Française* (Ecole des Hautes Etudes de la Marine, Paris, 1897–1898), pp. 71–72.

[90] Annuaire de la Marine; SHM, 1 CC 211 Ac 2: Lectures by Capitaine de frégate Degouy: *Marines étrangères 1ère Partie, Marines Anglaise, Allemande et Italienne* (Ecole des Hautes Etudes de la Marine, Paris, 1897–1898); SHM, 1 CC 211 Ac 6: Lectures by Lieutenant de vaisseau Charlier: *Marines étrangères 1898–1899* (Ecole des Hautes Etudes de la Marine, Paris, 1898–1899); Ropp: *The Development of a Modern Navy*, p. 357.

understanding of these matters. The traditionalists were frustrated by the fact that they were not able to influence public opinion to the same degree as the *jeune école*. The problem, according to the traditionalists, was that the French population was liable to get carried away by the facile, comforting message preached by the *jeune école*.

> The ideas of the *jeune école* pleased the French public, generally inclined to gladly believe that an invention will win, suddenly, with little cost and almost no effort, command of the seas for her navy, [a navy] that they, moreover, hardly appreciate or understand.[91]

The allegation that the proponents of the *jeune école* were not real sailors was of course an effective way to exclude them as disqualified from participation in discussions on naval affairs. The problem with such an approach was how to explain that important parts of the theory of the *jeune école* had been elaborated by the experienced sailor Théophile Aube. Houette's solution was to make a clear distinction between the journalist Charmes, and the seasoned sailor Aube. He claimed that the latter should have distanced himself from the enthusiasm of Charmes.[92]

Houette also used more matter-of-fact arguments in his effort to convince his students of the weak points in the theories of the *jeune école*. He examined thoroughly the different aspects of commerce warfare, and used a potential *guerre de course* against Germany and Great Britain as examples. He accused the *jeune école* of ignoring a vital factor, in this case the fact that the neutral countries depended on a well-functioning seaborne trade system. The first attacks on German shipping would most certainly force Germany to turn to neutral shipping in order to ensure the necessary flow of goods to and from Germany. Most probably, the Germans would turn to the world's leading merchant fleet, the British. Attacking British commerce would, however, be to challenge the world's most powerful navy, and thus to change the situation radically to the disadvantage of France. The sole option for the French Navy was therefore to stick to traditional fleet warfare against Germany, Houette concluded.[93]

Houette did not believe commercial warfare against Great Britain was likely to succeed, either. His argument was twofold. First, he obvi-

---

[91] SHM, 1 CC Aa6: Lectures by Capitaine de frégate Houette: *Stratégie maritime Française* (Ecole des Hautes Etudes de la Marine, Paris, 1897–1898), p. 44.
[92] *Ibid.*, p. 43.
[93] *Ibid.*, pp. 155–156.

ously did not fully accept that blockade was impossible in the era of steam and self-propelled torpedoes. He argued that the harbours of metropolitan France and bases in the French possessions would be blockaded, or at least that the British would be capable of conducting some kind of surveillance operations against French ships in port. Secondly, he argued that *guerre de course* would not only threaten the seaborne commerce of belligerent nations. It would threaten the general world trade system. The neutrals would not accept this, Houette countered. His arguments were very much an echo of Bourgois's case against violating international law. Both argued that international law was upheld because it was in someone's interest to do so. In this case it was in the neutral powers' interest. Bourgois had predicted that the neutral countries would rally against France, and declare French warships to be pirates. Houette argued that neutral countries would deny French ships access to neutral ports to bunker.[94] Logistical problems would hence undermine a war effort based on *guerre de course*.

The most interesting *jeune école* career officer in the pre-Fashoda years, besides Fournier, was Commander, later Admiral, Degouy. His arena was primarily the staff college where he gave lectures which contained his operational recommendations for war against Britain and the Triple Alliance. His ideas on how Great Britain should be fought were a combination of Aube's and Fournier's prescriptions.

Degouy argued that industrial warfare would be the only realistic way of fighting Great Britain. The term *guerre industrielle* had replaced the term *guerre de course* as the key word in the vocabulary of the *jeune école*, and it was also generally adopted in French naval circles as a term to describe characteristics of a possible future war between European powers. It reflected a more widespread notion that future wars would see nations mobilising the whole of society to support the war effort, and that national industrial capacity would be decisive to the outcome of the war. While many in the 1880s and early 1890s had interpreted Aube's and Charmes's arguments for *guerre de course* as merely a continuation of the French tradition of commerce raiding, although in a more radical formulation, there was from the mid-1890s a growing awareness that *guerre de course* had an objective beyond what the term itself implied. The consequences for modern warfare of the far-reaching industrialisation that now encompassed most of Western Europe were more and more

---

[94] *Ibid.*, pp. 156–159.

present in strategic discussions in the French Navy. The term "industrial warfare" was a more accurate expression of the relationship between the evolution of Western societies and modern warfare.[95]

The Navy's task in industrial warfare would, however, still be to raid seaborne trade and coastal cities and infrastructure. Degouy insisted that the French Navy should deploy in order to take the initiative early in a conflict with Great Britain. The war should be brought to the British Isles at the outset.[96] This should be done through early attacks on British coastal defence, military harbours, and by threatening to bombard the coast. The main objective at this stage of the war was to disturb British mobilisation.

Degouy maintained that the theatre of operations would be the Atlantic, the Channel and the North Sea. The best starting point for operations against Great Britain was clearly Brest, he argued. Degouy thus took a clear stand in a discussion that emerged as a major issue within the French Navy in the mid-1890s. The French Navy's main base had been Toulon with its squadron of battleships, and there had been no substantial controversies within the Navy concerning where the majority of the naval ships should have their home base. Even Aube, although he initiated some minor reorganisations of where the different ships should be stationed, did not push for a major shift towards Brest. An increased focus on the Atlantic could, however, be seen from 1889 when the first organised battleship formation, Battleship Division North, was stationed in Brest. It was enlarged to become the Northern Squadron in 1892. The rank of the commander-in-chief was raised from rear admiral to vice admiral, and hence corresponded to that of the commander-in-chief of the Mediterranean Squadron.

---

[95] See for instance SHM,1 CC Aa 4: Lectures by Contre-amiral E. Fournier: *Stratégie navale, 4ème Fascicule* (Division Navale constituant l'Ecole supérieure de guerre, 1896), pp. 9–10; SHM, 1 CC 211 Ac 2: Lectures by Capitaine de frégate Degouy: *Marines étrangères, 1ère Partie, Marines Anglaise, Allemande et Italienne* (Ecole des Hautes Etudes de la Marine, Paris, 1897–1898) pp. 19–20; SHM, BB8-2424/5: Conseil Supérieur de la Marine: *Séances du 11 Janvier 1899*; SHM, 1 CC 198 Aa 26: Lectures by Capitain de vaisseau Darrieus: *Stratégie et Tactique. 3ème Fascicule. L'utilisation* (Ecole Supérieure de Marine, Paris, 1906), p. 9.

[96] SHM, 1 CC 211 Ac 2: Lectures by Capitaine de frégate Degouy: *Marines étrangères, 1ère Partie, Marines Anglaise, Allemande et Italienne* (Ecole des Hautes Etudes de la Marine, Paris, 1897–1898), pp. 219–227. Degouy did not discuss who would start the war; neither did other *jeune école* writers. The aggressive party was generally perceived to be Britain, and Degouy most probably foresaw a rapid reaction to British aggression.

The rank of the commander-in-chief did, however, not mean that the Northern Squadron was anywhere near the Mediterranean Squadron in terms of naval capabilities. As late as 1898 the Northern Squadron consisted of not more than one battleship, two armoured cruisers, four armoured coastal defence vessels, one cruiser 1st class, one cruiser 2nd class and destroyers and torpedo boats, whereas the Mediterranean Squadron consisted of nine battleships, two armoured cruisers, two cruisers 1st class, three cruisers 2nd class, and destroyers, torpedo boats and gunboats.[97]

The fact that the bulk of the French Navy was stationed in the Mediterranean raised not only military problems, but also political and diplomatic dilemmas. Naval units are highly mobile and a transfer of the Mediterranean Fleet to Brest in peacetime would in itself not be a practical problem. In times of tension, however, the transfer of naval forces of the size of the Mediterranean Fleet to a position very close to British waters could very easily be interpreted as an aggressive act, even if it was meant as a defensive measure, and a crisis could unintentionally escalate into a war. Degouy argued that such a situation could be avoided if the bulk of the French fleet was permanently stationed on the Atlantic coast.[98] Diplomatic misunderstandings would be prevented, and France would have a credible capacity for offensive operations against Britain.

Given the way the Northern Fleet was composed, Degouy saw no mission for the larger warships of the fleet (battleship and coastal defence ships) other than to secure the approaches to Brest, Cherbourg and Dunkirk so that the faster ships could conduct offensive operations. Although Degouy placed a lot of emphasis on the operations against the British Isles, it was still commerce raiding he emphasised as the most effective way of fighting Great Britain. As did most *jeune école* proponents, Degouy started with a description of the importance of the British merchant fleet for British society, and explained the composition of the fleet. Still in 1895, three fifths of the British merchant navy consisted of sailing ships. Only very few of the steam ships could

---

[97] Annuaire de la Marine; Lecalve, Franck and Roche, Jean-Michel: *Liste des bâtiments de la flotte de guerre française, de 1700 à nos jours* (La Société Française d'Histoire Maritime, October 2001).

[98] SHM, 1 CC 211 Ac 2: Lectures by Capitaine de frégate Degouy: *Marines étrangères, 1ère Partie, Marines Anglaise, Allemande et Italienne* (Ecole des Hautes Etudes de la Marine, Paris, 1897–1898), pp. 219–227.

make more than 18 knots. The vast majority of the steam ships were tramp steamers with a speed of between 8–12 knots.

Degouy was also one of the few officers who saw that the German Navy would soon represent the major challenge from the Triple Alliance. This was due to the slow but steady build-up of the German Navy and the decline of the Italian one. He insisted that the maritime theatre of operations could not be disconnected from the army's theatre of operations, and he sketched out how the Navy could assist the Army in a joint effort in case of war with the Triple Alliance. He claimed that the German plan for attack on France and Russia had been presented by Emperor Wilhelm in a speech at the Naval Academy in Kiel two years earlier. The main element of the plan was to overwhelm the best-prepared enemy by a swift operation carried out by 1.200.000 well trained and effectively commanded men. Then a considerable part of this enormous force was to turn against the second front, which in the meantime had been held by 200.000 men. The German campaign would be characterised by a vigorous offensive in order to obtain a shocking effect on the enemies, both on land and at sea. This plan should not be surprising to anyone, Degouy concluded.[99]

Degouy was well aware that it was not the general opinion in the French Navy that the North Sea and the Baltic should be the principal theatres of operations for the Navy in a war against the Triple Alliance. Still, he maintained that the French Navy should concentrate her operations there in order to best support the army and the overall aims of the war. There the Navy should establish bases on the islands to support the blockading operations and offensive operations against fortified harbours like Kiel, Swinemünde, Danzig, and Pillau.[100]

---

[99] SHM, 1 CC 211 Ac 2: Lectures by Capitaine de frégate Degouy: *Marines étrangères, 1ère Partie, Marines Anglaise, Allemande et Italienne* (Ecole des Hautes Etudes de la Marine, Paris, 1897–1898), pp. 362–363. The possibilities of a two-front continental war against France and Russia were prevalent in German military thinking and planning in the 1890s. Count Alfred von Schlieffen expressed himself as early as August 1892 in favour of trying to gain a first swift victory against France which he perceived to be the most dangerous enemy, though the famous Schlieffen plan was not yet fully worked out when Degouy held his lecture. The same type of reasoning was also present within the German Navy in the 1890s. As long as the German fleet was superior to either the Russian Baltic Fleet or the French Northern Fleet, the objective would be to deploy as fast as possible against one of the opponents and try to defeat it before turning to face the other. The problem was that the German Navy did not have the necessary strength to defeat either of them. See Ivo Nikolai Lambi: *The Navy and German Power Politics, 1862–1914* (Boston, 1984), pp. 58, 84–86.

[100] SHM, 1 CC 211 Ac 2: Lectures by Capitaine de frégate Degouy: *Marines étrangères,*

International Law

The perennial problem for the proponents of the *jeune école* was the incompatibility of effective industrial warfare and international law. From the mid-1890s they no longer claimed, as Aube, Charmes, Commandant Z, and Montéchant had done, that international law was irrelevant. Both officers and civilians with *jeune école* sympathies had problems in coming to terms with the clash of interests that international law and effective trade warfare represented. Those who tried to discuss the problem very often attempted to show that this kind of warfare could be carried out within the rules of international law. Sometimes they just ignored whether certain actions would be in accordance with international law or not. The most notable exceptions to this trend were Lockroy and Fournier. Lockroy wrote in *La marine de guerre. Six mois rue Royal* that he did not believe that international law would be respected "when nations will be engaged in a deadly struggle, upon the outcome of which depend not only their liberty, but maybe even their existence, [...].[101] As will be shown later, Fournier, who in his early writings avoided discussing the dilemmas concerning commerce warfare and international law, after the Fashoda crises explicitly rejected that commerce warfare should be conducted according to international law.

From the mid-1890s it was the naval staff college that served as the main arena in which such questions naturally would be discussed. It was an obvious topic to discuss in the lectures on strategy and tactics, but international law was also a separate subject in the college's curriculum. The strategy of the *jeune école* and the dilemmas of industrial warfare were very often the point of departure for the lectures. Several of the lectures were striking examples of the difficulties that sympathisers of the *jeune école* encountered when they tried to make the idea of commerce warfare conform with international law.

This problem can be seen in Degouy's attempt to define contraband. The Declaration of Paris of 1856 had made enemy merchandise in neutral ships exempt from capture, with the exception of contraband of war, which was not defined. That implied that every power constituted itself a judge of what was contraband. Arms and ammunition were clearly contraband, but what about foodstuffs? There was no lack of

---

1ère Partie, Marines Anglaise, Allemande et Italienne (Ecole des Hautes Etudes de la Marine, Paris, 1897–1898), pp. 374–376.

[101] Edouard Lockroy: *La marine de guerre. Six mois rue Royale* (Paris, 1897), p. 13.

indications that food would be defined as contraband. In the Franco-Chinese war of 1884–85 and again in 1893, when France was enforcing a "pacific blockade" of Siam, rice was declared contraband.[102] Preventing deliveries of foodstuffs to Great Britain would most probably cause severe problems for the population, which after all was the objective of the kind of warfare preached by the *jeune école*. Degouy constructed an argument, based on the *jeune école*'s postulate that modern warfare would involve the whole machinery of modern society, that defined foodstuffs carried to Britain as contraband:

> It is common knowledge that English soil does not produce enough to feed its inhabitants—among whom figure all the men who constitute the armed forces, on land or at sea. To secure imports of foodstuffs is consequently to provide for the immediate and direct sustenance of these armed forces, in other words to make them contraband of war.[103]

Defining which goods were contraband or not, was a recurring question in international maritime law. Although it was complicated and the handling of the problem could have serious consequences, especially in relation to the neutrals, it did not in the same degree violate the principles of international law as Aube's and Charmes's prescription for merciless commerce raiding would. Degouy's reasoning around contraband did not indicate that he was of the opinion that ships carrying contraband could be sunk without warning. His discussions of what kind of protection international law gave non-combatants against attacks was, however, not consistent. This inconsistency is clear in his attempt to describe international law in regard to convoy systems and offensive mine-laying. His analysis of the convoy system was based on the condition that non-combatants would be much better protected by international law than combatants. His proposal for offensive mine-laying, on the other hand, did not recognize any such distinction.

The backdrop to Degouy' reasoning on these matters was the interest shown by French naval officers in the writings of the British Commander (later Admiral) George Alexander Ballard and his proposals for a convoy system to ensure the safety of the merchant marine. Degouy had an optimistic view on how the combination of fast cruisers and

---

[102] Marder: *The Anatomy of British Sea Power*, p. 89; Offer: *The First World War*, p. 271.
[103] SHM, 1 CC 211 Ac 2: Lectures by Capitaine de frégate Degouy: *Marines étrangères, 1ère Partie, Marines Anglaise, Allemande et Italienne* (Ecole des Hautes Etudes de la Marine, Paris, 1897–1898), p. 26.

larger torpedo boats (*avisos torpilleurs*) could effectively disperse a convoy, and due to their high speed could choose the right moment to attack individual ships. An important aspect of the convoy system, according to Degouy, was that it conferred combatant status on a ship which sailing alone clearly would have been a non-combatant:

> We notice that, from the moment that merchant ships sail in convoy, protected by warships, they become "ipso facto" subject to all means of warfare. They are *military convoys* like the ones one does not hesitate to attack in land warfare.[104]

There was in his reasoning an implicit recognition that merchant vessels as such were initially non-combatants and that they could not be hunted down and sunk. Their status changed, however, as soon as they operated within a military formation. Then they were, in legal terms, acceptable targets just like ordinary warships.[105]

Degouy's need to explain why merchant vessels in a specific context would be legally accepted targets for all means of warfare, appears inconsistent when seen against the background of his recommendation, in the same lecture, of offensive mine-laying in the narrow approaches to British ports. Mines could not discriminate between warships and merchantmen, ships sailing in convoy or independently, or between neutral ships and ships from belligerent nations. Still Degouy found offensive mine-laying an acceptable way to fight, admittedly with some qualifications: "It is quite interesting to ask oneself what will happen to traffic under national or foreign flag to and from English ports if we succeed in laying these mines—after having warned the neutrals of course—and if a single merchant ship is sunk."[106]

The specialists in international law who gave lectures at the staff college were also unable to give the students any conclusive advice on the limits of industrial warfare in relation to international law. The point of departure for the lectures on this subject was the debate between Aube and Bourgois in 1885–1886. In his lecture on international maritime law, *sous-commisaire* Brière, rejected the very idea, popular among

---

[104] *Ibid.*, p. 226.
[105] Marder claims in his book, *The Anatomy of British Sea Power*, p. 87, that the use of torpedo boats against merchant ships sailing in convoy would be "perfectly legitimate." He does not, however, explain why it would be legitimate.
[106] SHM, 1 CC 211 Ac 2: Lectures by Capitaine de frégate Degouy: *Marines étrangères, 1ère Partie, Marine Anglaise, Allemande et Italienne* (Ecole des Hautes Etudes de la Marine, Paris, 1897–1898), p. 223.

the *jeune école* sympathisers, that civilian resources that contributed to the overall military effort, or that had a military potential, could be legitimate targets. For example, he denounced the idea that passenger liners could be legitimate targets because they had attributes (i.e. high speed) that made them suitable for conversion to warships.[107] Brière would not accept a logic of pre-emptive attack on ships that might later be armed: "then one must also admit the legitimacy of massacring women and children under the pretext that they might, if necessary, take up arms."[108]

Brière argued generally for a strict adherence to international law, but also stressed that the principles for a just and fair war should be followed regardless of whether they were codified by law or not. He rejected the claim that any way of fighting that was not explicitly contrary to international law was acceptable. He stressed to his students that just and fair war was not a matter of whether certain means of warfare were illegal or not: "law does not make justice, it recognizes it, and in the absence of law, justice remains."[109]

Despite this reasoning by Brière, he did make an exception for maritime bombardment. This attitude on Brière's part is somewhat surprising. The Declaration of Brussels of 1874 stated that: "Open towns, agglomerations of dwellings, or villages which are not defended can neither be attacked nor bombarded."[110] Not all of the 15 European states which attended the conference that prepared the Declaration of Brussels were willing to accept it as a binding convention, and it was thus not ratified.[111] Brière did claim that it was formally established that bombardment of an open city, which did not house military units or in which the inhabitants had not shown any intention to defend the city

---

[107] SHM, 1 CC 222 Acc 1: Lectures by Sous-Commissaire Brière, Commissaire de Division: *Droit international maritime* (Division Navale constituant l'Ecole supérieure de guerre, 1896), pp. 105–107. As discussed in Chapter I, the British Admiralty had since the 1887–88 estimates been subsidising a large number of fast ocean steamers for use as auxiliary cruisers in wartime. See also Marder: *The Anatomy of British Sea Power*, pp. 102–103.

[108] SHM, 1 CC 222 Acc 1: Lectures by Sous-Commissaire Brière, Commissaire de Division: *Droit international maritime* (Division Navale constituant l'Ecole supérieure de guerre, 1896), pp. 105–107.

[109] *Ibid.*, pp. 2–3.

[110] Project of an International Declaration concerning the Laws and Customs of War, Brussels, August 27, 1874, article 15.

[111] Bombardment by naval forces of undefended ports, towns, villages, dwellings, or buildings was forbidden by the Hague Convention of 1907, which was signed by France. *Bombardment by Naval Forces in Time of War (Hague IX)*, October 18, 1907, Article 1.

by raising barricades or fortifications, would be a flagrant violation of international law. However, customary law did open up for maritime bombardment, he claimed. The aim of maritime bombardment against open cities would be to ruin the commerce of the enemy.[112]

Brière's reference to customary law seems somewhat inconsistent with his other arguments. He put customary law above what he himself had claimed was a formally established law. This he did despite the fact that bombardment of unfortified coastal towns and places had generally been considered taboo in the nineteenth century.[113] The one historical example of the ethical dilemmas of bombardment of open cities that Brière chose to mention was Admiral Bouet-Willaumez's refusal to bombard the small Pomeranian town of Kolberg in 1870.[114] One explanation for why Brière argued for the legality of maritime bombardment is most probably that the idea that trade was a legitimate target was strongly established within French naval thought. Even those who from a moral point of view disagreed with the *jeune école*'s radical view on international law, seem to have had a flexible view on international law when it came to commercial warfare. This kind of pragmatic interpretation of international law with regard to commercial warfare was even more evident in the lectures of Brière's successor at the French naval staff college, professor Wilhelm.

Professor Wilhelm's description of the main aspects of modern warfare concurred with those of the *jeune école*. His examination of the development of warfare from the sixteenth century until the 1890s is also in agreement with the analysis of modern historians who have tried to come to terms with the changing aspects of war in the latter half of the nineteenth century. Professor Wilhelm claimed that the sixteenth century saw the appearance of regular armies, and that wars were fought between governments and that they primarily involved the belligerents. Wars conformed to the theories of international law. The Crimean War was, according to Professor Wilhelm, very close to the ideal type of a limited war conducted in accordance with international law. It was the Franco-Prussian War that represented a breach with the

---

[112] SHM, 1 CC 222 Acc 1: Lectures by Sous-Commissaire Brière, Commissaire de Division: *Droit international maritime* (Division Navale constituant l'Ecole supérieure de guerre, 1896), p. 109.

[113] Marder: *The Anatomy of British Sea Power*, p. 76.

[114] SHM, 1 CC 222 Acc 1: Lectures by Sous-Commissaire Brière, Commissaire de Division: *Droit international maritime* (Division Navale constituant l'Ecole supérieure de guerre, 1896), p. 109.

past, and inaugurated a new era of warfare. He claimed that the manner in which Prussia fought the war had set a standard. All European states would have to mobilise their resources to become *la nation armée*. Nations would fight nations, and the attacked nation would have no choice but to defend itself with all means and in all ways:

> War will involve all men, and aim at the political, industrial and commercial ruin of the defeated, at the annihilation of all her [enemy's] forces and all her economic resources. The attacked nations are thus obliged to defend themselves with vigour because it is for them a question of life or death. If a war threatens the existence of a people, the legitimate necessities of its defence demand that it do everything to ruin what is important for the enemy (nationality (sic), finance, industry, trade).[115]

Based on his interpretation of the historical shift in warfare, professor Wilhelm tried to adjudicate between the views of Aube and Bourgois concerning the legal limits of commerce warfare at sea. He accused Aube of having too practical an approach to the problem, while Bourgois was too theoretical. Aube's recommendation of merciless commerce warfare would be both a breach of international law and contradict the very idea of legal warfare, according to professor Wilhelm. It would also harm the reputation of France. Admiral Bourgois was too restrained in his theoretical world. He had not taken note of the changes in warfare, and could certainly not have read Bismarck and von der Goltz. Professor Wilhelm recommended a position somewhere between the most prominent writers on commercial warfare in the French Navy at the time. He concluded that the capture of the merchantman was a right of the belligerent, but that the life of the crew should be saved.[116]

From Lockroy's First Period as Minister of Marine to the Fashoda Crisis

Lockroy was the first reform-minded Minister of Marine to fill the office since Aube. He was fascinated by Fournier's strategic thinking and his propositions for the future composition of the French fleet. This triggered an initiative to push the Superior Council into discussing vital strategic questions. This was the first time since Aube's ministry that the Superior Council was asked to debate and give advice on fundamental

---

[115] SHM, 1 CC 222 Acc 10: Lectures by Mr Wilhelm, Professeur à l'Ecole libre des sciences politiques. Chef du service du Contentieux de la Marine: *Droit maritime international* (Ecole des Hautes Etudes de la Marine, 1898), pp. 169–172.
[116] *Ibid.*, pp. 181–183.

questions concerning French naval strategy and the organisation of the Navy. Lockroy asked the admirals seven questions. The first was of a general character and addressed what the principal missions of the French Navy should be. The second and third question were attempts to examine to what extent the admirals on the Superior Council shared Fournier's ideas on the economic, tactical and strategic advantages a homogenous fleet of cruisers could provide. The four last questions were of no strategic significance.[117]

The admirals were not inclined to describe the Royal Navy as the principle enemy for the French Navy. They still insisted that Italy was the most probable enemy, and a redoubtable one, that the French Navy should prepare itself to fight. Several admirals also warned that the Italian Navy had been strengthened in recent years. This alleged fact forced the French Navy to concentrate in the Mediterranean, they claimed. Still the French admirals were confident that they could crush the Italian Navy, and their proposed strategy in case of war against the Triple Alliance was an offensive in the Mediterranean against the Italian Navy and coastal defence in the Channel against the German Navy.

Although the Triple Alliance was considered the most likely antagonist, Great Britain was not excluded as a possible adversary. A couple of admirals mentioned the possibility that the Royal Navy could join the Triple Alliance in their naval efforts, but most of the members of the Council ruled out such a situation as a premise for war planning. If France and Britain were to fight each other, it would be in a situation where they were the only two belligerents. There was a clear consensus among the admirals that the French Navy could not challenge the Royal Navy in fleet warfare, and that the French Navy would have to resort to commerce warfare. First of all they called for cruisers to raid seaborne trade, but some also argued in favour of attacks on British ports. They were not explicit as to how this should be done, and there was no tendency to embrace the proposal of Aube, Charmes and Fournier that the French fleet should specialize in this kind of warfare.

---

[117] SHM, BB8-2424/4. Lockroy's letter posing the questions is dated 18 March 1896. The answers are all filed in BB8-2424/4: Letters from Vice Admiral Prouhet, 17 June 1896, Vice Admiral Brown de Colsto(u)n, 2 April 1896, Vice Admiral Parrayon, no date, Vice Admiral Puech, 2 April 1896, Vice Admiral Régnault de Prémesnil, 28 March 1896, Vice Admiral Duperré, 17 June 1896, Rear Admiral Touchard, no date, Vice Admiral Barrera, 30 March 1896, Vice Admiral de la Jaille, 9 April 1896, Vice Admiral Gervais 12 April 1896. The letters dated June are probably answers to a letter from Lockroy's successor demanding a copy of the letters sent to Lockroy.

The admirals maintained vigorously that the French Navy should reflect the composition of the fleets of their probable foes. As long as Italy had battleships, the French Navy must have them too.

The Superior Council's logic led to a de facto resignation with regard to any ambition to challenge the Royal Navy. There was a clear consensus that France would not in any foreseeable future be able to face up to the British battle fleet. The total rejection of fighting the Italian Navy with anything but battleships left the French Navy with only limited means to build a fleet of cruisers that could mount a substantial threat to British trade and thus her economy. The bottom line of the Council's deliberations was that French naval war planning should have as a prerequisite that Italy would be the most likely enemy, and a that a battle fleet was required to fight the Italian Navy. In a war against Britain, the French Navy would have to defend the French coast and overseas possessions as best they could. The cost of a battleship fleet was, however, such that not very much could be spent on ships dedicated for cruiser warfare against Britain.

It seems that the very fact that Great Britain was viewed as such a redoubtable enemy helped push the admirals on the Superior Council to focus on an enemy the French Navy actually could beat, the Italian Navy. The majority of the admirals demonstrated no real wish to discuss in more detail how the French Navy should face the Royal Navy. The repeated references to commerce warfare as the way to fight Britain had the character of being a ritual rather than a carefully thought-out strategy. This also explains why the modalities of commercial warfare under existing international law were hardly ever deliberated.

A consequence of the admirals' insistence on having a fleet mirroring the composition of the fleet of the French Navy's potential enemies was that Fournier's idea of a homogenous fleet did not find much support.[118] This view was further strengthened by the admirals' argument that the Triple Alliance and Great Britain should be met with two different strategies, one based on classical fleet warfare with battleships and the other on commercial warfare conducted by cruisers. The Council also

---

[118] The question posed by Lockroy was somewhat oddly formulated. He asked the admirals on the Superior Council whether it would be advantageous to have a homogenous fleet with regard to speed. Some admirals limited their answers to discuss only speed, but most of the admirals understood the questions as whether they supported a homogenous fleet in the sense that Fournier advocated.

put up as a general argument that the French Navy should be composed of what they regarded as the pillars of any navy: battleships, cruisers and torpedo boats. This ruled out Fournier's proposal of a fleet consisting of only one type or class of ships. It was also added that the idea of a multipurpose ship with top all-over technical and war-fighting capabilities was unrealistic: "A ship good at everything, having at the same time and to the same extent, speed, offensive capabilities, defensive capabilities and a [vast] operational radius, is obviously nothing but a Utopian idea beyond discussion."[119]

The government of Léon Bourgeois had to resign in April 1896 shortly after Lockroy had put his questions to the Superior Council. Lockroy continued his efforts to reform the French Navy from his position as a Member of Parliament, and the concurrence of his ideas with Fournier's was even more evident in Lockroy's parliamentary work than it had been in his first period as Minister of Marine. In 1897 he proposed a law for Parliament that corresponded very much with the ideas forwarded by Fournier. The essence of his proposal was a plan for the construction of new cruisers, a system of overseas ports to serve the French cruiser fleet, and repair and upgrading of parts of the existing fleet. The Navy Commission of the Parliament, of which Lockroy was a member, supported his plan. In their report to the Parliament, where they examined both Lockroy's project and the French president's proposal for a new naval construction programme, the commission elaborated the strategic reasoning behind the Lockroy proposal.

The commission emphasized that the proposal to establish and improve naval bases in Tunisia, Algeria, Saigon, Madagascar, Dakar, Gorée and Martinique to support the cruiser fleet was to secure for the French Navy a possibility to conduct offensive warfare. They argued that to have a navy with a potentially good radius of action, but without any overseas bases to support their operations:

> is to admit that, even when attacked, we will withdraw to a strictly defensive posture. It is to renounce in advance the pursuit of the aggressor, it is to deprive us of the possibility to carry the war to him and hit his vulnerable spots and his trade. It is, in a sense, to reduce France to a besieged place where the commander would choose as his tactic to abandon all possibilities of escape, and that in order to be sure to stick fully

---

[119] SHM, BB8-2424/4: *Le Vice-Amiral Duperré, Président du Conseil des Travaux, à Monsieur le Ministre de la Marine*, 17 June 1896.

to the principle, would deprive himself of all opportunities to profit from favourable circumstances. That is a recipe for sure defeat.[120]

The commission did not leave any doubt as to who the enemy would be and what strategy should be followed in such a war:

> To neglect the strategic positions, the fantastic bases that our overseas territories in the Atlantic and the Indian Ocean offer us, that is not only to accept in advance the loss of these areas, but it is even more, in case of a war with England, to give her all the chances against us by reassuring her of the fate of her trade and of her supplies and deliberately depriving ourselves of any possibility of diverting operations against those of her colonial possessions where considerable blows can be delivered against her. It is to deprive France of her best weapon in a conflict with our eternal rival.[121]

Another interesting element in the Commission's arguments was its insistence on the construction of torpedo boats, torpedo destroyers and remarkably enough, submarines. Lockroy expanded on the proposal to build submarines three years later in his book *La défense navale*. He stressed that the technical problems of sailing submarines were sufficiently cleared up, and one could thus without worry start constructing a great number of submarines. Lockroy had the same expectations for the submarines' offensive capacities against a blockading force as the early *jeune école* advocates had of the torpedo boat: "After the experiences made, one can be sure that it will be impossible to impose any blockade in front of an area defended by submarines."[122] As Aube had envisaged swarms of torpedo boats defending the littorals against enemy attacks and landings, Lockroy predicted that the submarines could fill that role in a future war. He argued that France was well ahead of other navies in the development and use of submarines.[123]

Although Lockroy praised the torpedo boat, he admitted that the French Navy had experienced technical difficulties with the torpedo boats that were not yet completely solved. He argued that the torpedo boats could carry out terrible raids against enemy ports, and he underlined their tactical advantages in a way that very much resembled the

---

[120] SHM, BB8-1901: *No. 2514, Chambre des députés, Rapport fait au nom de la Commission del la Marine, Annexe au Procès-verbal de la séance du 12 juin 1897*, p. 3.
[121] *Ibid.*, p. 4.
[122] Edouard Lockroy: *La défense navale* (Paris, 1900), p. 82.
[123] Lockroy's description of the French lead in submarine development and construction was correct.

arguments of Aube and Charmes. The torpedo boats would be impossible to distinguish in the dark with the lapping of the waves, in the fine and dense rain that was typical for the coast of Normandy and Flanders, or in foggy weather. Lockroy summed up his praise of the torpedo boats, in the rather chauvinistic manner typical of the *jeune école*, by stating that the torpedo boats "constitute a typical French weapon, because, in order to conduct operations with them, it is necessary to be daring, to have a kind of heroic madness. With these [boats], our officers will work miracles."[124]

Lockroy predicted that in future wars the belligerents would rather put their effort into harassing their opponent and attacking his vital interests than to fight great naval battles. And he stated that it was commercial warfare that would be the way to victory.[125] He advocated, in accordance with Fournier's ideas, that the French Navy should prepare to conduct commercial warfare, and that it thus should build modern cruisers.[126] He found Fournier's concept of a homogeneous fleet attractive, but difficult to carry out given the existing fleet and the funding of the Navy. He found a reduction to five types of ships more realistic: battleships (*unités de combat*) of 10–12,000 tons, commerce-raiders of 4–5,000 tons, torpedo destroyers of 300–1,000 tons, torpedo boats of 100 tons and finally submarines.[127] His priorities in regard to the importance of cruisers were, however, clear. He managed, both through his position as Minister of Marine and Member of Parliament, to shift the priorities of the French Navy's building programme away from battleships and towards armoured cruisers.

Although Fournier's and Lockroy's efforts to shift the priorities towards a greater emphasis on cruisers did not meet Fournier's original idea of a homogeneous fleet of cruisers, the tendency was clear enough to raise considerable concerns in the Royal Navy.[128] Since the *Dupuy de Lôme*, France had built four more armoured cruisers. In 1896–97, however, the development of the armoured cruiser in the French Navy was pushed ahead, largely at the expense of battleship constructions. Lockroy and his allies in the Parliament managed to change the 1896

---

[124] Edouard Lockroy: *La marine de guerre. Six mois rue Royale* (Paris, 1897), p. 35.
[125] *Ibid.*, p. 31.
[126] *Ibid.*, p. 27.
[127] *Ibid.*, pp. 92–93.
[128] Marder: *The Anatomy of British Sea Power*, pp. 283–287; N.A. Lambert: *Sir John Fisher's Naval Revolution*, pp. 21–29.

budget proposal and replaced the second ship of the *D'Entrecasteaux* class with a new model cruiser named *Jeanne d'Arc*. The cruiser was substantially bigger than those proposed by Fournier, but she had capabilities that matched Fournier's strategic vision. With her high speed and long range she was purposely designed for raiding commerce on the high seas. The great length of her hull coupled with a huge coal capacity would, in theory, enable the *Jeanne d'Arc* to outpace and outdistance any more powerful adversary.

The battle of Yalu had further demonstrated to the French naval officers and engineers the weakness of unarmoured cruisers. The French had already been building armoured cruisers, but it was now, due to great improvements in the manufacture of armour, possible to protect considerable areas of the hull on first-class cruisers while keeping the size and cost of the ships within reasonable limits. This meant that the hull of the *Jeanne d'Arc*, and all subsequent French side-armoured cruisers, was in effect shotproof against the armour piercing shells fired from the 6-inch guns that composed the main batteries of the British cruisers with the speed to catch them.[129]

At first the British did not pay much attention to the French development of the side-armoured cruiser. It was not until 1897 when the tug of war between the conservative Minister of Marine, Admiral Besnard, and Parliament led to the construction of three 9,500 tons Fournier-inspired armoured cruisers of the *Montcalm* class that the Admiralty reacted.[130] It realized with concern that the new French cruisers outclassed even the newest British cruisers and, in effect, rendered obsolete the Royal Navy's fleet of trade protection vessels. In July 1897, the First Lord of the Admiralty, George Goschen, informed the Chancellor of the Exchequer that "in view of the extra exertions made by France specially in respect of fast cruisers" the Navy required money to lay down four

---

[129] N.A. Lambert: *Sir John Fisher's Naval Revolution*, p. 21.

[130] After Lockroy returned to office in June 1898, he and Fournier planned five slightly improved *Montcalms*, the *Gloire* class. These completed what became a formidable group of eleven relatively homogeneous armoured cruisers begun between 1897 and 1899. Ropp: *The Development of a Modern Navy*, p. 288. The priority given to cruisers in the French Navy could also be seen in the Programme of 1898, which consisted of only one modification to the Programme of 1896; it increased the number of cruisers for European waters from 12 to 18, and augmented the total number of armoured cruisers to 25. SHM, BB8-2424/6: EMG: *Rapport présenté à la Section Permanente du Conseil Supérieur de la Marine, sur le programme de constitution de la Flotte tel qu'il résulte d'avis émis par le Conseil ou de décisions prises par les Ministres depuis le mois de décembre 1896*, 25 April 1905.

large cruisers with the necessary speed to run down the French vessels.[131] The House of Commons granted the sum three days later.

The Admiralty was not alone in raising concern over the French construction programme. In February 1898 the Commander-in-Chief of Britain's premier Mediterranean Squadron pushed for four or five cruisers that could defend the Mediterranean trade route against the new French armoured cruisers.[132] Later the same month Goschen explained the seriousness of the situation to the Cabinet:

> The French, so far as their policy can be gauged, have begun to recognise that it is by cruisers rather than battleships that they can damage us most. What their efforts on battleships have been had been seen from the facts which I have described, but in the new and vast programme which is now awaiting the sanction of the Chamber there is only one new battleship to be laid down in 1898. Their first class cruiser programme, on the other hand, is most formidable.[133]

To meet the challenge posed by the French armoured cruisers, the Admiralty, in early 1898, laid down the Royal Navy's first class of armoured cruisers. The French threat appeared even more challenging when the Royal Navy learned that even the Russian Navy in 1898 initiated an ambitious cruiser programme. Despite the fact that the Franco-Russian challenge raised serious concerns in the Royal Navy, at that time hardly any recognition in the French Navy could be seen that the alliance with Russia would have any significant impact on the French-British balance of naval power.

Summary

The *jeune école*'s position in the French Navy in the post-Aube era can be divided into two distinct periods. In the first period, before the appointment of Lockroy as minister in 1895, no prominent *jeune école* officers or politicians held influential positions in the French Navy. *Jeune école* writers and officers, like Commandant Z, Montéchant, and Lieutenant X, were, however, active in public debate and these theoretically strong officers and writers elaborated the thoughts of Aube and Charmes and brought them to a wider audience. More important, perhaps, these

---

[131] Quoted in N.A. Lambert: *Sir John Fisher's Naval Revolution*, p. 22.
[132] Marder: *The Anatomy of British Sea Power*, p. 287.
[133] Quoted in N.A. Lambert: *Sir John Fisher's Naval Revolution*, p. 22.

heirs of Aube and Charmes maintained the *jeune école* as a distinct and coherent alternative to the dominant, traditionalist naval thought. The second period saw a comeback for the *jeune école* in French naval politics and was marked by strong personalities like Lockroy and Fournier, who both held influential positions. They were eager to reform the French Navy and were both inspired by the *jeune école*.

The heirs of Aube and Charmes did not deviate very much from the founders' theories. They viewed a future war as a conflict in which the whole nation would mobilise for the war effort, and where it would be legitimate to attack any part of this effort. The task of the military planners would therefore be to identify the weak links in the chain of the economic, social, political and military system that constituted the enemy's overall potential to wage war. It was against this weak link that French military resources should be aimed. This should be planned for in peacetime and the Navy should be organised accordingly. The weak link was public and political support for the war. Commandant Z, Montéchant and Lieutenant X shared the focus of Aube and Charmes on Great Britain as the major challenge to France. Great Britain's dependence on trade was its Achilles heel, and trade warfare was thus the logical answer.

A certain evolution occurred in ideas concerning how to fight Germany and Italy. The new generation of the *jeune école* were more confident than their predecessors that the French Navy could be an effective tool to undermine German and Italian popular support for a war against France. They recognized that the growth in German commerce, which emerged as a distant but significant challenge to the British during the 1890s, made raiding a possible weapon against Germany as well as Great Britain. They thus began to meet the old criticism that a programme focusing on commerce raiding would have no effect on a continental enemy.

Trade warfare was not viewed as an option against Italy. Sheer intimidation and terror by bombarding coastal cities could achieve the same result as commerce raiding against Great Britain, and to some extent Germany. The young state was perceived as lacking national cohesion, and the heirs of Aube and Charmes were convinced that the Italians could be bullied into political surrender. The aim was to undermine popular support for war; trade warfare and bombardment of cities would both have that effect.

Both with regard to the theatre of operations to which the French Navy should give priority and to the composition of the fleet there were an evolution in ideas from the predecessors to the heirs. Whereas Aube and Charmes envisaged the French Navy cruising the seven seas hunting British merchantmen, their successors argued that the French Navy should concentrate in European waters. Much of British and German trade would pass close to French waters. France could benefit from this geographical advantage and construct a fleet that was designed to operate in the littorals. By focusing on operations close to France, the importance of the fact that the small torpedo boats lacked seaworthiness on the high seas was reduced. Speed and numbers, which was a mantra of the *jeune école*, could thus be obtained. Although the heirs argued for the virtues of small boats, they proposed to build torpedo boats and torpedo-cannon boats that were larger than those proposed by Aube and Charmes. Commandant Z and Montéchant also argued for a number of big cruisers.

Commandant Z, Montéchant and Lieutenant X were, however, eager to underline that what they proposed were minor alterations of the theories of Aube and Charmes. Strategy they argued:

> rests on a certain number of principles, some which vary with time and scientific insight, others that are laws of military reason [...] and which have an almost eternal validity [...] It is the axioms of war to attack the weak spots of the enemy in strength, to organise in order to oppose one's own fresh forces at the point where the opponent is exhausted.[134]

It was hence these eternal military truths that had *guerre de course* and bombardment of cities as their logical conclusion.

The *jeune école* from the mid-1890s was different from the *jeune école* of the late 1880s and early 1890s in two fundamental and interlinked areas. This was illustrated by the lectures at the French staff college, the discussions within the Superior Council, political discussions and staff work. The *jeune école* had evolved into a theory with a wider support within the Navy, and simultaneously the theory as it was represented at the time made fewer extreme claims of the kind that had been so controversial under Aube and Charmes. The more moderate appearance of the theory probably explains some of the wider diffusion and acceptance of what was perceived to be the ideas of the *jeune école*.

The *jeune école*'s basic analysis of future wars remained fundamental for the new generation of the *jeune école*. There had been a growing

---

[134] Lieutenant X: Introduction to Commandant Z and H. Montéchant: *Essai de stratégie navale*, p. 14.

appreciation that future wars would be industrial wars, and that they would affect the whole of society. The notion that Great Britain was the most probable enemy was now also adopted outside the circles of the most eager colonialists. This was partly due to the approaching crisis over Sudan, and a slow, but perceptible recognition that the 1890s had seen a decline in Italian sea power. The idea that France, as an inferior naval power, would have to choose an alternative strategy to fleet warfare, and that a major element of this strategy would be attacks on British commerce, was still a recognisable part of the new generation's theories. What made the *jeune école* of the mid-1890s and onward distinct from that of the founders, was primarily the interpretation of the practical and moral consequences of the proposed strategy. The more extreme manifestations of the theory, both concerning the force structure and the alleged irrelevance of international law in wartime, were relegated to the background.

The strong belief that some revolutionary technological invention would give France an overwhelming advantage compared to her possible enemies was not as outspoken as it had been in the era of Aube and Charmes. There was, however, still a firm belief that French genius could give the French Navy the upper hand in some areas of naval warfare, primarily in defensive coastal operations and offensive trade warfare. The new generation of the *jeune école*, though, tended to favour concepts and ships that were well proven, like Fournier's cruisers. There was, however, one exception. As we shall see later, the successful tests of submarines led some of the most prominent *jeune école* supporters to argue with the same optimistic enthusiasm that Aube and Charmes had shown concerning the alleged blessings of the torpedo boats.

Another significant change from the mid-1890s could be seen in the way the adherents of the *jeune école* argued with regard to international law. The somewhat fanatical logic preached by Aube, Charmes, Montéchant, Lieutenant X and others, that concluded that the end justified the means, did not find the same support. There was a clear consensus that the nature of war had changed, but few officers and civilians within the Navy defended the kind of merciless warfare and disregard of international law, that the founders of the *jeune école* had advocated. To base a campaign against Great Britain on commercial warfare, and conduct it within the limits of international law would, however, as Bourgois had demonstrated, probably not be effective. The reasoning of the new generation of the *jeune école* was very much characterised by the dilemma between effectiveness and morally based considerations. Two solutions were proposed to cope with this quandary. The most prevalent approach was to ignore the problem. Those who chose to study the problem of commerce warfare and international law very often ended up with a flexible interpretation of international law.

CHAPTER FOUR

THE FASHODA CRISIS AND THE DEVELOPMENT OF A MODERN NAVY

The *jeune école*'s return to power was aided by shifting alignments in international politics. Competing imperial projects in Africa caused a dramatic crisis between France and Great Britain. The relationship reached its nadir with the Fashoda Crisis in 1898. The naval establishment would, however, only reluctantly admit that the Royal Navy could turn out to be a more likely naval enemy of the French Navy than the navies of the Triple Alliance, especially the Italian. The very determined naval Minister of Marine, Lanessan, did manage to convince most of the admirals in the aftermath of the Fashoda crisis that the French Navy needed a thorough reform of its strategy, doctrines, material, organisation and the composition of the fleet, and that the Royal Navy should be the standard against which it should measure itself. Lanessan, aided by Admiral Fournier, designed a programme for modernising the French Navy that was inspired by the *jeune école*'s ideas of how to fight a superior enemy, but at the same time retained many of the traditional elements of naval policy. Lanessan's programme thus resembled many of the ideas put forward by the predecessor of the *jeune école*, Richild Grivel.

Confrontation between France and Great Britain

French ambitions to acquire an empire showed a remarkable continuity during the 19th century. Robert Tombs has identified four phases of expansion: from 1820 to 1848; the 1850s and 1860s; the 1880s; and from 1890 to the end of the First World War.[1] In the 1880s young republicans, led by Léon Gambetta and Jules Ferry, were determined to restore French greatness. They promised a "French India" somewhere near the Sahara desert. The defeat in 1870–71 had, however, created a widespread fear of any act that could lead to another major war. There was a strong, prevalent notion that the French military effort should

---

[1] Tombs: *France 1814–1914*, pp. 204–207.

be concentrated in Europe. Hence, Gambetta and Ferry's proposals met vigorous opposition in parliament and the press, leading to Ferry's political downfall in 1885. The ambivalence of public opinion in this period was, however, such that the abandonment of Egypt to British influence three years earlier, in 1882, had been so unpopular that it brought down the Freycinet government and poisoned Franco-British relations for a generation.

During the renewed expansionist wave from the 1890s, journalists and politicians increasingly backed the colonial lobby's views. The "scramble for Africa" convinced many that if colonies were important for France's European rivals, they must be valuable to her too. From the 1890s onwards those in charge of policy in Paris were the leaders of the *Parti Colonial*. The most prominent was Théophile Delcassé who was appointed under-secretary for colonies in 1893, later minister for colonies (1894–95) and foreign minister (1898–1905). In both Siam and West Africa Delcassé saw French expansion as a race against Great Britain. His most ambitious project was a plan to challenge the British presence in Egypt. In the context of African expansion the logical way to make this challenge was to take up a position near the headwaters of the Nile.

Delcassé had by the spring of 1893 decided on a plan to send an expedition to Fashoda on the White Nile. A first expedition was launched, but later called off. A second expedition, commanded by Captain Marchand, was authorised by the French cabinet in November 1895. A year later Great Britain decided to begin the reconquest of the Sudan and a large Anglo-Egyptian army, commanded by General Kitchner, started a slow progress towards the upper Nile. Signals of the future confrontation between France and Great Britain due to colonial rivalry were already evident. A few months before Marchand's departure, in March 1895, Sir Edward Grey, then under-secretary at the Foreign Office, gave a public warning in the House of Commons that a French expedition to the Upper Nile would be considered an unfriendly act. Still, successive French governments took little account of the possible outcome of the Fashoda expedition. Once the decision had been taken to send Marchand to the Nile, the purpose of the expedition was never again discussed by the French until after its arrival at Fashoda.[2]

---

[2] Andrew: *Théophile Delcassé*, pp. 44–45; Charles Zorgbibe: *Théophile Delcassé. Le grand Ministre des Affaires étrangères de la IIIe République* (Paris, 2001), pp. 93–123.

The situation grew tenser during 1897. This was primarily due to the Niger crisis, a dispute between France and Great Britain over a portion of the Niger River that had caused a war scare in February and March 1898. The climax of the British-French crisis occurred, however, when both Marchand and Kitchener reached Fashoda. After a marathon journey from the Congo to the Nile, the French colonial expedition of about 150 men reached Fashoda on 10 July 1898. On 18 September 1898 the advance guard of Kitchner's army of 20,000 men appeared near Fashoda after completing the reconquest of the Sudan.

Marchand refused to abandon his position, and the two military leaders referred the dispute to London and Paris. An intense diplomatic crisis developed, marked by violently nationalistic press campaigns and political statements on both sides. Only one outcome was possible given the military imbalance that existed on the spot and France's lack of naval and expeditionary capabilities that could support a French campaign.[3] On 3 November the French cabinet, realizing that France was not ready for war with Great Britain, gave the order for Marchand to withdraw.

Despite the predictable confrontation between Great Britain and France, the Fashoda crisis found the French Navy totally unprepared. As Ropp has pointed out, the state of the Navy in 1898 reflected confusion in French diplomacy, politics, and industry in general. Who was the chief enemy of the Navy: Italy, Great Britain or Germany? Should war against Great Britain be waged by the battle fleet or by cruisers, in the Mediterranean or in the Channel? Were the colonies worth defending directly?[4]

As we have seen, in the 1890s there were only rough ideas on how to fight Great Britain. No carefully worked out plans existed. The Commander-in-Chief of the Northern Fleet, as late as October 1897, made a point of the fact that he could not find that any plans had been worked out for a war against Great Britain. Nevertheless he chose to complete a plan on how to fight Germany as late as July 1898, just

---

[3] Renée Masson writes that the inferiority of the French Navy was perfectly well known by public opinion and the Government. He concludes his thorough comparison of the force ratio between the French Navy and the Royal Navy by stating that "Not only was the French fleet outclassed in numbers by the British fleet, but the inferiority was in many cases made worse by the low quality of the material and the faulty organisation of the naval bases." Renée Masson: *La Marine Française lors de la crise de Fachoda (1898–1899). D.E.S. d'histoire, Université de Paris, Faculté des Lettres* (Paris, 1955), pp. 22–46.

[4] Ropp: *The Development of a Modern Navy*, p. 292.

at the time when the crisis between Great Britain and France was intensifying.

The war plans for the Mediterranean had Italy as their focus. The Minister of Marine, Vice Admiral Besnard, in February 1897, ordered that a war plan against the Triple Alliance should be worked out. The plan did not differ substantially from previous plans. The battleships of the Mediterranean Squadron were to deploy to the Golfe-Juan and prepare an offensive against the Italian Navy, while cruisers should bombard the railway between Savonne and Vintimille.

As the talks over the Niger question failed and caused a war scare in early 1898, Besnard decided that an operations plan against Great Britain had to be worked out. The plan was completed in April and revealed France's weak position. The principle theatre of operation would be the Mediterranean. Although France on paper could mobilise 14 battleships in the Mediterranean, the planners had to admit that only six of them had the necessary capabilities that made them able to operate as a single naval force. The Royal Navy could muster 16 battleships in the Mediterranean. The six French battleships that were able to operate together should be deployed between Toulon and Alger, and they should try to engage the forces with bases in Gibraltar and Malta separately. The problems the Ministry of Marine had in coming up with a credible plan to fight the Royal Navy was underlined by the minister's reluctance to describe which actions should be taken if the Home Fleet combined the fleets in Gibraltar and Malta. Besnard limited himself to stating that if this should occur, then the Commander-in-Chief of the French Mediterranean Fleet should "himself judge which decisions to take."[5]

The Northern Fleet should act as "a fleet-in-being", and tie as large part of the Royal Navy as possible down in the Channel in order to relieve the French forces in the Mediterranean. The bulk of the Northern Fleet should stay in port in Brest and profit from any beneficial situation that could arise. The armoured cruisers *Dupuy de Lôme* and *Pothuau*, accompanied by the cruiser *Friant*, which had speed and weapons that matched the two other vessels, should "perturb the trade close to the British coast" but "avoid combat against a superior

---

[5] Quoted in R. Masson: *La Marine Française lors de la crise de Fachoda*, p. 55. For French naval dispositions during the Fashoda Crisis, see also Motte: *Une éducation géostratégique*, pp. 309–310.

force."[6] Another four divisions, each composed of a cruiser and one or two armed merchantmen, were to operate in the Atlantic.

The Besnard plan did not initiate any thorough examination of the imbalance in strength between the Royal Navy and the French Navy, and the measures that could be taken to reduce the consequences of this imbalance. The plan ignored the most threatening scenarios, or left the problems to be solved by subordinate commanders. Fournier, who was Commander-in-Chief of the Mediterranean Fleet during the Fashoda Crisis, worked out a more defensive and probably more realistic plan for how to fight Royal Navy in the Mediterranean than that of Besnard. The tactical instructions that he issued in November 1898 were based on the assumption that the French Navy would be forced to conduct offensive operations close to the harbour of Toulon. He was convinced that the British would fight in a line-ahead and with at least twice as many battleships as the French Mediterranean Fleet. Fournier stated that the only way to compensate for French inferiority would be by tactical genius, but he was rather vague on how this genius would manifest itself and change the balance of forces in favour of the French Mediterranean Fleet.[7]

The Franco-Russian alliance could in theory influence the imbalance between the French Navy and the Royal Navy, and the General Staff of the Ministry of Marine therefore studied carefully the capabilities of the Russian Navy and whether its ally could improve France's position at sea. The study concluded that the Russian Navy would not be of very much help to France in a war against Britain. The General Staff's harsh verdict was based on an assessment of the present order of battle of the Russian ships, the competence and effectiveness of the naval yards, the professional standard of the naval personnel and the geostrategic position of Russia.

The Russian Navy had 13 battleships that, if they had been of the same standard as modern British or French battleships, could have represented an important reinforcement of the French forces. The Russian battleships and cruisers had a significantly lower speed than the French. Not only did the Russian capital ships differ from the French in speed, artillery and protection, there was also a diversity of battleships and

---

[6] Quoted in R. Masson: *La Marine Française lors de la crise de Fachoda*, p. 55.
[7] SHM: BB4-2437: *Le Vice-Amiral Fournier, Commandant en Chef l'escadre de la Méditerranée à M. le Ministre de la Marine*, November 1898.

cruisers within the Russian fleet that made fleet operations difficult. The General Staff of the French Ministry of Marine explained the variety as being the result of a lack of an independent Russian naval strategy. Lacking an independent strategy, the Russian Navy chose to copy ships they saw being built in other navies.

Although the Russian Navy did try to copy foreign types, the final results turned out to be bad copies due the ineffectiveness of the Russian naval yards. The General Staff claimed that the long construction time led to continual changes during the construction period. There could be changes of boilers, the artillery or its position could be altered, and there could even be modifications in the superstructure of the vessels. This often caused inconveniences such as increased tonnage and draught. Not only did the ineffectiveness of the yards have consequences for the construction time, but also for necessary repairs. The General Staff estimated that repairs in Russian yards took twice the time of similar repairs in a French yard. The main reason for the ineffectiveness was the outmoded technology used at the yards, and it was alleged that the Russian employees generally were slow workers.

The General Staff's estimation of the ordinary Russian was apparently not very high, at least not as potential sailors:

> Although the Slav of the lower classes has serious shortcomings, although he is still very ignorant and generally a drunkard, he has nevertheless major qualities worthy of admiration. He has stamina, selflessness and devotion. When one has indicated to an individual the direction to follow, the goal to reach, he will not have any other thought than to follow that direction and reach that goal. These qualities make the Russian an admirable soldier; but it is one thing to attack the enemy bravely in hand-to-hand combat, and something quite different to attack him with the complicated machines that are modern naval vessels.[8]

The General Staff was also sceptical as to the qualities of the Russian Navy's officer corps: "[The] recruitment to the corps of cadets is difficult, the young from the nobility prefer the army where one can make career faster and with less effort."[9]

---

[8] SHM, 190 GG2 36–37: EMG 1ère Section: *Situation de la flotte russe*, 25 November 1898, pp. 8–9. Pertti Luntinen's study, *French Information on the Russian War Plans 1880–1914* (Jyväskylässä, 1984), provides no information on the French evaluation of the Russian Navy in the late 1890s, but his study of the French view of the Russian Army reveals the same stereotypes as those reflected in the quotation above.

[9] SHM, 190 GG2 36–37: EMG 1ère Section: *Situation de la flotte russe*, 25 November 1898, p. 9.

Russia's difficult maritime strategic position added to the General Staff's scepticism to whether the Russian Navy would be of any help. The two main Russian fleets in Europe were based in the Baltic and the Black Sea, which meant that both fleets would have to pass narrow straits controlled by other powers in order to join the French Navy. The General Staff assumed that the Baltic Fleet would be denied supplies in neutral countries, and would be easy prey for the Royal Navy as soon as it entered the North Sea. Logistical problems were, however, not the most serious problem for the Baltic Fleet at the time of the Fashoda crisis. As the Baltic freezes annually, the fleet was locked up and disarmed in port every year from 27 September to 13 May. The General Staff pointed to the fact that warships by treaty were denied passage of the Bosphorus and Dardanelles, and if the Black Sea Fleet tried to force a passage it risked being engaged by Turkish coastal batteries and the Royal Navy. The Mediterranean Fleet with its one battleship, one armoured gunboat and a few smaller vessels was not seen as a significant reinforcement for the French Navy.

The General Staff concluded that the résumé of their study "is as simple as it is disturbing:

1. The Russian Navy is at the present time not ready to support an offensive war in Europe.
2. The nation that would count on the Russian fleet as a serious support in European waters would be cruelly disappointed the day fighting started.
3. The situation will be changed and significantly improved in five or six years' time.[10]

The French Navy thus lacked both a credible ally that could help to counterbalance the Royal Navy, and it lacked a clear idea on how to fight Great Britain alone. It was not until the Fashoda crisis that the French naval leadership undertook a thorough and painful self-examination of French naval strategy and admitted that over the past decades it had lacked a strategy on how to face a superior navy. This self-examination did not, however, remove the confusion and disarray of the Navy.

The Fashoda crisis came in the midst of Lockroy's second period as Minister of Marine. The crisis prompted a meeting of the Superior Council. The Council was invited, on the basis of a memorandum worked out by Lockroy himself, to contribute to an in-depth discussion

---

[10] *Ibid.*, p. 18.

on French naval policy.[11] The memorandum had a somewhat incongruous character in two respects. First, France was facing an acute military crisis by confronting the world's most powerful navy. The feeling of imminent danger was present and Lockroy chose to open the meeting in the Superior Council by stating that he still hoped that peace could be maintained: "but any day, war may break out. The English seem determined to raise, one after another, all the questions that may lead to a conflict; it seems thus that they want, that they seek, this conflict."[12] Nevertheless, Lockroy chose to start his memorandum by discussing how a war against the Triple Alliance should be fought. Secondly, the memorandum was an unusual mixture of directions or guidelines on how the possible war should be fought, and at the same time an invitation to discuss long-term strategic problems.

Despite the fact that Lockroy found it necessary to maintain a focus on the Triple Alliance and especially the Italian Navy, he complained that the French government had not considered Great Britain as a possible enemy until the last few years, and added that the General Staff had not "until today studied [such a possibility] in a comprehensive and serious manner [...]".[13] Lockroy had, despite the fact that the General Staff had not paid much attention to a possible war with Britain, a fairly clear idea on how Britain should be fought. The guidelines he set out, not surprisingly, concurred with the ideas put forward by the *jeune école*. Lockroy based his guidelines on two premises that had also constituted the point of departure for Grivel and Aube's theories on how to fight the superior power of Britain. First, Lockroy stated that it was an absolute imperative for the French Navy "NOT TO ACCEPT ANY FLEET WARFARE." Lockroy had chosen to write this in capital

---

[11] SHM, BB8-2424/5: Letter from the Minister of Marine to the members of the Superior Council: *Memorandum sur la politique maritime de la France*, 3 December 1898. The chief of the General Staff of the Ministry of Marine, Vice Admiral Cavelier de Cuverville, told the meeting of the Superior Council that the memorandum was not written on his initiative. He also disclosed that he disagreed with several of Lockroy's conclusions. SHM, BB8-2424/5: Conseil Supérieur de la Marine: *Séances du 11 Janvier 1899*, p. 49.

[12] SHM, BB8-2424/5: Conseil Supérieur de la Marine. *Séances du 11 Janvier 1899*, p. 2. The French evacuation of Fashoda did not lead to any détente in the relation between France and Great Britain. The popular press wrote about a possible pre-emptive attack by the Royal Navy against the French Navy. The French foreign minister, Delcassé, still believed in early 1899, as Lockroy did, that a naval confrontation between France and Great Britain was likely to take place. Zorgbibe: *Théophile Delcassé*, pp. 122–123.

[13] SHM, BB8-2424/5: Letter from the Minister of Marine to the members of the Superior Council: *Memorandum sur la politique maritime de la France*, 3 December 1898.

letters to underline the importance of this point. The overwhelming disproportion between the battle fleets of the two navies was such that any attempt to accept battle was impossible, he maintained, and fleet warfare should thus be avoided at any cost.

His second premise was that it was Great Britain's dependence on trade that represented its only vulnerable point. Drawing on these two premises he outlined a strategy, identical to that put forward by Fournier, on how to fight a maritime war against Britain. The battle fleet should take a defensive posture, but conduct offensive operations when local superiority could be obtained. The cruisers were to conduct offensive operations against British trade. Lockroy emphasized that the cruisers would play the dominant role in a war against Britain.

Lockroy raised a third point that had been debated in naval circles for some years. He maintained that it would be in the French Navy's interest for the war to last as long as possible.[14] This argument was based on the assumption that a prolonged maritime war would be far more exhausting for British commercial interests than for the French. Lockroy added another argument of a more tactical nature. He maintained that the blockading ships would be exhausted performing their duty patrolling the coast, while French battleships under shelter of the coastal artillery fortresses could patiently wait, without getting tired, for the right moment to attack. This argument was not used by the flag officers. Lockroy, a civilian, probably underestimated the stress and lack of valuable training that inactivity over a long period could cause.

Although the Superior Council was assembled under the clear impression that war was likely to occur, the deliberations were characterised by the recurring confrontations between the traditionalists and the *jeune école* faction on strategy and how to organise the Navy. The discussions focused very much on how and where the fleet should be deployed. Each member was given two questionnaires in which they were to give their view on the roles to be attributed to the battle fleet and the cruisers and where they should be concentrated. The discussions concluded with very concrete advice from each admiral on both forms of warfare and where the battleships and cruisers should be deployed.

Fournier had been promoted to vice admiral and assigned the post as Commander-in-Chief of the Mediterranean Fleet. It was in this

---

[14] This was the other point that Lockroy chose to underline by using capital letters.

capacity that he was a member of the Superior Council. He was very active in the deliberations of the Council and his clear and explicit proposals on how to deploy the forces and how to conduct the expected war was a point of reference for its discussions. Fournier argued that the traditional French view, in which the Mediterranean was perceived as the strategic focal point, was based on a situation in which France was on good terms with Great Britain. The Fashoda crisis had showed that this was no longer the case, and the French Navy was now in a situation where their main adversary was in the north. He argued along with two out of a total of thirteen members of the Council that the French Navy should follow a strategy with a clear focus on Great Britain as the enemy.

The possibility of a war against Great Britain triggered a heated discussion on where the French Navy's ships should be stationed. Most of the members agreed that Brest was the best port for cruiser warfare given that the enemy was Great Britain. The really controversial question was where the battleships should be deployed. Fournier stressed that it was in the north that Great Britain was most vulnerable and it was thus there that the French Navy should concentrate its effort: "one can hit England on her head from Brest, whereas from Toulon one can only threaten her heel."[15]

Brest was not only preferable due to its location close to the entrance of British ports. The port itself had tactical advantages compared to Toulon, and these advantages were especially precious in a naval war against a superior enemy. Great Britain would most probably use its superior battle fleet to confine the French Navy in port. Toulon's problem, according to Fournier, was the fact that it had only one exit, and even that was a narrow one. It would thus be a fairly easy task for a superior force to maintain effective surveillance and see to it that no French vessel escaped the port. "At Brest, on the other hand", argued Fournier:

> we have the great advantage of possessing three spaced out channels for carrying out offensive operations, or launching cruisers on the high sea undetected by the enemy; we can further make the return of these cruisers easier by appropriate diversions.[16]

---

[15] SHM, BB8-2424/5: Conseil Supérieur de la Marine: *Séances du 11 Janvier 1899*, p. 11.
[16] *Ibid.*, p. 10.

Brest was also an obvious choice, according to Fournier, in order to support a third way of threatening Great Britain. Fournier suggested that the French armed forces should make all necessary preparations for a landing on the British coast in order to arouse fear in Great Britain. In order to make this threat credible, considerable forces would have to be deployed close to the British coast. A concentration of French naval forces around the naval base in Brest was therefore necessary.

Fournier thus proposed a strategy comprising three different operations. One would be to prepare, but not necessarily carry out, a landing on the British coast. A second was to attack major British naval vessels in situations where the French battleships could gain local dominance. The third, and the main effort, according to Fournier, should be trade warfare. His description of how commerce raids should be conducted and the effect they would have on Great Britain echoed the *jeune école* ideas as they were developed by Aube and Charmes. Fournier stressed that the cruisers should patrol the waters close to British ports and there capture or destroy British merchantmen. Whereas he earlier had been vague about aspects of international law, Fournier now stated that commerce warfare had to be carried out "relentlessly and without mercy [...]."[17]

Fournier's willingness to carry commercial warfare to its conclusion was further illustrated by his view on the role that mines could play as a weapon in trade warfare. He rejected the allegations that the use of mines would be a violation of international law. He claimed that all powers equipped their ships with mines, a measure that showed that the right to use this weapon in war was implicitly recognized. He further claimed that the British would use mines for self-protection on the high seas. Fournier asked his colleagues in the Council rhetorically how the British, who intended to use mines, could refuse the French the right to use the same weapon in British territorial waters. What was important, Fournier maintained, was that the neutrals were warned about the danger they would run if they tried to enter British waters.[18]

---

[17] *Ibid.*, p. 12.

[18] *Ibid.*, pp. 12, 31–32. Matters concerning the laying of automatic submarine contact mines were addressed several years later at the Hague Conference of 1907. The use of mines was not forbidden, but article 2 in *Hague VIII, Laying of Automatic Submarine Contact Mines*, 8 October 1907, states that "It is forbidden to lay automatic contact mines off the coast and ports of the enemy, with the sole object of intercepting commercial shipping."

Fournier stressed the importance of the psychological aspects of commercial warfare. The use of mines to stop seaborne trade was particularly well suited to highlight the psychological effect of commercial warfare. Fournier claimed that even if the French refrained from using mines, the neutral merchantmen would hesitate to enter British ports and insurance rates would increase immensely. It was the fear of what harm the French Navy could inflict on trade to and from British ports that would produce economic consequences rather than the damage the French Navy actually inflicted on the merchantmen. It would also be a psychological blow to the British people when they were informed that neutral shipping entering or leaving British ports was exposed to the danger of mines.

As we have seen, Fournier was not operating in a vacuum when he advocated mines as an effective weapon in commerce warfare. Captain Degouy, in one of his lectures at the staff college before the Fashoda crisis, reasoned along the same lines as Fournier. He argued for an intense offensive as soon as hostilities had broken out. One of the offensive measures would be to mine narrow outlets, and Degouy emphasised, as Fournier did, the psychological effect these mines would have. He asked his students rhetorically what would happen "to the traffic to and from English ports by ships under British or foreign flag if we succeed in laying these mines—after having notified the neutrals, of course—and if one single merchantman is sunk."[19]

Fournier's contributions during the deliberations in the Council were very much a repetition of the arguments put forward by Aube and Charmes. He summed up the essentials of the *jeune école* theory when he argued for an incessant and merciless *guerre de course* involving cruiser and mine warfare, stating that "Our adversaries will then undoubtedly understand that the war will be conducted *à outrance* from our side and that we will not give them the satisfaction of playing their game [...]."[20] What was important for Fournier, as it had been for Aube and Charmes, was to choose a strategy that avoided a head-on attack on the strong points of a superior enemy. In order to intimidate Great Britain, the French had to choose an indirect approach and attack

---

[19] SHM, 1 CC 211 Ac 2: Lectures by M. le Capitaine de frégate Degouy: *Marines étrangères, 1ère Partie, Marines Anglaise, Allemande et Italienne* (Ecole des Hautes Etudes de la Marine, Paris, 1897–1898), p. 233.

[20] SHM, BB8-2424/5: Conseil Supérieur de la Marine: *Séances du 11 Janvier 1899*, p. 12.

what was perceived to be the basis for a modern, industrialised society instead of attacking Great Britain's strong point, the Royal Navy. That such warfare had to be carried to its logical extreme was perceived as nothing but a regrettable fact by Fournier and his supporters. It was a necessary measure for such a strategy to meet the intended result.

Fournier, partly due to the fact that he was Commander-in-Chief of the Mediterranean Fleet, but primarily because he presented a consistent alternative to the failed French naval policy, turned the debate into a question of whether the individual members were for or against his proposals. Several of the members of the Superior Council opposed commerce-raiding on the grounds that it was impracticable without violating international law, a consequence they found difficult to accept. It was first of all neutral shipping that was viewed as a problem. To stop contraband, if they ever could agree on a definition, carried aboard neutral ships would be time-consuming and consequently place the visiting vessel in an exposed and dangerous position. Perhaps the most outspoken critic of commercial warfare, Vice Admiral Humann, condemned "industrial warfare [as] an unrealistic idea (*une utopie*), a pure illusion."[21]

The proposal to prepare for a landing of army units on the British coast was met with some scepticism among some of the admirals on the Superior Council. Lockroy supported Fournier's idea and let the Superior Council know that the Government envisaged a possible cooperation with the army. The Minister of War had, according to Lockroy, expressed concerns regarding the logistics if a landing were to take place. Another serious worry for the army was what position the Germans would take in the case of an Anglo-French conflict. The army was reluctant to deploy forces to the west coast unless there was some tacit agreement with Germany securing France's eastern border.[22] Some of the scepticism expressed by the Minister of War and a few of the admirals on the Superior Council was, however, grounded in a misunderstanding of Fournier's proposal. He did not imply that a landing necessarily should be carried out. Fournier and a number of the admirals on the Superior Council emphasised that the main objective of gathering troops in northwestern France would be to make the British believe that such a landing on the British coast could take place.

---

[21] *Ibid.*, p. 32.
[22] *Ibid.*, p. 28.

This deception plan should have a twofold effect on Great Britain. First, preparations for an invasion were meant to arouse fear among the British population. Secondly, such deception could tie down British navy and army forces.[23]

The main reason why the majority of the Superior Council ended up recommending more or less a status quo, with the battle fleet stationed in Toulon while a limited number of cruisers should conduct occasional raids against British commerce, was the argument that the Triple Alliance could still pose a threat to France. Commercial warfare should thus be no more than a secondary operation with the limited aim of disturbing British trade.

Italy, the Perfect Enemy

Despite the repeatedly-stated worry of several of the participants in the Superior Council's meeting that war with Great Britain could break out any moment, both the minister and the majority of the admirals stressed Italy's role as a possible enemy as well. How can this preoccupation with Italy be explained? Did Italy pose a credible naval threat to France, or could the French naval establishment's focus on the Italian Navy have arisen from other motives?

As has been shown, the Italian naval budget dropped significantly from the late 1880s onwards, and its fighting power followed suit.[24] The Italian Navy in 1889 was, if not equal to the French, at least the third

---

[23] *Ibid.*, pp. 15, 53.

[24] Comparisons of relative naval strengths were very complicated as the navies became more influenced by industrial technology. The period discussed in this study was characterised by rapid technological change. Technological breakthroughs or improvements could render relatively new vessels more or less obsolete in a short time. The diversity of the ships of same type contributed to the difficulties in comparing the relative strength, although a more reliable classification of battleships could be noticed from the late 1880s and 1890s. For a discussion on comparisons of the relative strength of navies in this period, see George Modelski and William R. Thompson: *Seapower in Global Politics, 1494–1993* (London, 1988), pp. 73–75.

The method used in this study integrates the four following approaches: comparisons of orders of battle based on different naval lists and documents (i.e. *Annuaire de la Marine* for the different years) of that period from the respective navies and works by other historians; the orders of battle made by the French Navy's General Staff and other French naval authorities; comparisons of investments in new constructions; and subjective, unquantified, considerations of the relative strength made by French naval planners. These four approaches provide for the most part concurring results.

most powerful in the world. Ten years later it had fallen to seventh place. The decline of the Italian Navy was not sudden, and one could perhaps not expect that the French immediately noticed the weakening of the Italian Navy. The comparisons that were made between the French and Italian order of battle and how it had evolved during the 1890s reveal, however, that the French Navy had a fairly good idea of the relative strength of the two navies, and they pointed to the fact that France was increasingly superior to the Italian Navy throughout the 1890s.[25] Tables drawn up by the General Staff comparing both the total naval expenditures and investments in new constructions in the same period for the major European powers confirmed this development. Whereas the Italian investments in new constructions were 86% of the French investments in 1890–91, they were not more than 27% of French investments in new constructions in 1898–99. Whereas the French Navy almost tripled the nominal spending on new ships through the 1890s, the Italian Navy reduced its annual spending in the same period.[26] The consequences could be seen in the order of battle of the Mediterranean Fleets of the two navies. While most of the Italian battleships of the Mediterranean Fleet were launched in the 1880s, all the French battleships (and armoured cruisers, cruisers

---

[25] SHM, 1 CC 211 Ac 2: Lectures by Capitaine de frégate Degouy: *Marines étrangères, 1ère Partie, Marine Anglaise, Allemande et Italienne* (Ecole des Hautes Etudes de la Marine, Paris, 1897–1898), pp. 381–382. A comparison, made by the General Staff in 1898, between the total order of battle of the three navies of the Triple Alliance with that of the French Navy, showed that France was almost equal to the Triple Alliance in battleships, but seriously behind in armoured cruisers. If armoured cruisers under construction were counted, however, the total displacement of the French armoured cruiser fleet would be no more than 20.000 tons less than that of the Triple Alliance. SHM, 190 GG2 36–37: Study by the General Staff of the French Navy, Titre III, 30 September 1898. To list the displacement of types of ships was a common way to compare order of battle, despite the fact that such comparisons have obvious limitations. The above-mentioned comparison conceals the fact that the French Navy had spent more on new constructions during most of the 1890s than the Triple Alliance. When the money spent on new constructions by the Triple Alliance eventually surpassed that of France in the budget year 1899–1900, it was due to the German naval build up and not to new Italian constructions. See SHM, 190 GG2 36–37: Etat-Major Général 1ère Section: *Budget totaux, dépenses pour les constructions neuves (crédits ordinaires et extraordinaires) et effectifs des Marines européennes*, 6 May 1899.

[26] SHM, 190 GG2 36–37: Etat-Major Général 1ère Section: *Budget totaux, dépenses pour les constructions neuves (crédits ordinaires et extraordinaires) et effectifs des Marines européennes*, 6 May 1899.

1st and 2nd class) were launched in the 1890s.[27] British spending on new ships, on the other hand, was more than twice that of France by the end of the decade.[28]

The operational plans worked out by the General Staff also suggest that the French Navy had gained a fairly good insight into the status of the Italian Navy, and the planning was characterised by a strong confidence in French superiority already from the early 1890s. French self-confidence was also reflected in the somewhat patronizing manner in which some French naval officers viewed the Italian Navy: "The weaknesses that our rather frequent contacts [with the Italian Navy] reveal, and that cause on our part, a kind of mocking, smiling contempt, are impossible not to notice."[29]

Serious doubts were also expressed concerning the French Navy's focus on the Italian Navy and the Mediterranean even in a context where the Triple Alliance was seen as the only probable constellation of enemies. From the budget year 1895–96 Germany was spending more than Italy on its navy, and German investments in new ships rose to approximately twice those of the Italian Navy from the budget year 1897–98.[30]

The gradual decline of the Italian Navy and the strengthening of the German Navy did not influence French strategy against the Triple Alliance, although, as we have seen, a few French admirals urged from the mid-1890s a shift in attention from Italy to Germany as the most redoubtable naval enemy among the powers constituting the Triple Alliance. The strategy that the French Navy had followed since the establishment of the Triple Alliance was characterised as "Offensive in the Mediterranean. Defensive offensive in the North", and as late

---

[27] SHM, 190 GG2 36–37: EMG 1ère section: *Emplacement des navires de guerre italiens dans la Méditerranée*, 1 March 1899; Annuaire de la Marine; Lecalve and Roche: *Liste des bâtiments de la flotte de guerre française*.

[28] SHM, 190 GG2 36–37: État-Major Général 1ère Section: *Budget totaux, dépenses pour les constructions neuves (crédits ordinaires et extraordinaires) et effectifs des Marines européennes*, 6 May 1899.

[29] SHM, 1 CC 211 Ac 2: Lectures by Capitaine de frégate Degouy 1897–1898: *Marines étrangères, 1ère Partie, Marine Anglaise, Allemande et Italienne* (École des Hautes Études de la Marine, Paris, 1897–1898), pp. 381–382. See also Commandant Z and H. Montéchant: *Les guerres navales de demain*, pp. 108–114.

[30] SHM, 190 GG2 36–37: État-Major Général 1ère Section: *Budget totaux, dépenses pour les constructions neuves (crédits ordinaires et extraordinaires) et effectifs des Marines européennes*, 6 May 1899.

as December 1898 it was confirmed by Lockroy as the one to be followed.[31]

The criticism directed at this strategy was, however, not only founded on the changes in relative strength levels between the French, Italian and the German Navy. Degouy, who was the sharpest critic of French naval strategy against the Triple Alliance, argued that the established strategy disconnected the maritime theatre of operations from the army's theatre of operations and thus from the most dangerous threat posed by the Triple Alliance: the German Army. He questioned what good French naval superiority in the Mediterranean would serve the overall military objectives in a war against the Triple Alliance. His answer was that it would have no effect on the German campaign in eastern France if the French Navy should succeed in luring the Italian fleet to a decisive battle. The total defeat of the Italian fleet would not divert a single German army unit away from their main objective, he claimed. If one wished to divert the German forces from Champagne or Lorraine, one would have to conduct offensive operations in the North and the Baltic Seas. Degouy's conclusion was a rather harsh verdict on French naval priorities: "the actual distribution of our forces is already, and will increasingly be, wrong."[32]

The political relations between France and Italy cannot explain the French Navy's focus on Italy as the most probable enemy in the late 1890s. The relations between the unified Italy and the Third Republic had indeed been strained for most of the period up to the mid-1890s. The Triple Alliance that Italy joined in 1882 was primarily directed against France. Article two in the treaty even named France as a potential aggressor.[33] A certain francophobia was apparent in Italian business circles and sections of the Italian press, especially in those close to Crispi, and a corresponding italophobia could be seen in France. The right and the extreme right especially displayed such attitudes.[34]

A *rapprochement* between the neighbours was, however, noticeable from 1896. After the fall of Crispi, the Italian Foreign Ministry attempted

---

[31] SHM, BB8-2424/5: Letter from the Minister of Marine to the members of the Superior Council: *Memorandum sur la politique maritime de la France*, 3 December 1898.

[32] SHM, 1 CC 211 Ac 2: Lectures by Capitaine de frégate Degouy: *Marines étrangères, I ère Partie, Marine Anglaise, Allemande et Italienne* (Ecole des Hautes Etudes de la Marine, Paris, 1897–1898), pp. 481–484.

[33] François Garelli: *Histoires des relations Franco-Italiennes* (Paris, 1999), p. 233.

[34] *Ibid.*, pp. 238–241.

to improve the relationship with France. Initiatives were taken to settle disagreements over West Africa and Tripolitania. From early 1897 the French and Italian governments entered into close cooperation concerning the dispute over the status of Crete, and the two nations signed agreements concerning Tunisia in September 1897. More importantly, the Italian government assured the French government during the Fashoda crisis that it would stay neutral in case of war. On 21 November, a few days after the Fashoda crisis was resolved, a trade agreement was signed between the two nations in Paris, and in April 1899, during the king's visit to Cagliari, French naval vessels made a port call to Sardinia to honour him.[35] Thus, although there were controversies between Italy and France, a significant improvement in their relations had occurred a couple of years before the Fashoda crisis. Relations between France and Italy were improving at the time when relations between France and Great Britain were close to war. Still, the French Navy chose to present Italy as a probable enemy, depriving itself of the possibility to prepare to fight Great Britain more effectively.

The French naval establishment's preoccupation with Italy in a situation where a conflict with the superior Royal Navy seemed possible can thus not be explained by an aggressive Italian foreign policy or an Italian naval build-up threatening France. There is also reason to question the strategic rationale for the French Navy's focus on the Italian Navy and the Mediterranean even if a war against the Triple Alliance had been the most probable scenario. The Italian Navy seemed to remain the traditionalists' favourite enemy. The most likely reason for this is probably that the Italian Navy was a perfect enemy for the supporters of battleships. There was a clear correlation between a preference for battleships and fleet warfare, a critical attitude towards commercial warfare, a strong conviction that the fleet should be concentrated in the Mediterranean with Toulon as base and a perception of Italy as a probable and formidable enemy.[36] A war against Italy would mean that the French Navy could benefit from the advantages of a superior navy. Her battle fleet could be used to achieve command of the seas over the Italian Navy. The Italian Navy was thus an enemy that legitimised

---

[35] *Ibid.*, pp. 241–244.
[36] There was an equally clear correspondence between an inclination for *guerre de course*, a critical view of fleet warfare, an opinion that the fleet should be stationed in Brest and a view that Great Britain was the enemy the French Navy should plan to fight.

heavy investments in a French battle fleet. The total of the three navies of the Triple Alliance was traditionally perceived to be inferior to the French, and a negative change in that balance could, from the battleship supporters' perspective, arouse public backing for an increase in battleship construction. The Royal Navy's dominance in battleships, on the other hand, had the opposite effect. The British lead was beyond the reach of France, and it was thus not effective in raising support for an increased construction of battleships.[37]

After Fashoda

It was not until Lanessan was appointed Minister of Marine, in June 1899, when a more coherent French naval strategy began to take form. Shortly after he entered office, Lanessan finished a confidential report on the status of the French Navy. It consisted of a critical and thorough analysis of the Navy's priorities, or rather lack of priorities over the preceding years. Critical reports on a predecessor's priorities were not unusual in French naval politics. What was new was that Lanessan outlined a plan for the systematic modernisation of the French Navy that was accepted by the Parliament.

Lanessan's Analysis

Lanessan's criticism was twofold. First, it was a criticism of what he saw as the French Navy's single-minded focus on the Triple Alliance and especially the Italian Navy ever since the Alliance was established. Secondly, he presented an insightful analysis of an inflexible naval organisation that continued to do what it always had done, and that was unable to decide on priorities.

Lanessan saw the French naval establishment's ignorance of the threat posed by Great Britain and British sea power as a demonstration both of a lack of understanding of the historical relationship between the two countries and an inability to analyse contemporary international politics. He underlined that historically Great Britain had been the maritime nation that had been most hostile to France. Lanessan compared the

---

[37] See i.e. SHM, 1 CC 195 aa 6: Lectures by Capitaine de frégate Houette: *Marine Française. Stratégie, Tactique. 1ère Partie. Stratégie Marine Française* (Ecole des Hautes Etudes de la Marine, Paris, 1897–1898), p. 93.

preceding years with the period in the mid-eighteenth century when there was a political *rapprochement* between France and Great Britain. At the time, he argued, French naval forces:

> were allowed to collapse, forgetting that the friendship between peoples will not be solid and enduring if it is not cemented by a reciprocal respect for each others' strength, especially when these people are, like France and Great Britain, in a state of economic and colonial rivalry at almost every spot of the world.[38]

Lanessan warned those who might have been interested in a *rapprochement* with Great Britain that it would also be in their interest to see a considerable build up of French naval forces, "because of all nations, England is, unquestionably, the one that most rigorously follows "a policy of interest" and that has respect and sympathy for the strong."[39]

It further seemed that the naval planners had ignored the colonial rivalry between France and Great Britain which had intensified from the early 1890s. Since the Triple Alliance was established, Lanessan claimed, it was "almost an absolute rule that one should not concern oneself with England. One dismissed the very idea of war with this power, and consequently, one did not in any way think of organising our navy with the prospect of such a war."[40] In a report to the president of the republic, Lanessan claimed that the main reason for the deplorable situation of the French Navy was that it long ago had renounced any ambition to prepare for a potential conflict with Great Britain. One had instead concentrated on what happened to the Italian Navy, and the French fleet had been constructed to match the Italian.[41]

The obsessive focus on an inferior enemy was probably an important reason why the structural and organisational dysfunctions of the Navy could grow without raising much concern. The possibility of confrontation with a superior enemy forced the French Navy to tackle these problems, and it was Lanessan who had the necessary political courage to identify the dysfunctions and implement the required reforms.

Lanessan harshly criticised the naval construction programmes of the previous fifteen years. Naval construction had been characterised by a wish to have a large fleet in order to give the impression of strength,

---

[38] SHM, BB4-2437: Memorandum by Lanessan: *Note sur la situation et les besoins de notre marine*, November 1899, pp. 2–3.
[39] *Ibid.*, p. 4.
[40] *Ibid.*, p. 3.
[41] J.-L. de Lanessan: *Histoire de l'entente cordiale franco-anglaise* (Paris, 1916), p. 203.

and numbers had been the sole overall rationale behind the construction of war ships. No coherent strategy had provided guidance for the construction. Lanessan identified a number of unfortunate consequences that followed from the aimless production of a large number of units, and he came up with several explanations as to why the French Navy had ended up in such a situation.[42]

The combination of economic restraints and the wish to have a large number of ships had forced the French Navy to stay below the ideal size for the type of warship under construction. This made it difficult to combine all the different qualities that the actual type of ship ideally should possess. The result was that all ships of the type had some major weaknesses in one or several of its functions. Some lacked speed, others endurance, sufficient protection, or adequate weaponry, and some were inferior in all these functions. The French Navy thus ended up with second or third-rate ships, and many of them had to be condemned after a few years, not because they were old, but because of their inferior operational performances.

Another characteristic of the fleet was the numerous classes of ships within the same category or type of ships. In addition there were a number of batches for each class of ships. To have several classes and batches of cruisers for example was not in itself extraordinary or unsound for a major navy, most had this. Lanessan's point was that this variety of classes did not necessarily have any technological, tactical or strategic rationale. It was rather, he claimed, a consequence of overzealous and ambitious engineers, all determined to create new classes: "Everyone wanted to leave his imprint on an original piece of work [...]."[43]

The variations among of types and classes of ships had serious consequences. Firstly it raised construction costs. Production of a series of identical ships would certainly be a lot cheaper than producing only originals. Secondly, variety called for a complex system for training the crews. It also made a smooth rotation of crews impossible. The crews would have to be retrained before they could operate another ship. One thing was the waste of time and money this represented, it also led to a number of accidents and breakdowns, according to Lanessan. He

---

[42] SHM, BB4-2437: Memorandum by Lanessan: *Note sur la situation et les besoins de notre marine*, November 1899, pp. 49–53.

[43] *Ibid.*, p. 50.

admitted that the establishment of the *Direction technique des constructions navales* had improved the situation somewhat. But still the variations represented a great problem for the French Navy.[44]

The reasons for the diversity of ships and the military irrelevance of some of them could also be traced to a shipbuilding industry that was unable, or unwilling, to adapt to the demands of a modern navy. There was political pressure to keep the workers at the naval yards employed. As soon as a ship was launched, the construction of a new one should commence. Lanessan's programme disclosed that this practice had unintended consequences with regard to the kinds of ships that could be built. Docks in many yards were too small for the warships that the naval programme prescribed. The problem was highlighted when it was proposed to build a series of dispatch cruisers, so-called *estafettes*. Lanessan's overall approach to the programme dictated that the French Navy should concentrate on a small number of types of ship with a high war fighting capability, or "combatants" as Lanessan labelled them. Dispatch cruisers did not fall into this category, and Lanessan was thus sceptical about the proposals to build them.

The majority of the admirals had initially shared Lanessan's opinion, and the urge to build the dispatch cruisers originated with the naval yards and the Director of Naval Constructions. He had explained to Lanessan that the construction of dispatch cruisers was necessary in order to keep the workers at the naval yard at Rochefort employed. The yard was soon to launch the ship they had under construction. If they were not given the task of building new dispatch cruisers, they would soon be out of work since the yard was not equipped to build large cruisers and battleships.[45] The Director of Naval Construction some days later found support among the majority of the admirals on the Superior Council. Although they shared Lanessan's view that the new programme should give priority to real fighting ships, they had great problems accepting they could not have it all. Seven admirals voted for the construction of five dispatch cruisers, while four voted against.[46]

There was also a tendency within the French Navy to accept a lower quality of naval ships stationed in the colonies than for those operating out of French ports. Vessels designated for imperial constabulary duties

---

[44] *Ibid.*, pp. 50–51.
[45] *Ibid.*, p. 52.
[46] SHM, BB8-2424/5: Conseil Supérieur de la Marine: *Séance du 29 novembre 1899*.

were naturally different from warships designed to fight a European naval power. It was the idea that protected cruisers of 2nd or 3rd class would suffice to protect the colonies that Lanessan found unacceptable. In a war against Great Britain, these ships would have to fight real warships, and the British ships stationed overseas were superior to the French. The construction of a great number of second-rate warships, under the pretext that they should serve in the colonies, was a waste of money, Lanessan argued. He claimed that their first concern if war broke out would be to seek a safe haven in a French overseas port. Lanessan concluded that the defence of the colonies would have been much better if the money spent on protected cruisers 2nd and 3rd class had been used to build real fighting ships.[47]

We have seen how Fournier's proposal to construct a homogeneous fleet mostly consisting of one class of cruisers was an extreme way to think of cost effective mass production for a navy. It represented an effort to match the Royal Navy by efficient production. The French Navy, however, had a production line with a variety of ships that made constructions unnecessarily expensive. To cope with the costs it had two options, either to reduce the number of ships under construction or to reduce the size and capabilities of the new constructions. The last option was the one with most unfortunate consequences, according to Lanessan. He demonstrated that the Superior Council had repeatedly reduced the requirements for new ships in the course of the planning process in order to reduce expenses. Each ship or class of ships thus ended up, not only as inferior to the corresponding type of France's naval rivals, but also inferior to the requirements that the Superior Council had originally decided. Lanessan insisted that any naval ship launched should have at least the same quality and capabilities as the best units of the same type of any foreign navy.

The Reform

Lanessan left no doubt that the French Navy should plan and organise to fight Great Britain. He reminded the Superior Council that the Fashoda crisis had been a revelation and that:

---

[47] SHM, BB4-2437: Memorandum by Lanessan: *Note sur la situation et les besoins de notre marine*, November 1899, p. 53.

> whatever political contingencies that may arise, the need to organise our fleet in view of a possible conflict with England appears inescapable to any reflective mind [...] And this navy should be organised in such a way that Great Britain can no longer impose her will, neither in the political nor in the economic field.[48]

Lanessan's insistence on organising the French Navy for a possible conflict with Great Britain was, however, not solely based on threat assessments. He pushed the argument one step further. He insisted that by using the most advanced and powerful navy of the world as a standard against which to measure itself, the French Navy would have nothing to fear from the navies of the Triple Alliance.

In addition to an insistence on the quality of every single naval unit, Lanessan maintained, as the discussion regarding the dispatch cruisers illustrated, that the French Navy should concentrate on what he regarded as the core elements of a first-rank navy. There were in his view four types of ships that constituted the core elements: battleships, armoured cruisers, destroyers and torpedo boats.[49] The French Navy should limit itself to construct these four types, and all of the new constructions should be the best of their kind:

> If we build battleships, they shall have nothing to fear from the strongest battleships of other navies. When it comes to armoured cruisers, they must be at least as fast, as well protected, as well armed and given an operational radius as good as any foreign armoured cruiser of the same type. Every one of our destroyers should have, if possible, better seagoing capabilities, be at least faster than all the destroyers of our rivals, and the same should be true for every one of our high-seas torpedo boats.[50]

Lanessan was well aware that France could not afford, or at least would not give priority to building the same number of these ships as Britain could. Still, it was only by building units of equal or better quality than those of the Royal Navy that "we will give France a fleet, that under given circumstances, will be able to fight honourably with that of England, and victoriously with that of the German Triple Alliance."[51]

---

[48] *Ibid.*, pp. 4–5.

[49] Lanessan did not mention submarines, but the Programme of 1900 had a planned order of battle of 38 submarines. This implied the construction of 26 submarines in the period 1900–1906. Although submarines were being introduced in increasing numbers into different navies, they were still not considered reliable and were hence not regarded as core elements of a navy.

[50] SHM, BB4-2437: Memorandum by Lanessan: *Note sur la situation et les besoins de notre marine*, November 1899, pp. 71–72.

[51] *Ibid.*, p. 72.

However, Lanessan was not content with an honourable defeat by Great Britain. To avoid a predictable defeat against a numerically superior enemy, which the *jeune école* since the time of Aube had claimed would be the outcome if the French Navy chose to stick to the traditional composition of the fleet, Lanessan proposed to organise the French fleet in order to force the Royal Navy to disperse its units. That would, he argued, give units of the French Navy liberty of action. The emphasis on dispersing the elements of the battle fleet and cruisers for individual raids made naval bases an important part of naval thought.

The idea that it would be possible to force the Royal Navy to spread its units was based on a widespread perception in the French Navy of how the Royal Navy would choose to fight. Britain would try to establish a kind of advanced maritime frontier in French waters, and try to dominate both the Channel and the Mediterranean. Confident in the superiority of the Royal Navy, the British would send the majority of their naval ships to blockade ports and most probably attack those military ports that had weak defence installations. The numbers and locations of French naval bases and ports would hence decide the complexity of the Royal Navy's mission.

One of the important measures taken by Lanessan was to establish two major fleets, one in the Mediterranean and one in the Channel. At first glance this seemed nothing new. A squadron under the command of a vice admiral was in place both in Toulon and Brest. The squadron in Brest that was established in 1892 was, however, a battleship squadron only in name and not in fact up to 1899, when the number of battleships was increased from one to six.[52]

Brest was not only close to Great Britain; it was also France's best port from the perspective of protection against bombardment from the open sea. Further, it had, as Fournier had emphasised, three separate channels that made enemy surveillance of the port difficult. Brest was thus an ideal port from which the French Navy could initiate offensive operations against single units or small groups of British warships. Equally important was the assumption that the geography of Brest facilitated the launching of raids against British commerce and the return of the cruisers.[53]

---

[52] Annuaire de la Marine.
[53] SHM, BB8-2424/5: Conseil Supérieur de la Marine: *Séances du 11 Janvier 1899*, p. 10.

The port of Toulon could not provide sufficient protection against bombardment or even against a determined attack by torpedo boats or cruisers. There was also only one channel out, and it would thus be difficult to leave port without having to face a superior British fleet waiting outside. The Mediterranean Fleet could hence be forced to leave Toulon before hostilities broke out in order to avoid a battle that could be disastrous for the French Navy. To compensate for the weaknesses of Toulon, Lanessan would speed up the works at Bizerte in Tunisia, and, in 1900, he managed to convince the Parliament to grant money for a complete arsenal.[54] He saw Bizerte as the key to future operations in the Mediterranean, and compared the role of Bizerte in the Mediterranean to that of Brest in the Channel. Bizerte offered a good strategic position in relation to Malta, Sicily, Sardinia and the route to Egypt. A naval stronghold in Bizerte also opened up the possibility of benefiting from the strong position of the French army in the region. In a joint navy and army operation France could threaten Malta in a war against Great Britain, and Sicily and Sardinia if the enemy were the Triple Alliance.

With Bizerte, Toulon and Brest as the major bases, the French Navy could threaten the British Isles, British colonies, their naval bases and important trade routes. Neither of these bases could thus be ignored, and given the geographical distance between them, it would force the Royal Navy to disperse its units. An effective use of minor bases, offensive torpedo boat bases and protected anchorages would further aid in dispersing the Royal Navy. The bases in Lorient and Rochefort on the Atlantic were safe from bombardment. Lanessan would improve the access to these two ports and upgrade the yards there so they could be a real alternative to Toulon and Cherbourg if they were blockaded.[55]

To complete the effort to force Britain to divide her fleets and to enhance the strength of the main French fleets, torpedo boats were scattered in small bases along the coast. The torpedo boats, and also destroyers and even submarines as they became operational, would help to push the British battleship formations further out to sea by

---

[54] SHM, BB4-2437: Memorandum by Lanessan: *Note sur la situation et les besoins de notre marine*, November 1899, pp. 76–77; Ropp: *The Development of a Modern Navy*, pp. 337–338.

[55] SHM, BB4-2437: Memorandum by Lanessan: *Note sur la situation et les besoins de notre marine*, November 1899, pp. 72–77. In the north, the works at Brest, Rochefort and Cherbourg were completed under the law. Ropp: *The Development of a Modern Navy*, p. 336.

night attacks.[56] This offensive use of small, fast boats, or invisible craft in the case of submarines, against battle fleets was the realisation of ideas advocated by the *jeune école*. These boats could be guided by a complex system of bases and havens, which could in turn be guided by the telegraph and semaphores in a coordinated war of concentration, dispersion and reconcentration.

What was new, however, was the proposed use of the combination of groups of torpedo boats scattered at bases along the coast and improved communications technology in order to support a squadron moving from base to base. Ropp has described how a squadron would be able to pick up offensive torpedo boat flotillas, already organised but not able to go far to sea:

> A fleet with a dozen destroyers would find eight additional torpedo boats at Ajaccio, ready to aid the fleet in any operations in the Corsican region, with whose waters they were thoroughly familiar. The Ajaccio boats did not have sufficient range to accompany the fleet to Bizerte, but the fleet would pick up another set of sixteen boats permanently stationed there, and so on.[57]

The new organisation provided five offensive torpedo boat groups outside the regular naval ports. The torpedo boats would also have a function in attacking convoys in the Mediterranean. The bases in Ajaccio, Bizerte, and Oran (in Algeria) were well suited to intercept convoys. The torpedo boat group in Dunkirk was to block the Channel against either an English or a German force. The Navy also created a new base at Lézardrieux, at the northern tip of Brittany. Its task was to attack Channel convoys or the anchorages at Falmouth and the Isles of Scilly.[58]

The Lanessan programme established an integrated system of major and minor havens for cruisers and light craft of all kinds in France and North Africa. France's coastal defences no longer consisted of a few major bases. This defensive system was a prerequisite for the offensive system tailored for use against Great Britain that Lanessan proposed and that the Superior Council agreed to. The offensive system was a combination of fleet warfare and commerce warfare. The anticipated dispersion of the Royal Navy's units in order to control the different

---

[56] SHM, BB4-2437: Memorandum by Lanessan: *Note sur la situation et les besoins de notre marine*, November 1899, p. 74.
[57] Ropp: *The Development of a Modern Navy*, p. 342.
[58] *Ibid.*, p. 342.

naval bases, combined with harassing operations from smaller units, would enhance the chances for battleships and cruisers to leave port and to return safely. Fleet warfare could thus be conducted in situations where French forces found themselves in a situation of local superiority, something the French planners reckoned would occur as long as the Royal Navy had to spread its resources in an effort to control both the Channel and the Mediterranean.

Commerce warfare, the other cornerstone in the new strategy, led Lanessan and the Superior Council to conclude that priority should be given to the Channel, not only regarding cruisers but also battleships. Brest should be France's major naval base. The discussion as to whether the main naval force should be in Toulon or Brest had been going on ever since the crisis with Britain had begun. The admirals' new approach since the heated discussion in the Superior Council in January 1899 was probably due to the change of naval tactics that was prescribed. There was agreement that commerce warfare would be important in order to confront Great Britain. But unlike the warfare preached by the *jeune école* using independently operating torpedo boats or cruisers to attack British commerce, the new tactics prescribed that the battleships and armoured cruisers should support cruisers, including lightly armed auxiliary cruisers, in conducting trade warfare. This tactic presupposed the stationing of an effective battle fleet in Brest. Lanessan thus proposed to form two battleships squadrons at Brest.[59] The battleships and armoured cruisers at Brest would be fast enough to operate in support of the cruisers. The fleet in Brest should consist of two squadrons of battleships capable of making 18 knots, three cruiser divisions of which one should make 23 knots, the second 21 knots and the third 18–19 knots. The armoured cruisers that were under construction were to join the fleet in Brest, and Lanessan proposed an extensive construction programme of destroyers and torpedo boats to complete the naval force in the Channel.

The mission of the Mediterranean Fleet would primarily be to force the Royal Navy to keep a substantial force in the Mediterranean and thus reduce the potential British dominance of the Channel. The Mediterranean Fleet should play a secondary role to that of the Northern Fleet, and would thus also be second in strength. While the planned

---

[59] SHM, BB4-2437: Memorandum by Lanessan: *Note sur la situation et les besoins de notre marine*, November 1899, pp. 81–83.

new battleships should be part of the battleships squadrons in Brest, the older ones should be transferred to the Mediterranean.[60]

In order to realise these plans Lanessan asked Parliament to increase the fleet to a strength of 28 battleships, 24 armoured cruisers, 52 destroyers, 263 torpedo boats, and 38 submarines. To do this, France would have to build 6 battleships, 5 armoured cruisers, 28 destroyers, 112 torpedo boats, and 26 submarines over the next eight years. The Parliament not only accepted the programme, but also reduced the time limit to seven years, added 50 million francs for submarines and torpedo boats (on an amendment by the later allegedly *jeune école* Minister of Marine, Pelletan) and relaxed the usual accounting rules to permit unspent sums to be carried over to later years. As Ropp has noted, the approval of the Fleet Law by the Parliament was the first indication of a new unity in French naval policy.[61]

The strategy proposed by Lanessan and accepted by the Superior Council was a combination of the naval theories that had competed and caused disarray in the French Navy over the previous 20–25 years. The divisions between the traditionalists and the *jeune école* were less sharp. There was a general understanding that the French Navy could not, in a conflict with Great Britain, go in for either industrial warfare or fleet warfare. Industrial warfare should rather be complementary to fleet warfare, the two ways of fighting a war would support each other. Commerce warfare remained a key element in the new French naval strategy. There existed, however, within the French Navy two different motivations or arguments as to why commerce warfare would still be important in a war against Great Britain. On the one hand there was the *jeune école* argument that trade warfare in itself could have a decisive political impact. On the other hand, the traditionalists saw commercial warfare as primarily a means to divert the resources of the Royal Navy:

> Commerce warfare as the only means of fighting [Great Britain] will not lead to any political result. The raiders will soon be destroyed and commerce warfare ended. But used as a supplement, it can contribute to forcing the enemy to disperse his forces in order to protect his trade.[62]

---

[60] *Ibid.*, p. 83.
[61] Ropp: *The Development of a Modern Navy*, p. 329.
[62] SHM, 1cc 196 Aa 13: Lectures by Capitaine de frégate Aubry: *Tactique et Stratégie. 1ère Partie* (Ecole Supérieure de Marine, Paris, 1902), pp. 437–438. See also SHM, 1 CC 196 Aa 11 bis: Lectures by Capitaine de frégate Rouyer: *Tactique et Stratégie, 2ème*

To force the Royal Navy to spread its units turned out to be the main focus of the new strategy. The scattering of major and minor naval bases along the French and North African coasts, and commercial warfare were both means to achieve such an objective. The alliance with Russia was soon also to be seen as a further effective means of tying down British forces. This represented a significant change of perspective when compared to French naval planning in the early 1890s and up to the Fashoda crisis. The Russian Navy, if it succeeded in entering the Mediterranean through the Dardanelles, could force the Royal Navy to dedicate additional forces to protect Egypt. Russian ships could also tie down the Royal Navy in the China Sea and carry out commerce raiding in the Indian Ocean.[63] The more positive view of the Russian naval potential was due to the ambitious plan of 1898 to strengthen the Russian Navy within a period of 5–6 years.[64]

Even so the Russian fleet was still viewed as playing a secondary role in a naval war against Great Britain. The somewhat sceptical French opinion of the capabilities of the Russian Navy did not correspond with the British analysis of the Russian Navy and the naval potential of the Franco-Russian alliance. The Russian plans announced in 1898 made the Admiralty request an immediate supplementary appropriation to pay for four battleships and four armoured cruisers and more would be required the following year. But as Nicholas Lambert has pointed out: "the Admiralty's approach to meeting the Franco-Russian challenge by maintaining a numerically superior fleet of battleships and cruisers was, by the turn of the century, running into the limits of the British state's willingness or ability to pay."[65]

It was not only the possibility of facing the second- and third-ranking naval powers that worried the Royal Navy. The French strategy with its emphasis on measures to force the Royal Navy to spread its resources and thus open up opportunities for raids by cruisers also caused concern. Senior naval officers had come to the conclusion that a close blockade of enemy ports would be dangerous when the enemy

---

Partie (Ecole Supérieure de Marine, Paris, 1901), pp. 471–474; and SHM, 1 CC 197 Aa 21: Lectures by Capitaine de vaisseau Rouyer: *Tactique et Stratégie, 3ᵉ Fascicule* (École Supérieure de Marine, Paris, 1905), p. 128.

[63] SHM, 1 CC 196 Aa 11 bis: Lectures by Capitaine de frégate Rouyer: *Tactique et Stratégie, 2ᵉᵐᵉ Partie* (École Supérieure de Marine, Paris, 1901), pp. 471–474.

[64] SHM, 190 GG2 36–37: EMG 1ᵉʳᵉ Section: *Situation de la flotte russe*, 25 November 1898, pp. 18–20.

[65] N.A. Lambert: *Sir John Fisher's Naval Revolution*, pp. 23–24.

had a large number of torpedo boats. The blockading ships would be forced to take station further out with the obvious result that without the provision of more warships the net surrounding the blockaded port would have to be wider. This would in turn make it easier for raiders to escape undetected, especially at night. A very explicit confirmation of the Admiralty's grasp of the French strategy, the measures already taken according to the strategy, and the threat that it could pose to Great Britain, was provided in a Cabinet memorandum circulated in January 1901:

> The French coast of the Channel is now studded with torpedo boat stations, and this development of what is known as the "Défense Mobile" has for its object to make it impossible for British battleships to blockade any of the French naval ports owing to the danger to which they would be exposed by torpedo-boats and submarines. The blockade of the French ports by a British fleet being thus rendered, in their view impracticable, the idea of the French strategists is that from these ports could issue by night their powerful fast new armoured cruisers, which would then proceed to place themselves upon our trade routes and do great damage to our mercantile marine. None of the large fleet of unarmoured cruisers which are allocated for the protection of our commerce on the various trade routes would be capable of meeting any of these new armoured cruisers, but as the preceding tables will have shown, we have already begun to build the ships that could do so, though not yet in sufficient numbers.[66]

The Admiralty's problem was the approaching financial limitations to naval efficacy. The cost of building armoured cruisers in sufficient numbers to protect British trade and at the same time preserve naval supremacy through a large battleship fleet strained the British state finances.[67]

The theoretical heritage of Aube and the *jeune école*'s predecessor, Richild Grivel, was obvious in many parts of the new French strategy. Aube's arguments for a concentration on commercial warfare to fight Great Britain found little support. The breakthrough for his ideas was somewhat paradoxically within fleet warfare. In the war of fleet against fleet, the new strategy involved Aube's principle of dispersing the French naval forces among numerous bases and suddenly concentrating them at the right moment to attain at least numerical equality. The influence

---

[66] Quoted in *ibid.*, pp. 28–29.
[67] *Ibid.*, p. 29.

of Grivel was apparent in the basic postulate that the French fleet should contain elements of both fleet warfare and commercial warfare, and that the choice of the kind of operations would depend upon the enemy to be met. With such a composition the Navy could stick to fleet warfare against an inferior enemy and a combination of fleet warfare and commercial warfare against a superior enemy.

SUMMARY

The race for colonies in the 1890s led to a dramatic confrontation between France and Great Britain. Despite the fact that a tense situation between the two countries, due to colonial rivalry in Africa, had evolved over the preceding couple of years, the Fashoda crisis found the French Navy totally unprepared for a conflict with Great Britain. French naval war planning had focused on the Triple Alliance. The Fashoda crisis prompted a meeting in the Superior Council where the Minister of Marine, Lockroy, and the admirals displayed the same confusion that had characterised French naval planning over the preceding years. They could not agree on who the enemy would be or how the war should be fought. In a memorandum from the Minister of Marine to the members of the Superior Council setting the agenda for the meeting, he started with a discussion on how a war against the Triple Alliance should be fought before he sketched the principles on how Great Britain should be met. Lockroy argued that the French Navy should fight Great Britain according to the principles advocated by the *jeune école*. The meeting of the Superior Council, however, developed into the usual confrontation between those promoting *jeune école* ideas on the one side and the traditionalists on the other. The majority ended up recommending a status quo with the battle fleet stationed in the Mediterranean while a limited number of cruisers should make occasional raids against British commerce. The argument for this solution was that the Triple Alliance still could pose a threat to France.

This almost single-minded focus on the Italian Navy, even when France was in the midst of a serious confrontation with Great Britain, cannot be explained by the actual development of the force ratio between the Italian Navy and the French Navy or by deteriorating political relations between the countries. The French Navy was increasingly superior to the Italian Navy throughout the 1890s, and the political relations between the two countries had improved over the years immediately preceding the Fashoda crisis. Italy's role as a kind of favourite enemy for the traditionalists can probably be explained by the fact that an inferior navy would be an argument in favour of a battleship fleet and for maintaining the status quo in the organisation and deployment of the French Navy.

The Fashoda crisis did eventually pull French naval leaders out of their complacent self-image as leaders of a first-rank naval power. It was Lanessan who had the courage and determination to seek a combination of the theories of the *jeune école* and the traditionalists and form a strategy of the weak that could achieve a certain consensus within the top ranks of the Navy and gain support in the Parliament.

Ropp has described the French naval programme of 1900 as almost equally important to the other big naval programme of 1900, the German naval law (Tirpitz' second), not in the history of international relations, but in the history of naval policy.[68] The fact that the *jeune école* and the traditionalists, both among politicians and naval officers, after decades of controversies agreed on a coherent strategy, base structure and force composition was very much due to the impact of the Fashoda crisis. The change of attitude was most significant among the traditionalists. The *jeune école* had claimed all the way that France should plan for a possible conflict with Great Britain. The traditionalists' view had been that the French Navy would have to take a defensive posture and even seek refuge in port in order to avoid a defeat if war should break out with Great Britain. The public debate during and after the Fashoda crisis had, however, convinced them that a purely defensive approach would be unacceptable to public opinion. Most top officers were convinced that the battle fleet would sooner or later be forced by public opinion to leave the protected harbours and take up the fight.[69] The new strategy and the Programme of 1900 could give the French Navy hope for more than an honourable defeat.

---

[68] Ropp: *The Development of a Modern Navy*, p. 328.

[69] Lanessan had asked all the admirals to give their opinion in writing on how the French Navy should best organise itself and act so that France could avoid another humiliating retreat when confronted with the might of British forces. See SHM, BB4-2437: Memorandum by Lanessan: *Note sur la situation et les besoins de notre marine*, November 1899, pp. 78–86.

CHAPTER FIVE

THE REVITALISATION OF THE *JEUNE ÉCOLE*

There were two distinct developments in the post-Lanessan period that influenced the *jeune école* in a contradictory way: The development of the submarine and the signing of the Entente Cordiale. The *jeune école* had ever since Aube's period as Minister of Marine been a driving force behind the development of the submarine. Progress in submarine construction had been so promising that the *jeune école* in the first years of the twentieth century started to argue for a strategy in which the submarine would represent the offensive capacity of the French Navy. The submarine was seen as perfect for operations against British sea lines of communication. The Fashoda crisis in 1898 and French sympathies for the Boer cause during the Boer war (1899–1902) nurtured the anti-British sentiments that were a precondition for the *jeune école* theory. A few years later, France and Great Britain signed the Entente Cordiale and a closer alliance between the two nations developed. The conflict scenario that was a prerequisite for the *jeune école*'s strategic solutions was thus gradually removed.

CHANGING ALLIANCES AMONG THE EUROPEAN POWERS

The Fashoda crisis in 1898 represented a low point in French-British relations. The Boer War, when Great Britain waged war against the Boer republics of the Transvaal and the Orange Free State in South Africa in 1899–1902, prolonged the strained relations between France and Great Britain.

The British campaign against the Transvaal and the Orange Free State was initially unsuccessful. Troop reinforcements had to be sent out, which stripped Great Britain of its organized military forces. To protect the long sea lines of communication between Great Britain and South Africa was a very demanding task for the Royal Navy. A large portion of the cruiser fleet was diverted to patrol these vital sea lines of communication. The military resources Britain had to send to South Africa in order to secure victory in the Boer War thus made it vulnerable to foreign attack at home. The perception of being left more or less undefended contributed to an invasion scare among the British public.[1] It was feared that France, with her ally Russia, would take advantage of Great Britain's exposed situation, but a possible Franco-Russo-German coalition was also considered a possible threat. A German contribution to such a coalition was ruled out in March 1900 when Emperor William II rejected a Russian proposal for a three-power intervention to save the Boers.[2]

The British closely followed French and Russian naval manoeuvres and movements. When the French Mediterranean Fleet visited the Levant in October 1899, a visit that had been planned long before the outbreak of the Boer war, suspicions were raised as to whether the French fleet would join the Russian Black Sea fleet. The British Channel Fleet was subsequently deployed to Gibraltar. The British move served as a signal to the French Navy that the Royal Navy was able to protect Great Britain even though Britain was engaged in a war more than five thousand miles away.

The planned junction of the French Mediterranean Fleet and the Northern Fleet prior to the manoeuvres in the Channel and the Bay of Biscay during the summer exercise in 1900 raised doubts about the French intentions. The annual army manoeuvres were to be held in the northern districts of France, well within easy reach of the French western coast. The manoeuvres were to involve four or five army corps. Marder refers to the *St. James's Gazette*, which was the first to write about the possible linkage between the naval and army manoeuvres. The *St. James's Gazette* suggested that it would be very easy, once the army units were in the field to entrain them and embark them for the invasion of England.[3] Articles in the French press had further fuelled the invasion scare by describing how troops could be transported across the Channel.[4]

The possibility of invading Great Britain, or of preparing to threaten invasion, was discussed from time to time in the top echelons of the French Navy. The French Army and Navy held modest combined manoeuvres in the Mediterranean in 1898 and a course in combined operations was instituted at the French services' respective staff colleges

---

[1] Marder: *The Anatomy of British Sea Power*, pp. 372–373.
[2] *Ibid.*, p. 375.
[3] *Ibid.*, p. 377.
[4] *Ibid.*, pp. 375–376; Ropp: *The Development of a Modern Navy*, p. 345.

the same year.⁵ Captain Davin, who taught tactics and strategy at the staff college when the invasion scare was at its peak, maintained to his students that "England has two weak points: Her trade [and] her territory."⁶ Davin was a devoted believer in the offensive, and claimed that the offensive was the essence of the French national character. He did not believe that commerce warfare would be sufficient to bring Great Britain to its knees. One should therefore hit at the heart of Great Britain and attack London, Davin told his students. He argued that history had shown that Great Britain always had feared seaborne attacks against its territory. Davin referred to Mahan's writings and stated that the isolation of the British Isles had made the British especially prone to an invasion scare. Davin concluded that Great Britain had an open coast of one hundred nautical miles that would make it possible to implement an invasion.⁷

There is, however, no clear indication that Davin's lectures reflected plans for France to take advantage of Great Britain's temporary weakness in 1899 and 1900. In the same series of lectures on strategy Davin proposed that combined operations in northern Prussia should be conducted in case of war against Germany.⁸

Preparations for an invasion of Great Britain were discussed in the Superior Council in the aftermath of the Fashoda crisis, and in later lectures at the staff college. The minutes from these discussions and the lectures do not reveal any plans to invade Great Britain in order to occupy larger parts of the country. In fact, they leave the impression that an invasion of Great Britain was not considered an option at all in the late 1890s and during the first years of the new century. What the discussions reflected was rather that preparations for an invasion should be used as a deception with the aim of tying down Royal Navy resources. Fournier was a spokesman for this approach in the discussions in the Superior Council in the aftermath of the Fashoda crisis, at a time when there still was a fear among the naval leadership that war between Great Britain and France could break out any moment. Instead of arguing for discreet preparations for a landing that would have reduced the risk of massive military opposition to the operation,

---

⁵ Ropp: *The Development of a Modern Navy*, p. 345.
⁶ SHM, 1 CC Aa 10: Lectures by Capitaine de vaisseau Davin: *Tactique et stratégie* (Ecole Supérieure de Marine, Paris, 1900), p. 566.
⁷ *Ibid.*, pp. 566–567.
⁸ *Ibid.*, p. 581.

he argued that the preparations should be overt and convincing with the aim of arousing fear in Great Britain that an actual landing would take place. This would force both the Royal Navy and the British Army to take precautionary measures that would tie down their forces.

Admiral Parrayon was the only member of the Superior Council who categorically rejected Fournier's proposal stating that "a landing on the coasts of England is utopian."[9] Parrayon argued that the French Navy would not have enough ships to carry out such an operation. Admiral Regnault de Prémesnil agreed that an actual landing would be very difficult to carry out, but he supported that "ostensible preparations for a landing could produce some results."[10] The other admirals who commented on Fournier's proposal to create a diversion were more unconditional in their support of Fournier's idea. Admiral de Maigret argued that France by pretending that a landing was planned "would obtain, without much effort, the most considerable effects."[11] Both Admiral Sallandrouze de Lamornaix, who was Commander-in-Chief of the Northern Fleet, and Admiral Barréra, who was *préfet maritime* in Brest, supported the idea that preparations should be made in the north to make the British "believe in the threat of an invasion."[12] Admiral Cavelier de Cuverville, Chief of the General Staff, added to the general argument that concentrations of troops on the north-western coast of France would tie down British naval and army forces, and that it would also have a considerable impact on public opinion in Great Britain. The message to the British public would be that a war with France could cost dearly.[13]

That preparations for a landing on the British coast could be no more than part of a plan of deception was also made clear in the War Minister's response to the Minister of Marine's request for army cooperation. The Minister of War answered that the army would be more than glad to assist the Navy if it was only a question of concentrating troops on the Channel coast, but he was very reluctant to entertain any idea of conducting an actual landing on the British coast. One

---

[9] SHM, BB8-2424/5: Conseil Supérieur de la Marine: *Séances du 11 Janvier 1899*, pp. 33–34.
[10] *Ibid.*, p. 35.
[11] *Ibid.*, p. 19.
[12] Quotation from Admiral Barréra, SHM, BB8-2424/5: Conseil Supérieur de la Marine. *Séances du 11 Janvier 1899*, p. 26. Admiral Sallandrouze de Lamornaix's arguments is found in the same document on p. 24.
[13] *Ibid.*, p. 53.

thing was the difficulties concerning the cross-Channel transfer of the troops and the landing, but the real problems started when the troops were to be resupplied on an almost daily basis, the Minister of War warned.[14]

Discussions on deceptive invasion schemes that were intended to tie down Royal Navy forces were rather frequent in the French Navy. Both the *jeune école* and the traditionalists were well aware that an inferior navy would have to develop ways of dispersing the units of the superior navy in order to create conditions for local superiority. As late as 1906, two years after the Entente Cordiale was concluded, Captain Darrieus, in one of his lectures at the staff college, argued strongly in favour of the effectiveness of deceptive landing preparations as a means of creating local superiority against Royal Navy. He also tried to specify what such an operation would involve in men and ships in order to convince the British authorities and the public that an invasion was probable. An Army of 150.000 men would have to be assembled at Dunkirk. He estimated that each steamship that was to carry soldiers on the five-hour crossing would carry from 1500–2000 men, an operation that would require a total of 75 to 100 ships. Such a force would give the impression that a landing operation actually would take place, and it would "inevitably arouse enough worries in England and force the Admiralty to strip the other spots in order to keep a sufficiently imposing fleet in the Channel and the Straits of Dover to safeguard the coasts of Great Britain."[15]

Most of the British invasion scares between 1870 and 1914 had no basis in actual preparations by continental states.[16] John Gooch argues that it was General Burgoyne in 1846 who came up with an analysis that set precedence for the dynamics of later invasion scares. Burgoyne drew up a scenario, against the backdrop of French and British conflicts of interest in areas of the globe ranging from North Africa to Tahiti, in which Britain was assumed to fight under very unfavourable terms. With no explanation he postulated that the French Navy could achieve naval superiority in the Channel for long enough to transfer up to 150.000 troops. With Britain's 10.000 troops the result was given. The invasion scare mounted when the Duke of Wellington, in an article in

---

[14] *Ibid.*, pp. 66–67.
[15] SHM, 1 CC 198 Aa 26: Lectures by Capitaine de vaisseau Darrieus: *Stratégie et Tactique. 3ᵉ Fascicule. L'utilisation* (École Supérieure de Marine, Paris, 1906), p. 37.
[16] Ropp: *The Development of a Modern Navy*, p. 344.

the *Morning Chronicle* in January 1848, supported Burgoyne and depicted a scenario stimulating the public's imagination when he wrote that: "excepting immediately under the fire of Dover Castle, there is not a spot on the coast on which infantry might not be thrown on shore at any time of tide, with any wind and in any weather."[17] Gooch describes how this first invasion panic since the days of Napoleon Bonaparte set the pattern which successors would follow:

> The alarm had been sounded by a great public figure of the day; it had rested upon little if any searching considerations of the implications of the technological developments which underpinned it; and there was missing from it any attempt to view the issue from the enemy's perspective and establish whether he would or even could invade.[18]

Newspapers very often indulged in scaremongering, triggering and escalating the invasion scares. A.J.A. Morris gives a vivid and illustrating example of the dynamics of the 1900 invasion scare:

> In the appropriate month of April 1900, Maxse [editor of the *National Review*] affirmed as a certainty to his readers that the French General Staff *knew* that they could land 50,000 troops in England. What was more, the military attachés of a number of foreign nations were busily telling their governments that England was practically defenceless. Following the inexorable laws of invasion arithmetic, Maxse's 50,000 became in the *Daily Mail* 80,000 with 400 guns thrown in for good measure. Then *Public Opinion* unblushingly told its readers that it had been reliably informed by a French naval captain that the true figure was 90,000. Suddenly elderly gentlemen in the home counties became aware of a veritable plague of French military cyclists choking the country lanes while the suburbs of London groaned with hordes of highly suspicious aliens obviously waiting only to be summoned by an invader to commit countless acts of sabotage.[19]

High-ranking British naval or army officers usually contributed to the invasion scares that from time to time occurred in the British press. This seems not to be the case of the 1900 invasion scare. Neither the Admiralty nor the Government seemed to take very seriously the

---

[17] Quoted in John Gooch: *The Prospect of War. Studies in British Defence Policy 1847–1942* (London, 1981), p. 2.
[18] Quoted in *ibid.*, p. 3. Gooch gives a very good description of the invasion scares from 1848–1914 on pp. 1–15.
[19] A.J.A. Morris: *The Scaremongers. The Advocacy of War and Rearmament 1896–1914* (London, 1984), p. 101.

alarms raised of a surprise invasion.[20] Yet, the Government was not totally unaffected by the invasion scare, and even the Prime Minister, Lord Salisbury, who was no supporter of invasion scares, held a speech in May in which he praised the virtues of every Englishman making himself fit to meet any invader by joining a rifle club. Rifle shooting was a most popular hobby among the invasion polemicists.[21] Since no invasion occurred, the scare of a French invasion faded during the summer and autumn 1900. The very fact that invasion scares occurred from time to time, however, supports the arguments of those who favoured deceptive operations. British public opinion seemed likely to swallow the bait.

The invasion scare of 1900 also reflects the mistrust that existed between France and Great Britain by the turn of the century. Yet, a few years later France and Great Britain concluded the Entente Cordiale. A major precondition for the shift in British foreign policy towards a *rapprochement* with France was the traumatic experience of the Boer war. Britain had sent 390.000 soldiers to South Africa in order to defeat 80.000 Boers and had succeeded only after two-and-a-half years. It revealed British military weakness and underlined her diplomatic isolation. Both French and British observers and politicians concluded that the Boer war had made Great Britain wiser and reduced the belief in "Splendid Isolation".[22] The worsening Russo-Japanese situation and Great Britain's inability to come to an understanding with Russia, unrest in Morocco, the possibility of a Far Eastern war and an ambitious and self-assertive German foreign policy were additional factors contributing to a reorientation of British foreign policy.[23]

A very clear symbol of the more ambitious German foreign policy from the turn of the century was the build-up of its navy. This naval expansionism had its root cause, as Paul Kennedy has pointed out, in the rapid industrialization of Germany and its consequent interest in overseas markets, colonies and power politics.[24] The Tirpitz Plan was a clear manifestation of the shift of German foreign policy. Tirpitz strongly believed in the political importance of sea power in peacetime.

---

[20] Marder: *The Anatomy of British Sea Power*, pp. 378–380; Ropp: *The Development of a Modern Navy*, p. 347.

[21] Morris: *The Scaremongers*, p. 102.

[22] Andrew: *Théophile Delcassé*, p. 203.

[23] Zara S. Steiner and Keith Neilson: *Britain and the Origins of the First World War* (Houndmills, 2003), p. 31.

[24] Kennedy: *The Rise and Fall of British Naval Mastery*, p. 214.

His ideas led him to identify Great Britain as a new rival that had to be made to respect German naval strength. His ideas were formulated as early as 1895. Tirpitz was appointed State Secretary of the *Reichsmarineamt* in 1897, and already in his first meeting with the Kaiser he sketched his foreign policy analysis and his recommended ambitions for the German Navy:

> For Germany the most dangerous enemy at the present time is England. It is also the enemy against which we most urgently require a certain measure of naval force as a political power factor [...] our fleet must be so constructed that it can unfold its greatest military potential between Heligoland and the Thames [...] The military situation against England demands battleships in as great number as possible.[25]

Tirpitz's strategy was based on a battleship fleet that should not only be able to defend the German coast but also have the strength to threaten the maritime superiority of the most powerful existing fleet. The first Navy Law of 1898 envisaged a fleet of 19 battleships. The second Navy Law of 1900 doubled this to 38. The fleet would, according to the second Navy Law of 1900, also include 14 large armoured cruisers, 34 small cruisers and 96 destroyers.[26]

The German naval build-up and the rhetoric that accompanied it represented an overt challenge to Great Britain, but it took some time before British authorities started to show concern regarding the German naval bills. There was a worsening in the relationship between Great Britain and Germany in the years 1900–02. The German press was very critical of Britain's war in South Africa, and the British setbacks were applauded. An increasing awareness of the German naval build-up coupled with the deteriorating relations between the countries led to a growing suspicion in Great Britain regarding German aims. Kennedy claims that the years 1901–1902 represent a watershed in British attitudes towards Germany, and he argues that a conviction that there existed a German threat was not only present among right-wing journalists, but could also be found among influential officials in the Navy, the Army, and the Foreign Office. In 1902 the Admiralty informed the Cabinet that they were convinced that "the German Navy was being

---

[25] Paul Kennedy: *The Rise of the Anglo-German Antagonism 1860–1914* (London, 1980), p. 224.
[26] Hobson: *Imperialism at Sea*, p. 297; Kennedy; *The Rise and Fall of British Naval Mastery*, p. 214; Marder: *The Anatomy of British Sea Power*, p. 456.

built up from the point of view of a war with us [...]."[27] The Cabinet accepted in April 1902 a proposal from the Admiralty to buy the land necessary for a North Sea naval base. The size of the battlefleet to be stationed there was to "be practically determined by the power of the German Navy."[28] The army also started to reconsider its view on Germany. The War Office had in its planning hitherto been almost exclusively occupied with the Franco-Russian challenge outside Europe. The new awareness of a potential German threat was partly triggered by a considerable discussion in German newspapers on the feasibility of an invasion of Great Britain.[29]

Kennedy has pointed out that a logical answer to the German naval build-up, consistent with British naval thinking over the preceding years, would be to establish a *Three* Power Standard.[30] Such a solution would demand a substantial increase in the naval budget. The cost of maintaining a margin of superiority over the French and Russian navies and of keeping pace with technological changes would further increase demands on British finances. Naval expenditure was already spiralling. The enormous increase in the defence budget due the Boer War had severely strained British finances. The cost of supporting forces in a distant conflict led to an enormous increase in government spending. Instead of the usual surplus, budgets now showed massive deficits, a situation that consequently led to a dramatic rise in taxes. Aaron L. Friedberg has in his study on the relative decline of Great Britain in the period 1895–1905 pointed to the fact that the Boer War was a catalytic rather than a causal event in regard to Great Britain's economical difficulties. The British economic growth rate was persistently less than that of her leading challengers. Despite an increase in existing taxes and the introduction of new taxes, the limits of Britain's financial power had been reached and to some extent exceeded. Friedberg states that by 1904 there was a "widespread agreement within the Government that spending on armaments would have to be reduced in real terms, regardless of the defensive needs of the empire,"[31] and he writes that in the period 1900–1905 "decisions regarding alliances

---

[27] Quoted in Kennedy: *The Rise and Fall of British Naval Mastery* p. 215; see also Marder: *The Anatomy of British Sea Power*, p. 464.
[28] Quoted in Paul Kennedy: *The Rise of the Anglo-German Antagonism*, p. 252.
[29] *Ibid.*, p. 252.
[30] Kennedy: *The Rise and Fall of British Naval Mastery*, p. 215.
[31] Aaron L. Friedberg: *The Weary Titan. Britain and the Experience of Relative Decline, 1895–1905* (Princeton, New Jersey, 1988), p. 107.

and the organisation and deployment of both the army and navy were profoundly influenced by a desire to control and, if possible, to reduce government spending."[32] One alternative would be a *rapprochement* with France and Russia, a solution that members of the Foreign Office and the public were beginning to air.[33]

The animosity that was developing between Great Britain and Germany was not unambiguous, neither from a British nor from a French perspective. In 1901–1902 there was in France even a fear of a potential hostile coalition between Germany and Great Britain. At the same time there was also a realisation that France could not afford hostility with both the strongest naval power and the strongest military power in Europe. There were few influential persons in France who argued for a *rapprochement* between France and Britain before 1903, but by the beginning of 1903 there were more and more signs in the French press that sympathy was on the side of the British in the antagonistic relationship that was developing between Great Britain and Germany. Differences between Britain and Germany over a joint expedition to force a settlement of financial defaults on Venezuela through the use of naval pressure in the winter of 1902–03 worsened relations between the two countries. The German commander, who acted independently, opened fire on a Venezuelan fort thus provoking the United States and at the same time disquieting British authorities who were anxious to be on good terms with the United States.[34] The Venezuelan affair and the open antagonism towards Germany in the British press in the aftermath of the affair, contributed to the change of the French perception of Great Britain. *The Times* underlined this change in a report on 11 March from a foreign policy debate in the French Chamber:

> It is evident from the altered tone of French public utterances respecting England within the past couple of months that the moral of the Venezuelan affair, and of the attitude of the British nation towards Germany, has not been lost upon politicians of all shades of opinion in this country. It is a lesson, therefore, that has been doubly learned, and it is gratifying to find that it has not been lost even on Anglophobe exponents of French opinion, whom today we heard and hardly recognised. African, Asiatic,

---

[32] *Ibid.*, p. 90. For Great Britain's economic difficulties and the implications for the defence budget, see also Kennedy: *The Rise of the Anglo-German Antagonism*, p. 229; and Steiner and Neilson: *Britain and the Origins of the First World War*, p. 32.

[33] Kennedy: *The Rise and Fall of British Naval Mastery*, p. 215.

[34] Marder: *The Anatomy of British Sea Power*, pp. 465–466; Andrew: *Théophile Delcassé*, pp. 204–205.

and European questions can now be discussed here without animus towards England.[35]

The German ambassador to London noticed the same change of sentiments three months later: "The Anglo-French rapprochement is the product of a common aversion to Germany [...] Without the estrangement of England and Germany a mood of Anglophilia would have been impossible in France."[36] The shifting attitudes helped pave the way for settling colonial disputes between France and Great Britain. Both the processes towards solutions of the disputes and the solutions themselves reinforced the *rapprochement* between France and Great Britain.

The French foreign minister, Delcassé, considered that France's future role should be that of a Mediterranean power stretching from Algeria and Tunisia in the north to French Congo in the south. Full French control over Morocco fitted such a design. Initially, Delcassé had hoped for German support, along with that of Italy and Spain, in gaining recognition for French control over Morocco. As late as 1901 envoys were sent to Berlin in order to seek an arrangement, but no agreement was reached.[37] Delcassé had throughout his period in office feared that Germany would try to establish herself as a Mediterranean power. He was convinced by 1903 that Germany would try to accomplish her Mediterranean ambitions by gaining a foothold in Morocco rather than in the Adriatic as he previously had thought. German economic interests in Morocco were practically nil. But Morocco's geostrategic position fitted in with the Wilhelmine *Weltpolitik* and made it attractive to Germany.[38] By the spring of 1903 Delcassé had accepted the idea promoted by the *Comité de l'Afrique Française* and by the leader of the *Parti colonial*,[39] Eugène Etienne, of seeking an agreement with Great Britain based on bartering Egypt against Morocco.[40]

The basis of The Entente Cordiale was an agreement settling colonial differences between the two countries in three main areas. First, a treaty

---

[35] Quoted in Andrew: *Théophile Delcassé*, p. 205.
[36] Quoted in *ibid.*, p. 205.
[37] John F.V. Keiger: *France and the Origins of The First World War* (Houndmills, 1983), p. 18.
[38] Motte: *Une éducation géostratégique*, p. 371; Kennedy: *The rise of the Anglo-German antagonism*, pp. 223–250.
[39] Delcassé was appointed Foreign Minister in 1898 as the candidate of the *Parti colonial*.
[40] Andrew: *Théophile Delcassé*, pp. 51–52, 136–137; Keiger: *France and the Origins of The First World War*, p. 18; Zorgbibe: *Théophile Delcassé*, pp. 174–176.

was signed that resolved Anglo-French differences over Newfoundland and West and Central Africa. Secondly, there was a treaty that dealt with Siam and the New Hebrides. Thirdly, a treaty based on an exchange of interests in Egypt and Morocco was signed. France agreed not to obstruct British actions in Egypt, while Great Britain agreed to give France more or less a free hand in Morocco. Secret clauses provided for a future protectorate by France over Morocco and by Britain over Egypt. An important aspect from a naval strategic point of view was France's agreement both to accept a Spanish sphere of influence in Morocco and the non-fortification of most of Morocco's Mediterranean coast. Great Britain's concern for the safety of the Straits was thus taken care of.[41]

The Entente did not include any general policy agreement between Great Britain and France. It was restricted to solving the above-mentioned overseas differences between the two nations. Delcassé hoped that the agreement would be the beginning of a lasting shift in the coalitions of the European powers, but generally, French politicians did not at the time consider it a landmark in Anglo-French relations. It was above all viewed as an agreement giving France the possibility to control Morocco. In hindsight, however, one can see that the Entente Cordiale paved the way for closer links between the two nations.[42]

The Moroccan crisis in 1905–1906 triggered military conversations between France and Great Britain based on the Entente Cordiale. The talks started in late 1905 as unofficial military and naval talks. The staff conversations, originally intended to cover the immediate danger of military conflict between France and Germany in 1905–1906 over the Morocco dispute, turned official from early 1906 and became a permanent part of the entente.[43] The naval talks were in the first years restricted to the bureaucratic level, and they were neither frequent nor substantial.[44] Few politicians knew of the staff conversations. The lack of involvement of the governments both in France and Great Britain was reflected in Foreign Minister Grey's comment during the Agadir Crisis in 1911: "What they settled [the military talks] I never

---

[41] Andrew: *Théophile Delcassé*, pp. 212–213; Marder: *The Anatomy of British Sea Power*, pp. 473–474; Keiger: *France and the Origins of The First World War*, pp. 19–20.
[42] Andrew: *Théophile Delcassé*, p. 213; Zorgbibe: *Théophile Delcassé*, pp. 186–187.
[43] Samuel R. Williamson, Jr.: *The Politics of Grand Strategy. Britain and France Prepare for War, 1904–1914* (London—Atlantic Highlands, NJ, 1969, 1990), pp. 59–88.
[44] *Ibid.*, p. 320.

knew—the position being that the Government was quite free, but that the military people knew what to do, if the word was given."[45] The Agadir crises spurred detailed talks on military and naval preparations, and in late 1912 and early 1913 the French naval attaché shuttled constantly between London and Paris as the respective naval staffs worked out detailed plans for naval cooperation. Both navies planned for two options; either they would fight alone or in entente cooperation, and plans were made for a division of responsibility between the two navies in the Channel and the Mediterranean.[46]

Samuel R. Williamson has given a succinct summary of the consequences of the German naval armament and ambitious foreign policy on French-British naval cooperation:

> Yet the Channel and the Mediterranean arrangements suggest that neither admiralty, wanted, expected, or [sic] could afford to go it entirely alone against the Triple Alliance. Admiral von Tirpitz' naval program had prompted what no British or French diplomat would have even contemplated ten years before—the forging of a virtual Anglo-French alliance.[47]

THE SUBMARINE[48] AND THE *JEUNE ÉCOLE*

The *rapprochement* between France and Great Britain coincided in time with improvements in submarine construction, making it the preferred offensive weapon in the *jeune école*'s constant search for ways to neutralize the Royal Navy's superiority in capital ships. The idea of constructing a ship that could dive and sail submerged was of old date. The French Navy constructed its first experimental submarine, the *Plongeur*,

---

[45] Quoted in Christopher M. Andrew: "The Entente Cordiale from its Origins to 1914" in Neville Waits (ed.): *Troubled Neighbours* (London, 1971), p. 30.
[46] Williamson Jr.: *The Politics of Grand Strategy*, pp. 320–324.
[47] *Ibid.*, p. 324.
[48] No distinction is made between pure submarines and submersibles in this chapter. Both are referred to as submarines. The strategic and to a large extent the tactical implications of these two vessels were the same, and the submersibles were replaced by pure submarines as soon as technological progress allowed satisfactory speed and endurance for the submarines. The term submersible was introduced to broader use in the naval vocabulary in the late 19th century (admiral Bourgois had, however, already used the term in 1872 in his proposals to the *Conseil des Travaux*). It described a vessel able to descend below the surface during the attacking phase in order to protect itself by a layer of water. The conning tower, the funnel and the intake of air were above water while the rest of the boat was under water.

as early as 1863.[49] It was, however, not until the 1880s that efforts to construct submarines intensified, and it was France and Russia that invested energy in the construction of submarines. An increased focus on submarines from the 1880s must be seen in connection with the development of the self-propelled torpedo and torpedo boats. One of the weaknesses of the torpedo boat was the difficulties it met when trying to come within effective firing range in daytime, especially as surface vessels were armed with light rapid-firing guns and machine guns. The torpedo boat had to seek cover by operating during nighttime or in periods of low visibility due to rain or fog. The problem was that the torpedo boats were handicapped by the same low visibility that gave them their precarious protection. The difficulty was to see without being seen. In land warfare the units could benefit from the irregularities of the terrain and mask their tactical operations. Navies did not have the same possibilities in operations outside the littorals. The flatness of the scene of operations denied such possibilities. Yet if a ship could slip below the surface of the waves for some time, it would achieve an advantage that had no analogy on land.

Two months after his arrival in office in 1886, Aube opened an official competition for designs for a submarine. In the same year he signed an order to build a submarine from the plans of Gustav Zédé. These plans were essentially modifications of an original design worked out by the recently deceased Dupuy de Lôme.

Aube's decision led ultimately to the construction of France's first viable underwater craft, the *Gymnote*.[50] Launched in 1888, it was an experimental boat built as cheaply as possible. *Gymnote* displaced only 30 tons and had no military apparatus at all. While most submarines of the time, like the Holland no. 1 (1881) and the Nordenfelt series (1885–90) were steam-propelled even under water, the *Gymnote* was the first to use an electric storage battery. While it made seven knots when surfaced, the maximum speed submerged was a little over four knots. It could cruise for four hours submerged at slow speed, and the living

---

[49] In 1859 naval engineers were invited to propose designs for a submarine. Three projects were presented for the *Conseil des Travaux*. The design by Charles Brun was chosen and the submarine was given the name *Plongeur*. The first trials were conducted in 1863. Henri Le Masson: *Du Nautilus (1800) au Redoutable (Histoire critique du sous-marin dans la marine française)* (Paris, 1969), pp. 52–59.

[50] Aube also ordered the construction of the five meters long submarine *Goubet* with a crew of two persons.

conditions were considered to be good for the crew of five persons.[51] The trials of 1888 to 1890 were so promising that the Navy decided to build two real fighting submarines. Both the 267-ton *Gustave Zédé* and the 142-ton *Morse* were equipped with torpedo tubes. These two boats, however, revealed so many difficulties due to their increased size that they were initially viewed as comparative failures.[52]

While the two submarines were under construction the *Gymnote* was used to study their possible tactical employment. The studies were carried out by Lieutenant (later Vice Admiral) Darrieus, partly according to a test program developed by his predecessor, Baudry de Lacantinerie. The tests confirmed a capability both to follow a moving target and to force a blockade. A number of shortcomings were also revealed. The submarine had no conning tower, which deprived the commander of a good and safe position from where he could command the ship in surfaced position. The freeboard was not more than ten centimetres, which made a close passage of even a small steamer dangerous. There were also other major technical challenges concerning the engine, batteries, periscope, and gyroscope and considerable efforts had to be made to solve them. Ways to overcome these deficiencies were found, and eight years of methodical experiments with the *Gymnote*, without any serious accidents, helped pave the way for the acceptance of the submarine.

Gustave Zédé was laid up as early as 1893. Its batteries were more or less destroyed and it could only navigate in a surfaced position. It was estimated to take one year to put it back in operational status, but no decision was taken until Lockroy entered office. He decided shortly after entering office to return the *Gustave Zédé* to operational status.[53] Lockroy also instituted a public contest to construct a true submarine capable of military use. Only a few requirements that the submarine should meet were stipulated: The speed should be 12 knots, the operational radius should be 100 nautical miles at a speed of eight knots, and at least ten nautical miles at eight knots submerged. The submarine should carry two torpedoes and the displacement should not be more than 200 tons.[54] The criteria were far from draconian, and important

---

[51] Le Masson: *Du Nautilus (1800) au Redoutable*, p. 95.
[52] Ropp: *The Development of a Modern Navy*, p. 350.
[53] Lockroy: *La Marine de Guerre*, p. 345.
[54] Le Masson: *Du Nautilus (1800) au Redoutable*, p. 135. Lockroy mentions in his memoirs that the displacement should be not more than 100 tons. Lockroy: *La Marine*

parameters like operational radius surfaced and submerged were far below the performances of the *Gustave Zédé*.

The design submitted by the engineer Maxime Laubeuf, who won the 1896 competition, which finally ended up as the *Narval* exceeded the performances of its predecessors. The new submarine merged the French electric and the American Holland types of propulsion to what became the more or less standard submarine, a vessel with a petroleum-fuelled steam engine for surface navigation and batteries for underwater cruising. The *Narval* was launched in 1899 and set off on extensive technical and tactical tests. The tests proved that the submarine could transit surfaced for 500 nautical miles at 6.5 knots, which meant that it could stay on patrol for three days. It could further make 60 nautical miles submerged at 3.25 knots and 11 nautical miles at five knots before it had to surface in order to recharge the batteries (which was done through the petroleum-fuelled engines and dynamos while transiting surfaced). No other contemporary submarine, either in France or elsewhere, could show such promising accomplishments.[55]

Both the *Narval* and the *Gustave Zédé* carried out tactical operations to prove their ability to approach and attack from a submerged position ships at anchor or ships sailing at slow speed. In 1898, the *Gustave Zédé* conducted several torpedo firings against the battleship *Magenta*. In the manoeuvres of 1901 the *Gustave Zédé* conducted an astounding attack against the battleships blockading the ports of Ajaccio, torpedoing the flagship *Charles Martel*. The achievement received a lot of public attention, and boasting on the part of the *jeune école*. Whether the *Gustave Zédé*'s exploits both in 1898 and 1901 were such an unconditional success was disputed, especially among British experts.[56] A more significant but less noticed achievement was the *Narval*'s submerged penetration through the narrows in to Brest the same year. Before it entered Brest it had cruised surfaced and submerged off the coast of Brittany for

---

de Guerre, p. 341. Henri Le Masson's figures concerning the displacement concurs with the actual displacement of the *Narval*.

[55] Le Masson: *Du Nautilus (1800) au Redoutable*, p. 147.

[56] The critics maintained that the manoeuvres were made under conditions that bore little resemblance to those of war. i.e. the submarine was in the 1901 manoeuvre towed all the way from Toulon to two miles off Ajaccio where it dived and torpedoed the *Charles-Martel*. See i.e. Marder: *The Anatomy of British Sea Power*, pp. 357–362; N.A. Lambert: *Sir John Fisher's Naval Revolution*, pp. 42–43; Ropp: *The Development of a Modern Navy*, p. 351. A more positive evaluation of the attack, based on the same factual description of the events, was given by the commanding officer of the Gustave Zédé, quoted in Le Masson: *Du Nautilus (1800) au Redoutable*, pp. 121–122.

48 hours. A few days later it left Brest and transited submerged for 12 consecutive hours before it arrived at Cherbourg.[57] The operational radius of the *Narval* indicated that the latest submarines could be used for more than local defence.

Ropp claims that the development of the submarine in France was not the result of the propaganda of the *jeune école*, but of patient experimentation by a long series of naval officers. His argument is based on the statement that France's first practical submarine, the *Gymnote*, was the product of Dupuy de Lôme's last years.[58] There is in Ropp's argument an implicit assumption that Dupuy de Lôme was motivated by a purely technological interest. Ropp's argument ignores the fact that construction programmes are not developed in a vacuum disconnected from strategic and operational considerations and the usual political tug-of-war between different interests.

Dupuy de Lôme was not known as an active participant in the dispute between the traditionalists and the *jeune école*. He was, however, well aware of the arguments, and when in 1884 he learned of the successful trials of a very light but powerful electric motor used on the airship *La France*, Dupuy de Lôme told Zédé that "we are going to recommence the study of the of the submarine and we will end the conflict of the torpedo boats and the battleships by suppressing both of them [...]".[59] Dupuy de Lôme also had a vision of the context within which the submarine had a potential and should be used. He saw it as a means to land troops in Britain, an operation he thought would hit at the weak point of British defences.[60] His logic was not far from that of the *jeune école*, but it is not Dupuy de Lôme's strategic thinking that so closely links the early successful French construction of the submarines to the *jeune école*. The *jeune école*'s influence on the development of the submarines is apparent in the fact that *jeune école* ministers and officers encouraged the construction and experimentation of submarines. The *jeune école* also gradually developed an idea as to how the submarine could be an important asset that fitted into their strategic thinking.

Dupuy de Lôme's fundamental idea was to use electric propulsion when the submarine was submerged. He had not worked out any specific

---

[57] Le Masson: *Du Nautilus (1800) au Redoutable*, pp. 150–151.
[58] Ropp: *The Development of a Modern Navy*, p. 349.
[59] Le Masson: *Du Nautilus (1800) au Redoutable*, p. 93. Ropp has also quoted this remark. Ropp: *The Development of a Modern Navy*, p. 349.
[60] Le Masson: *Du Nautilus (1800) au Redoutable*, p. 349.

plans for a submarine before he died in 1885. It was his friend and professional companion over many years, Gustave Zédé, who drew up the plans for the *Gymnote*. Zédé had as early as 1883 presented his ideas on the construction of a submarine to Admiral Alexandre-Louis-François Peyron, the Minister of Marine, and in 1885 to Admiral Charles-Eugène Galiber, Peyron's successor. None of them demonstrated any enthusiasm for the project. Aube's positive view of the project and his decision to construct a submarine according to the design drawn up by Zédé was a logical follow up of arguments he had forwarded earlier. He had as early as 1882 argued positively for the potential of submarines.[61] Zédé underlined that Aube's appreciation of the potential of the submarine for modern naval warfare had been a prerequisite for the development of submarines in France. In a letter to Aube a few years after he had left the post as Minister of Marine Zédé wrote concerning the successful trials of the *Gymnote* that:

> you were the only one who understood the importance of the problem, and without your intervention I would never have dared to approach it. [...] I fear that we will not find today in the Navy the intelligent energy necessary to make good use of the lead that we, thanks to you, have at present over our neighbours.[62]

As we have seen, Lockroy initiated the next leap in French submarine construction and experimentation. He shared Aube's view that the naval establishment's opposition to innovations like the torpedo boat and the submarine was a result of an inherent scepticism towards anything new.[63] The determination of the most prominent *jeune école* officers and politicians to support the development of the submarine was also evident in Admiral Fournier's backing of Laubeuf when the tests of the *Narval* started in 1899. Laubeuf wrote that "at that moment, I could count on my ten fingers the number of my supporters. But among them were, fortunately for me, Admiral Gervais and Admiral Fournier."[64]

Ropp is right in the assumption that the development of the submarine in France was the result of patient experimentation by a long series of naval officers. The construction of the submarines and the experimentation, however, could only take place if they found support

---

[61] Aube: "La guerre maritime", p. 324.
[62] Quoted in Commandant Z and H. Montéchant: *Les guerres navales de demain*, p. 241.
[63] Lockroy: *La Marine de Guerre. Six mois Rue Royale*, p. 34.
[64] Quoted in Le Masson: *Du Nautilus (1800) au Redoutable*, p. 142.

among military and political decision-makers. It was not by accident that the most significant initiatives in submarine construction and experimentation in the 1880s and 1890s occurred under the patronage of three of the most prominent *jeune école* personalities; Aube, Lockroy and Fournier. They were all ardent supporters of the submarine, and one can see a gradual incorporation of the submarine into *jeune école* thinking as development progressed.

The earliest *jeune école* agitation for the submarine was characterised by a rather vague idea about its potential, and it was above all marked by a technological optimism characteristic of the *jeune école* and a hope of finding an easy way to level out the Royal Navy's superiority. Openness to technological innovations and alternative ways of fighting maritime war was an important part of their self-image, and the *jeune école* saw opposition to submarines as a reactionary reflex, an attitude they attributed to the traditionalists. It was in the 1880s and 1890s still the torpedo and the torpedo boat that in the *jeune école*'s arguments represented the technological wonder that would revolutionise naval warfare. The submarine was viewed as a variant of the torpedo boat with just another capability, the ability to cruise below the surface. The invisibility of the submarine was, however, thought to only marginally improve the merits of the torpedo boat that in the 1880s and early 1890s was assumed to be very hard to spot by the enemy due to its small size.

The role of the submarine was gradually emphasised in the writings of the *jeune école* throughout the 1890s and the first decade of the twentieth century. Commandant Z, Montéchant and Lieutenant X briefly touched upon possible roles for the submarine in their writings in the early 1890s. In *Les guerres navales de demain* from 1891 they stressed that it would take a long time before the use of submarines in naval operations would be more than a hypothetical possibility.[65] A clear optimism was, however, present concerning the potential of the submarine. Commandant Z and Montéchant claimed that if the submarine were "fitted with two ordinary self-propelled torpedoes, each loaded with 100 kilos [of explosives], we would possess the most formidable instrument of maritime warfare that one can possibly imagine. With 100 boats of this model, England will be at our mercy."[66] Lieutenant

---

[65] Commandant Z and H. Montéchant: *Les guerres navales de demain*, p. 33.
[66] Ibid., pp. 231–232.

X elaborated on the ideas of Commandant Z and Montéchant in the introduction to their *Essai de stratégie navale*, published in 1893. He depicted an offensive against Britain by "200 torpedo boats, 60 cruisers and some submarines [...]."[67] The role of the submarine would be the same as for the torpedo boats and cruisers; to attack British seaborne trade. The submarine would also have as its special mission to lay mines in British ports.

Lockroy, who was the politician who speeded up submarine construction and experimentation in France in the 1890s, viewed the submarine primarily as a torpedo boat that could dive. The torpedo boat was perfect for night operations, while the merit of the submarine was its ability to attack during daylight. In *La Marine de Guerre*, published in 1897, Lockroy argued that the submarine should conduct defensive operations close to its own ports. He also suggested that submarines should be deployed overseas to defend the French possessions.[68] In his *La Défense Navale* (1900) he still argued that the submarine was best suited for defensive operations close to French ports. Lockroy had been optimistic on behalf of the submarine ever since the early 1890s, and he now argued that most problems concerning submerged cruising had been solved and that one "without fear could start to construct a large number of submarines."[69]

One of the problems the Navy was on the verge of solving was that of the periscope. *Gustave Zédé's* attack on the *Magenta* in 1898 illustrated the problem of not having a periscope. Without a periscope, the only possible way to see anything was to poke the conning tower itself out of the water. During the eleven minutes that the attack lasted, the *Gustave Zédé* had to emerge and thus expose her conning tower five times in order to correct her position. The shortest time interval that the tower was exposed was a half-minute while the longest exposure lasted one and a half minutes.[70] Although the small conning tower could be difficult to spot and certainly to hit, the periscope represented a significant improvement of the submarine's capability to operate undetected close to the enemy.

---

[67] Lieutenant X: Introduction to Commandant Z and H. Montéchant: *Essai de stratégie navale*, p. 64.
[68] Lockroy: *La Marine de Guerre*, pp. 32–34.
[69] Lockroy: *La Défense Navale*, p. 82.
[70] *Ibid.*, pp. 251–252.

The technical and operational improvements convinced Lockroy that it would be impossible to impose a blockade of French ports if a number of submarines were deployed in their vicinity. He also envisaged patrolling submarines in the littorals that could deny any attempt to conduct landings on French territory. He further had great hopes regarding Laubeuf's *Narval*, which was built on Lockroy's initiative. In his second period as minister, Lockroy ordered four more of the same type to be built. The improvement in range that the *Narval* represented, proved to Lockroy that the submarine also had a potential for offensive operations, although he did not elaborate on what kind of offensive operations they were suited for.[71]

An increased optimism regarding the offensive potential of submarines could be noted in the lectures given at the French naval staff college. Captain Davin, who insisted that offensive warfare was deeply rooted in the French national character, envisaged in his lectures in 1900 that French submarines operating in the Irish Sea could stop the shipment of reservists from Ireland.[72] Commander Aubry, who, like Captain Davin, taught tactics and strategy at the staff college, also saw a clear potential for offensive submarine operations.

Aubry argued in his lectures in 1902 that the Royal Navy should be the standard against which the French Navy should measure itself for two reasons. First, if the French Navy prepared to fight the strongest navy, it would more likely be able to tackle second and third rank navies. Secondly, Commander Aubry was an ardent colonialist, and he warned against the decline of France if it did not pursue colonial expansion. An expansionist foreign policy might easily lead to a confrontation with the leading power of the time. A mixture of fleet warfare and commerce warfare was Aubry's recipe for fighting Great Britain. He did not have much confidence in the traditional *jeune école* ideas of conducting commerce raiding with fast surface vessels. Instead he argued that the submarines could be used to enforce what had traditionally been viewed as a British prerogative due to its command of the seas, a close blockade:

> Admit that in the not too distant future one succeeds in giving this kind of ship sufficient capabilities for it to cruise for some days at the approaches to

---

[71] *Ibid.*, p. 253.
[72] SHM, 1 CC Aa 10: Lectures by Capitaine de vaisseau Davin: *Tactique et stratégie* (École Supérieure de Marine, Paris, 1900), p. 555.

the enemy's commercial ports and there conduct an effective surveillance day and night. One could thus declare an effective blockade upheld by a few of these ships and inform all ships that enter the belligerents' territorial waters that they expose themselves to the risk of being sunk.

If the neutrals followed this line of thinking, if some neutral ships were sunk attempting to gain access to a blockaded enemy port, this would undoubtedly have serious consequences for the supplies of the country because the numbers of ships that are needed [to supply Great Britain] are considerable and it will be difficult to supply England in a covert way.[73]

Commander Aubry underlined that France had still some way to go before it would have a sufficient number of capable submarines that could conduct such offensive operations. He also raised some concern about the legal aspects of a blockade conducted by submarines. The Declaration of Paris of 1856 stated that blockades, in order to be binding, must be effective. The blockading power was obliged to maintain a force strong enough to prevent access to the coast of the enemy. A mere "paper blockade" would be a breach of international law. If the submarines of an inferior power were to conduct a blockade off the coast of the enemy, the submarines would have to operate much of the time submerged in order to survive in a hostile environment. Aubry admitted that such a blockade was not necessarily in accordance with what was thought of as an effective, visible blockade: "It is indeed a rather delicate question of international law: To accept a blockade by submarines will be to accept, so to speak, a simple declaration of blockade (*ce sera admettre le blocus pour ainsi dire sur parole*)."[74]

Paul Fontin (who earlier wrote under the pseudonym Commandant Z) argued in his *Les sous-marins et l'Angleterre* (1902) that France could relatively cheaply acquire an offensive capability by investing in a submarine fleet. He was convinced that the submarines could operate on the open sea, and he reminded his readers that the open sea in a war against Great Britain would be the Straits of Dover, the Channel and the western basin of the Mediterranean. Fontin here referred to what had been one of his and Montéchant's main arguments in the 1890s for an offensive strategy relying on high-seas torpedo boats: that France bordered the most important British trade routes and the operational

---

[73] SHM, 1 CC 196 Aa 13: Lectures by Capitaine de frégate Aubry: *Tactique et stratégie, 1ère Partie. Stratégie et Marine française* (École Supérieure de Marine, Paris, 1902), p. 419.
[74] *Ibid.*, p. 419.

areas of the Royal Navy. France's geographical position permitted its small vessels to operate on what was viewed as the high seas, but that was never far from a friendly coast. Fontin underlined that France controlled the opposing coasts of the western part of the Mediterranean and that they also controlled Corsica that lay as a hyphen connecting the two coasts. Fontin claimed that not only would it be impossible for British battleships to operate close to French ports, they would also be cut off from operating close to their own coast, especially the southern parts of England, due to the threat that French submarines would pose. "The submarine is, par excellence, the offensive weapon", Fontin concluded.[75]

The idea of using the submarine in offensive operations was energetically embraced by Vice Admiral Fournier who had been appointed Inspector General of the torpedo boat and the submarine flotillas in 1902. Fournier viewed the submarine as having an almost revolutionary impact on naval warfare. His optimism was partly based on experiences from the manoeuvres of 1902 and 1903,[76] the manoeuvres he himself led in 1905 and 1906,[77] and some small-scale manoeuvres off Toulon and Cherbourg.[78] Fournier's optimism was also part of an incipient trend among an increasing number of officers, not only in the French Navy, to appreciate the progress in submarine construction and their operational potential. Fournier, however, seemed more convinced than most that the development of the submarine was reaching perfection and that large-scale construction of submarines was justifiable. This optimism fitted into a pattern of thinking characteristic of the *jeune école*, and that contemporary officers ironically described as a conviction that some technological break-through would tip the military balance

---

[75] Paul Fontin: *Les sous-marins et l'Angleterre* (Paris, 1902), pp. 67–68.

[76] Vice Admiral Fournier: *La Politique Navale et la Flotte Française* (Paris, 1910), p. 152.

[77] Brière: *Le Vice-amiral Fournier*, p. 171.

[78] SHM, BB8-2424/6: Vice Admiral Fournier to the Minister of Marine: *Note sur l'importance du rôle des flottilles sous-marines dans la guerre navale et sur les conséquences de ce rôle, exceptionnellement favorable à la FRANCE*, 8 December 1905, p. 9. The year the manoeuvres were held is not mentioned in the memorandum in which they are referred to, but they must have been conducted in the period from 1902 to 1905. Paul Fontin refers to an exercise conducted on the initiative of Fournier in July 1902 when four submarines under escort of a torpedo boat left Cherbourg for Brest and succeeded in attacking the battleship *Fulminant* in the port of Brest. The crew aboard the *Fulminant* did not discover the four submarines before they surfaced approximately 400 meters from the battleship. Fontin: *Les sous-marins et l'Angleterre*, pp. 68–69.

in favour of France and that it was possible to obtain a cut-price advantage.[79]

When Fournier described the impact that a large scale introduction of submarines to the French Navy would have on naval warfare, his arguments resembled very much those forwarded by Aube and Charmes in the early and mid-1880s concerning the alleged qualities and potential of the self-propelled torpedoes and the autonomous torpedo boats:

> Until now we have not had other effective ways of stopping an enemy fleet than by meeting it with a similar fleet, using the same weapons and the same tactical measures to fight for victory. From now on it will be different, and we can already see that in a very near future ordinary submarines of 200–500 tons will have the possibility to dive at will in order to make themselves invisible and invulnerable to artillery fire when attacking and while escaping the enemy. They will be capable of disabling or destroying by surprise the most powerful surface ships, however fast they may be.
>
> Under these conditions, all maritime nations, even if they lack capital ships, will be able to repel any offensive attempt by enemy squadrons against the coast with much more certainty by using submarines than by using big surface ships. The success of these small units is due to their invisibility and the irresistible and immediately destructive power of their torpedoes, and not to a long and uncertain battle, where valour generally does not lead to victory without the help of numbers, superiority in tonnage, in armament and speed of the vessel, and finally luck.
>
> In the future a country will succeed in its naval offence and defence by adapting the use of submarines to its geographical position.
>
> Henceforth, this can be achieved by any country in a position to deploy these invisible assailants, some off the enemy ports, others on the sea routes and near straits. There are positions that the opposing fleet will be forced, in time of war, to sail and to cross so as to cover its merchant navy, to direct and protect reinforcements, in numerous convoys, towards its overseas positions, and finally—to ensure its domestic supplies.
>
> Such is the position of France, especially in regard to England, and it is this situation that will soon decide the maritime importance of our country,

---

[79] See i.e. SHM, 1 CC 197 Aa 21: Lectures by Capitaine de vaisseau Rouyer: *Tactique er Stratégie, 3ème Fascicule. Stratégie navale* (École Supérieure de Marine, Paris, 1905), pp. 129–131.

not the relative strength of our battle fleet, which will be incapable of ensuring such importance, even at the price of the greatest sacrifices.[80]

Probably the best illustration of the similarity between Fournier's reasoning and that of Aube and Charmes was Fournier's presentation of his view on the submarine's potential to cruise the seven seas. His arguments echoed Aube's and Charmes's very optimistic prophecies of the autonomous, seagoing torpedo boat in the 1880s. While most officers viewed the torpedo boats primarily as vessels tailored for operations close to the coast, Aube and Charmes described them as small vessels with the same potential as cruisers. In the 1890s and early 1900s the submarine in the French Navy was also primarily seen as a boat best suited for defensive operations close to the coast, although some, especially officers of the *jeune école*, argued for offensive operations off the coast of the British Isles. Fournier went further and characterised the submarine as "small submersible cruisers and torpedo boats."[81] The capability to cruise the seas with submarines would cut Britain's links to its colonies and prevent supplies from reaching the British Isles:

> The consequences of this submarine war will be disastrous for England, not only because the British archipelago will find itself starving since its convoys with supplies will not be able to arrive, but moreover, it will be impossible to bring reinforcements in the form of ships, troops and war material to Egypt, India and her principal colonies as well as to her naval bases.[82]

Fournier's enthusiasm for the submarine was built on three well-known *jeune école* principles. First, it assumed that Britain was the enemy with its dependence on safe sea lines of communication. Secondly, in order to realise the *jeune école* strategy, the French Navy needed a fleet of numerous, and consequently relatively cheap, vessels that could patrol the British trade routes. The submarine promised, according to Fournier, to possess these characteristics. Thirdly, France's geographical position

---

[80] SHM, BB8-2424/6: Vice Admiral Fournier to the Minister of Marine: *Programme naval à adopter dans l'ordre d'urgence que commandent les événements dans la mesure de nos ressources budgétaires pour répondre aux besoins de la sécurité nationale et de la stratégie navale de la France*, 10 May 1905, pp. 1–7.

[81] SHM, BB8-2424/6: Vice Admiral Fournier to the Minister of Marine: *Note sur l'importance du rôle des flottilles sous-marines dans la guerre navale et sur les conséquences de ce rôle, exceptionnellement favorable à la FRANCE*, 8 December 1905, p. 3.

[82] *Ibid.*, p. 3.

with its Atlantic and Mediterranean ports was viewed as a perfect point of departure for operations against British maritime activity.

Fournier's preoccupation with Great Britain was not in agreement with official French foreign policy. His initiatives to build a large submarine fleet as part of a strategy to fight Great Britain were taken more than a year after the Entente Cordiale was signed between Great Britain and France, and more than three years after diplomatic steps towards a *rapprochement* between the two traditional rivals had begun in 1902.

Fournier's apparent obsession with Great Britain was probably not an expression of Anglophobia that one could see demonstrated from time to time among French naval officers. Ropp claims that Fournier remained on the best personal terms with the British, and that he was selected to serve as president of the arbitration commission in the aftermath of the Dogger Bank incident in 1904 on account of his personal popularity in British naval circles.[83] What is evident from Fournier's writings is that he was a colonialist and an admirer of Britain's colonial achievements. French colonial ambitions were likely to be contrary to the interests of Great Britain. Fournier feared that conflicting interests could lead to a clash between the two, and his strategic reflections were based on these assumptions. Although the initial purpose of the Entente had been to improve the relations between the two countries by resolving their colonial disputes, Fournier must have been convinced that the rivalry between these two European powers was of such a fundamental character that it could not be eased by an agreement.

Fournier's reasoning was symptomatic of the naval colonialists' logic around the time when the Entente Cordiale was concluded. Captain (later Vice Admiral) Gabriel Darrieus, chose in his lectures at the staff college to ridicule the conclusion of the Entente Cordiale with what he labelled France's hereditary enemy. He argued that the Entente Cordiale was just another truce between two powers with permanently conflicting interests. The Entente Cordiale will last "as long as the economic development of France does not offend her neighbouring power", he claimed.[84] Darrieus insisted that the British were predestined to expand their empire continuously due to their location on an island charac-

---

[83] Ropp: *The Development of a Modern Navy*, p. 328.
[84] SHM, 1 CC 197 Aa 24: Lectures by Capitaine de vaisseau Darrieus: *Stratégie et Tactique. 1ère Fascicule. La doctrine* (École Supérieure de Marine, Paris, 1906), pp. 346–347. The lectures of Darrieus were later published. See Gabriel Darrieus: *La guerre sur mer. Stratégie et Tactique. La doctrine* (Paris, 1907).

terised by a harsh climate and that they were far from self-supporting in the essential commodities of a modern society. This explained the inflexible character of British politics, he argued, and

> we understand why preparation for war against England is a sacred duty for all countries inspired by the legitimate desire to extend their influence and progress beyond their maritime borders. It is thus a vital necessity for us, if we, as I hope, are to abandon the idea of remaining paralysed by our commercial weakness, and soon gain the place in the world economy that belongs to us.[85]

It was not only the colonialists and the supporters of the *jeune école* among the naval officers who had problems substituting Great Britain for Germany as the probable naval adversary. Captain Rouyer complained in one of his lectures in 1905 at the Staff College that it was difficult to know against whom the French Navy should plan to fight:

> Twenty years ago, everybody would have answered Germany; around twelve years ago some clear-sighted minds thought and said that it would be England; and now, even many of those who energetically supported that view think that the moment when a rupture with England could become imminent is gone and over, while a conflict with Germany is still possible.[86]

The teaching at the Staff College thus did not immediately adapt to the realities of French foreign policy. The scenarios that were presented described both Great Britain and Germany as possible enemies, and ways to fight each of them were discussed. But few expressed such a fundamental scepticism about the new agreement between France and Great Britain as Darrieus and Fournier did.

Fournier was convinced that Great Britain's conciliatory politics towards France was due to the threat that a large French submarine fleet would pose to British naval supremacy. The French submarines would be like the sword of Damocles, permanently threatening the Royal Navy and British maritime and colonial interest, Fournier argued.[87] He

---

[85] SHM, 1 CC 197 Aa 24: Lectures by Capitaine de vaisseau Darrieus: *Stratégie et Tactique. 1ᵉʳ Fascicule. La doctrine* (École Supérieure de Marine, Paris,1906), p. 372.

[86] SHM, 1 CC 197 Aa 21: Lectures by Capitaine de vaisseau Rouyer: *Tactique er Stratégie, 3ᵉᵐᵉ Fascicule. Stratégie navale* (École Supérieure de Marine, Paris, 1905), pp. 129–131.

[87] SHM, BB8-2424/6: Vice Admiral Fournier to the Minister of Marine: *Note sur l'importance du rôle des flottilles sous-marines dans la guerre navale et sur les conséquences de ce rôle, exceptionnellement favorable à la FRANCE*, 8 December 1905, p. 6.

suggested that it was the British anticipation of a major French effort to build a substantial French submarine fleet that had forced Britain to conclude the Entente Cordiale:

> Is it not already the salutary fear of our submarines, even the still distant and uncertain perspective [of a large construction programme], that recently has pushed England in the direction, that we thus must believe is sincere and lasting, of the Entente Cordiale with France?[88]

The progress in French submarine development did raise concern within the Royal Navy. An interesting aspect of the internal considerations of the Royal Navy was the worry that a high profile British effort to develop and construct submarines would encourage the general development of submarines. Vice Admiral Archibald Douglas, the Second Naval Lord, opined in January 1901 that it would be most unwise "to use the inventive powers of a country to develop and advance submarine warfare."[89] Rear Admiral Sir Arthur Wilson was equally clear in a memorandum he wrote in January 1901 that encouraging the development of submarines would be harmful to British interests. Wilson argued that French submarines were not yet capable of crossing the Channel, but he predicted in accordance with the *jeune école*'s arguments, that when such craft became available both Britain and France would find their warships and merchant fleets confined to port. He admitted that whereas it was essential for Great Britain to keep her overseas trade flowing, France was not so dependent on maintaining free access for their ships. Thus, he argued:

> The development of submarine warfare must be detrimental to a nation depending on navigation at the surface for its supplies of food and the necessaries of life. We cannot stop the invention in this direction [and] we cannot delay its introduction any longer, but we still should avoid doing anything to assist in its improvement in order that our means of trapping and destroying it may develop at a greater rate than the submarine boats themselves.[90]

Discussions within the Royal Navy over the next years revealed a deep concern about the potential threat that submarine warfare could pose

---

[88] SHM, BB8-2424/6: Vice Admiral Fournier to the Minister of Marine: *Programme naval à adopter dans l'ordre d'urgence que commandent les événements dans la mesure de nos ressources budgétaires pour répondre aux besoins de la sécurité nationale et de la stratégie navale de la France*, 10 May 1905, p. 12.
[89] Quoted in N.A. Lambert: *Sir John Fisher's Naval Revolution*, p. 48.
[90] Quoted in *ibid.*, p. 48.

to the traditional command of the seas imposed by the Royal Navy's capital ships. The descriptions of what challenges French submarine warfare could pose to Great Britain concurred very much with the optimistic scenarios propagated by the *jeune école*. The inspecting captain of submarines, Captain Reginald Bacon proclaimed that a group of three to five submarines would be sufficient to pose an insurmountable obstacle to a squadron operating in the vicinity of a port where these submarines were based. "The risks of allowing a large ship to approach such a port are so great that I unhesitatingly affirm that in war time it should never be allowed," he claimed.[91]

The First Sea Lord, Admiral Sir John Fisher, wrote in 1904 that the submarine had challenged the foundation of British strategic thinking:

> THE SUBMARINE IS THE COMING TYPE OF WAR VESSEL FOR SEA FIGHTING. And what is it that the coming of the submarine really means? It means that the whole foundation of our strategy [...] has broken down! The foundation of that strategy was blockade. The Fleet did not exist merely to win battles—that was the means not the end. The ultimate purpose of the Fleet was to make blockade possible for us and impossible for the enemy [...] Surface ships can no longer maintain or prevent blockade [...]. All our old ideas of strategy are simmering in the melting pot.[92]

Concern about French offensive use of submarines was also raised. A scenario in which twenty perfected French submarines operated in the narrow waters of the Channel was used to exemplify the threat that these craft could pose to British shipping.[93] The progress and the potential of submarines gradually convinced the Royal Navy that submarines should be an integrated and an important part of its inventory.

Despite the worry raised within the Royal Navy regarding the progress and potential of French submarine warfare, the conclusion of the Entente Cordiale can hardly be explained by British fears of French submarines, as Fournier suggested. The discussions within the military and political leadership of the Royal Navy centred on the problem of how to avoid encouraging the further development of the French submarine fleet, and which naval means could counter such a threat effectively. As we have seen, the Entente Cordiale was based on other arguments. Fournier's allegations must rather be understood as part of

---

[91] Quoted in *ibid.*, p. 53.
[92] Quoted in Tiller: *Seapower*, p. 63.
[93] N.A. Lambert: *Sir John Fisher's Naval Revolution*, p. 49.

an effort to convince the Minister of Marine of the potential of submarines and of the need for France to invest in a large-scale construction programme of submarines.

Although all Fournier's strategic reasoning centred on Great Britain as the enemy, he did assure the Minister of Marine that the submarine would be an effective weapon against any country acting contrary to French interests at sea. Fournier's memoranda were written at the time when the arms race between Great Britain and Germany was getting under way. Still, he did not pay much attention to the German Navy as a potential threat. He did, however, assure the Minister that French submarines would be able to destroy the German fleet either when passing the Straits of Dover or in the Channel.[94]

The French Navy needed a fleet of numerous submarines for Fournier's strategy to succeed. The balancing item was not surprisingly the battleships. Fournier argued that the next generation of battleships would displace at least 19,000 tons and have a price of close to 50 million francs. For that price, Fournier claimed, the French Navy could build 25 submarines, which would:

> constitute a flotilla capable of controlling either the Channel or the western basin of the Mediterranean and each unit will be capable of destroying or disabling a battleship, while [the battleship] will not be in position to sink the smaller submarine, if it is not by accident, despite its formidable and expensive armament.[95]

In the memorandum of May 1905 Fournier suggested a fleet of 100 long-range submarines. Some months later, in the memorandum of December 1905, Fournier had reduced the number to 90 submarines. In this memorandum he described the logic leading to the recommended number of submarines. He argued that France should have a battleship fleet that was one third of the battleship fleet of the Royal Navy. The French battleships should be as capable as the British. In order to even out the British predominance in battleships, it would be sufficient to have the same number of submarines as the number of

---

[94] SHM, BB8-2424/6: Vice Admiral Fournier to the Minister of Marine: *Note sur l'importance du rôle des flottilles sous-marines dans la guerre navale et sur les conséquences de ce rôle, exceptionnellement favorable à la FRANCE*, 8 December 1905, p. 6.

[95] SHM, BB8-2424/6: Vice Admiral Fournier to the Minister of Marine: *Programme naval à adopter dans l'ordre d'urgence que commandent les événements dans la mesure de nos ressources budgétaires pour répondre aux besoins de la sécurité nationale et de la stratégie navale de la France*, 10 May 1905, pp. 17–18.

British battleships exceeding the number of French battleships. Fournier ended up recommending a fleet of 36 battleships and 90 submarines. The submarines would replace some of the functions of the torpedo boats, and Fournier suggested a considerable reduction in the number of these boats. Fournier also insisted that the French Navy should build minesweepers in order to keep the ports out of which the submarines operated free from enemy mines. The importance that Fournier attributed to the introduction of the submarine in the French Navy was illustrated by his proposal to reorganise the Navy into three distinct fleets or flotillas: one for the battleships, a second for torpedo boats and destroyers and finally a third for the submarines.[96]

Fournier recommended that 40 submarines should be deployed to the Mediterranean and 24 to the Channel. The 40 submarines deployed to the Mediterranean would turn the western basin of the Mediterranean into a French lake, he argued.[97] He recommended in his proposal for a new programme that the operational range of the submarines should be between 2,500 and 3,000 nautical miles. That would be more than sufficient for operations in European waters. The demand for such an extended operational range was primarily due to the requirements of operations in the Far East. Fournier envisaged that the submarines should be able to cover the littorals from the Gulf of Tonkin to the Gulf of Siam and the southern basin of the Chinese Sea.[98]

Although the submarines were viewed as a significant reinforcement of the defence of the French colonies, it was primarily in European waters that they were to challenge the British hegemony on the seas. Fournier shared the geostrategic analysis already formulated by Vauban in the seventeenth century and adopted and further developed by Montéchant and Commandant Z. They had been convinced that France had a geostrategic advantage in commerce warfare compared to Great Britain and Germany. The French ports were viewed as perfect

---

[96] *Ibid.*, pp. 17–18, 22–23, 29–31, 45; SHM, BB8-2424/6: Vice Admiral Fournier to the Minister of Marine: *Note sur l'importance du rôle des flotilles sous-marines dans la guerre navale et sur les coneséquences de ce rôle, exceptionnellement favorable à la FRANCE*, 8 December 1905, pp. 7–8.

[97] SHM, BB8-2424/6: Vice Admiral Fournier to the Minister of Marine: *Programme naval à adopter dans l'ordre d'urgence que commandent les événements dans la mesure de nos ressources budgétaires pour répondre aux besoins de la sécurité nationale et de la stratégie navale de la France*, 10 May 1905, pp. 34–35.

[98] SHM, BB8-2424/6: Vice Admiral Fournier: *Annexe No 1. Programme sommaire d'un submersible de haute mer*, May 1905, pp. 2–3.

points of departure for attacks on British and German trade. Fournier echoed this opinion, and argued that the French ports in the Mediterranean and on the Atlantic coast were perfectly positioned for launching operations to block British ships in the Straits of Dover, Gibraltar, the channels or narrows on the route from Gibraltar to Malta and the British ports in the Mediterranean, and they could deploy outside the main ports of Great Britain. France's geographical position allowed the Navy to commence such operations at the very beginning of hostilities, Fournier argued, and it would allow France to achieve command of the seas even without aid from its battleships.

That the initial operations should be conducted without the support of the battleship fleet was logically consistent with Fournier's view that the submarine would be almost totally superior in battle against surface ships and the fact that the Royal Navy's battleship fleet was three times the size of the French. The French battleships should stay in port safe from both British submarines and battleships, while the French submarines would have "an overabundance of targets to disable or destroy due to the incessant movements of the enemy's fleet and supply convoys that the urgent necessity of a naval war brings to a head."[99] Fournier's conclusion regarding the proposed strategy, formed as a question, illustrates that he viewed the submarine as having the same revolutionary impact on naval warfare to the benefit of the inferior power that Aube and Charmes had predicted the torpedo boat would have:

> Such a tactic, would it not give France, at little cost and at almost no risk, a certain and decisive superiority over England that it can no longer expect from its battleship fleet, even if it were to be tripled and were to fight long, fierce battles with enormous sacrifices of all kinds—the hazards of battles, which may bring glory to our service, but which are necessarily futile and ruinous.[100]

The *jeune école* perspective on submarine warfare gradually faded away as Great Britain more clearly stood out as France's ally against an ambitious Germany. The French Navy, and particularly the *jeune école*, seemed, however, quite hesitant about shifting the focus onto Germany as the most immediate threat. The Navy's attitude differed significantly from that of the French Army. For the French Army a possible conflict

---

[99] SHM, BB8-2424/6: Vice Admiral Fournier to the Minister of Marine: *Note sur l'importance du rôle des flottilles sous-marines dans la guerre navale et sur les conséquences de ce rôle, exceptionnellement favorable à la FRANCE*, 8 December 1905, p. 4.
[100] *Ibid.*, pp. 4–5.

with Germany had been its natural focus. The humiliation of Fashoda had for a while made Great Britain seem as likely an enemy as Germany. The making and the strengthening of the Entente Cordiale turned Great Britain from a potential enemy into a probable ally. The improvements in Franco-Italian relations reduced the potential major enemies to one.[101] Although the French Army discussed plans on how to challenge the British, both by deceptive invasion preparations and an expedition against Egypt,[102] it never actually stopped directing its attention to the German menace.

Even though the Schlieffen plan did not find its final form until 1905, the French Army started to receive bits and pieces of intelligence regarding some of the key elements of the plan as early as 1900. The French military attaché in Berlin reported that teaching at the German military academies emphasised that the enemy should be engaged along one of its flanks. A year later a French member of the *Conseil Supérieur de la Guerre* publicly observed that German manoeuvres revealed a new German strategy whereby German forces would concentrate against the enemy's flanks in order to envelop it. This view was supported by the Belgian General Staff that let the French know that they expected that Germany would move through the Ardennes in south-eastern Belgium in case of war between Germany and France. In late 1903 and early 1904 French intelligence received documents presenting outlines of what later would be the Schlieffen Plan. A minimum number of troops would hold the eastern front against Russia, while the main part of the German Army would attack France through Belgium. There was some scepticism in the French General Staff concerning the reliability of these documents, but the General Staff found such a plan highly probable. The majority of the generals on the Superior Council disagreed with the assessment that the Germany Army would try a flanking move through Belgium. They were convinced that the existing war plan according to which

---

[101] Christopher M. Andrew: "France and the German Menace" in Ernest R. May (ed.) *Knowing One's Enemies. Intelligence Assessment before the Two World Wars* (Princeton, New Jersey, 1984) p. 127.

[102] The Minister of Marine, Lockroy, was informed by the Minister of War in the wake of the Fashoda crisis that a military expedition through Tripolitania was discussed. Lockroy told the Superior Council that such an operation would involve both political and military risks before arriving in the valley of the Nile. The French forces would have to violate neutral territory and would hence risk stirring up the whole of Europe against France. Further, the march through the desert from the borders of Tripolitania to the Nile Valley would place an enormous strain on the troops. SHM, BB8-2424/5: Conseil Supérieur de la Marine. *Séances du 11 Janvier 1899*, p. 67.

the French Army should concentrate along the Epinal—Toul—Verdun line west of Lorraine would be adequate.[103]

The discussions and considerations in the French Army differed significantly from those of the French Navy through these years. As illustrated by the short summary of some of the army deliberations above, the army kept their focus on Germany as a probable enemy even through the period where Britain was considered an equally likely enemy as Germany. The French Navy, on the other hand, rarely paid any interest to the German Navy until it was obvious that the Tirpitz Plan would be carried out and that the Entente Cordiale was signed.

The *jeune école* only very reluctantly shifted its focus away from Great Britain and the Royal Navy, but eventually Fournier engaged in the discussions over how a naval war against Germany should be fought. While the German threat had played an almost insignificant part in his memorandum of 1905 concerning submarine warfare, he wrote a memorandum to the Minister in 1906 devoted to how German aggression could be stopped. He argued that the submarines should play a vital role in stopping the German fleet in the Straits of Dover or in the Channel. The potential role of the submarines was the same as the First Sea Lord, Admiral Fisher, forwarded in conversations with the French naval attaché about the Moroccan conference and British naval preparations. Fisher was quite confident that the British Channel Squadron alone would crush the German Navy. All he wanted from the French Navy was their help to establish a submarine and destroyer cordon across the Straits of Dover.[104]

Fournier linked the use of submarines to the recurrent discussion as to whether the French battleships should be concentrated in one fleet, and in that case where. He claimed that the Germans would probably try to fight the Northern Fleet and the Mediterranean Fleet separately. The German fleet would first rush to Brest in order to prevent the ships there from joining the Mediterranean Fleet. Fournier argued that a concentration of the battleships in the Northern Fleet would be the most effective way to the stop the German Navy. To take up the fight

---

[103] Jan Karl Tanenbaum: "French Estimates of Germany's Operational War Plans" in Ernest R. May (ed.) *Knowing One's Enemies. Intelligence Assessment before the Two World Wars* (Princeton, New Jersey, 1984), pp. 150–156.

[104] Williamson Jr.: *The Politics of Grand Strategy*, pp. 68–69. I have found no indication that Fournier was aware of the First Sea Lord's view on the submarines capability to form an effective barrier across the Straits of Dover.

in the Channel would enable effective, combined operations with the battle fleet, torpedo boats and submarines.[105]

The General Staff of the Ministry of Marine agreed with Fournier that military logic would justify that the bulk of French naval forces were stationed in the north, but they claimed that such a solution would be politically unwise. It would signal, the General Staff claimed, that France saw a war against Germany as a duel between the two countries, while the other powers remained neutral. It could also send a politically unfortunate signal both to French and German public opinion, and the German press could exploit it. Instead, the General Staff argued, the focus should be on the Mediterranean. The General Staff based its arguments on the same strategic reasoning that had been so dominant within the French Navy before the Fashoda crisis. In a conflict with the Triple Alliance the French Navy should concentrate on, and secure the sea lines of communication with Algeria. Submarines and torpedo boats should conduct defensive coastal operations denying the German fleet access to the French Atlantic coast.[106]

A decision was soon taken to concentrate the battleships in the Mediterranean in case of a war with the Triple Alliance.[107] Plans were, however, made for the possible case where the other European powers stayed neutral in a conflict between Germany and France. In such a case the Northern Fleet should sail directly to the Mediterranean until the French Navy was mobilised, and then the united fleets should return to the Channel and in joint operations with the flotillas challenge the German fleet. The submarines should operate both as a coastal defence and as part of fleet operations.[108]

As the diplomatic and naval relations between Great Britain and France gradually improved, an understanding was reached in 1912–1913 between the two navies in case of war with Germany. The Royal Navy should have the complete responsibility for the defence of

---

[105] SHM, BB4-2437: Vice Admiral Fournier to the Minister of Marine: *Mesures préparatoires à prendre d'urgence dans la flotte française en prevision d'une brusque agression de l'Allemagne*, 18 January 1906.

[106] SHM, BB4-2437: Ministère de la Marine, EMG 3ème section: *Observations de l'État-Major Général au sujet de la note de M. Le Vice-Amiral Fournier sur les mesures préparatoires à prendre d'urgence en prévision d'une brusque aggression d'Allemagne*, January 1906.

[107] SHM, BB4-2437: Ministère de la Marine, EMG 3ème bureau: *Note 1—Au sujet des instructions de guerre des escadres*, 6 April 1907.

[108] SHM, BB4-2437: Le Ministre de la Marine à M. le Vice-amiral, Commandant en Chef l'Armée Navale: *Instructions pour le cas d'une guerre avec l'Allemagne, toutes les autres puissances restant neutres*, 11 May 1908.

the Straits of Dover. The French should as reinforcement keep some submarines available and operate a few torpedo boats between Calais and Boulogne. The French should have the responsibility for the lower Channel, reinforced by four British armoured cruisers. The main French naval effort should be in the Mediterranean. The plans for cooperation in the Mediterranean were less complete than for the Straits of Dover and the Channel. One reason was that Royal Navy could not promise to maintain a fixed number of ships in the Mediterranean. Yet, there were hopes that the Royal Navy would have enough ships to balance the Austrian fleet.[109]

Henri Le Masson has identified five kinds of submarine operations that the French Navy considered in the period before World War I:

– Attacks against the enemy's sea lines of communication
– Protection of the coast
– As a barrier in straits (i.e. the Straits of Dover)
– Actions against the enemy's coast (preferably the enemy's ports)
– Fleet operations

There were mainly two kinds of operations that seemed realistic, as Great Britain turned out to be an unlikely enemy: defensive operations near the coast and fleet operations. The idea of using submarines to erect a barrier was also mentioned from time to time. To erect a barrier in the straits seemed a logical and feasible operation, although the submarines with steam propulsion had difficulties operating submerged. Actions against the enemy coast and ports could have been an alternative, but as Henri le Masson points out, the submarines did not yet have the necessary qualities to conduct these kinds of operations. Attacks on the sea lines of communication were the kinds of operations that the French submarines were best suited to conduct, but the strategic situation with Germany as the probable enemy made this kind of operation unlikely.

Submarines in fleet operations were viewed as a feasible option, and four *escadrilles* were attached to the battle fleets. The idea of submarines in fleet operations was upheld yet the submarines could not make more than 10–11 knots when surfaced. Ideally they should have been able

---

[109] Masson: *Histoire de la Marine, tome II*, p. 188; Williamson Jr.: *The Politics of Grand Strategy*, pp. 322–324.

to reach a maximum speed of 20 knots and a transit speed of 15–16 knots surfaced and 13–14 knots submerged in order not to hamper the battleships they should accompany. After the manoeuvres in 1913, the division commander of the flotillas of the *Armée navale* concluded that the submarines were unsuitable for fleet warfare and proposed that they should rather be used for barrier operations and blockades. The other type of operation where the French Navy considered submarines to be a valuable asset was for protection of the coasts. This mission would, however, be difficult due to the fact that France has two extensive coasts with many ports that could be threatened, and that the submarines at the time had low tactical and strategic mobility. The majority of the submarines would risk not seeing the enemy at all.[110]

France continued its experimentation and development with new prototypes of submarines, and on the eve of World War I France had a larger submarine fleet than Great Britain and Germany. The French submarine fleet was, however, very heterogeneous, reflecting a lack of consensus on what kind of operations they should conduct and political and economically motivated changes to already adopted construction programmes.

The potential of the submarine had been vital for the renaissance of the ideas of the *jeune école* in the early 1900. The capabilities of the submarines were improved throughout the first decade of the twentieth century, although not as fast as the optimists of the *jeune école* had professed. It was, however, not the weak performances of the submarine that contributed to the decline of the *jeune école*. It was rather the fact that the French Navy was to face a different enemy that did not fit into the strategy of the *jeune école*, and that the constitutive enemy for the *jeune école* theory was France's most probable ally against Germany.

The Pelletan Regime

The 1902 election made the divisions within French politics very visible. Such mundane issues as income tax, pensions and tariffs were more or less absent from the political debate. The main issue was the fate of the church, a sensitive question that led to a polarisation of French politics. It was, as Robert Tombs has noticed, "Left against Right, the

---

[110] Le Masson: *Du Nautilus (1800) au Redoutable*, pp. 194–215.

Republic against its enemies."[111] The *bloc des gauches* won the election with a margin of more than 50 seats. Waldeck-Rousseau who represented a careful mix of republican anticlericalism and moderate social progress was replaced by Emile Combes who was a fierce anticlerical.[112] Camille Pelletan succeeded Lanessan as Minister of Marine in June 1902. Pelletan was passionately anticlerical and contributed actively to the division of church and state. He had, as Theodore Ropp writes, also an ambition to stamp out clericalism and aristocracy in the Navy.[113] This ambition he shared with the Minister of War, whose eagerness for further "republicanization" of the army eventually led to the fall of the Combes government. The Minister of War, General André, used his newly gained powers to promote officers with a republican record. He created a system where civil servants, freemasons (he was himself a freemason) and officers provided information on officers' and their families' religious and political affiliations. The information was noted on cards and used to favour republicans in promotion. There was, as Tomb has noted, nothing new about this procedure. But when the news of the card system leaked at the end of 1904, it led to the fall of the Combes government in early 1905.[114]

Pelletan had supported several of the positions of the *jeune école* as a Member of Parliament, and he was the architect behind the 50 million francs extension of credit to the Programme of 1900 in order to build more torpedo boats and submarines than originally envisaged in the programme.[115] Most historians have described Pelletan as a *jeune école* Minister of Marine. Theodore Ropp claims that the appointment of Pelletan brought the *jeune école* back to power for the last time.[116] Philippe Masson maintains that the *jeune école* found an interpreter of their theory in Pelletan,[117] while Martin Motte argues that "the *jeune école* was given, although discredited as a doctrine, an unexpected new lease of life" by the appointment of Pelletan.[118] Ray Walser writes that

---

[111] Tombs: *France 1814–1914*, pp. 468–469.
[112] Combes had a doctor's degree in theology but abandoned a clerical career and started to study medicine and engage in politics.
[113] Ropp: *The Development of a Modern Navy*, p. 325.
[114] Tombs: *France 1814–1914*, p. 470; Charles Sowerwine: *France since 1870. Culture, Politics and Society* (Houndmills, 2001), p. 85.
[115] Motte: *Une éducation géostratégique*, p. 365.
[116] Ropp: *The Development of a Modern Navy*, p. 325.
[117] Masson: *Histoire de la Marine*, p. 194.
[118] Motte: *Une éducation géostratégique*, p. 361.

Pelletan "stubbornly stuck to his belief in *jeune école* strategies,"[119] and Samuel R. Williamson, in his verdict on Pelletan's regime, concludes that Pelletan's successor "was unable to correct immediately the damage wrought by Pelletan's application of the outdated ideas of the *jeune école* to naval strategy and socialism to naval shipyards."[120]

Pelletan had undoubtedly acquired a reputation as an advocate and supporter of the *jeune école* from his position in Parliament. Some of his most marked initiatives in Parliament on naval policy were perceived as *jeune école* policy. He was seen as an admirer of admiral Aube, and the *jeune école*'s expectations of Pelletan's ministry were high. It is, however, far from obvious that his policy as minister agreed with the naval theories of the *jeune école*. On the contrary, Pelletan's proposals and decisions as minister revealed that they were not governed by any coherent idea except by that of provoking his political enemies. His initiatives were primarily characterised by a will to remove what he saw as reactionary elements in the Navy, e.g. personnel, organisational structures or types of ships. His agenda seemed to be to remove what he disliked or perceived as anti-republican, and not to transform the French Navy according to any particular naval theory, be it the *jeune école* or any other.

Many of the initiatives and decisions made by Pelletan during his ministry had primarily a symbolic value. His willingness to democratize the Navy found its expression in the names he proposed for ships. Instead of giving new ships traditional names such as *Dupleix*, *Suffren*, and *Dupuy de Lôme* he gave the six battleships of the Programme of 1900 the names *Patrie*, *République*, *Démocratie*, *Justice*, *Vérité* and *Liberté*, and the armoured cruisers names like *Jules-Ferry*, *Léon-Gambetta*, *Victor-Hugo*, *Jules-Michelet*, *Ernest-Renan*, *Edgar-Quinet* and *Waldeck-Rousseau*. His "democratic disposition" was demonstrated in his personnel policy by favouring in principle young officers from modest backgrounds for promotion, and by discriminating systematically against well-known Catholics.[121]

---

[119] Walser: *France's Search for a Battle Fleet*, p. 113. Walser offers a more nuanced description of Pelletan's alleged *jeune école* ministry. He writes, for example, that: "Pelletan's interests were more administrative than naval, particularly if they involved budgetary reductions", and that "The Minister strengthened his controls over the administration by centralizing the authority of his office, but he failed to utilize his position for any specific military objectives." *Ibid.*, p. 116 and 122.

[120] Williamson Jr.: *The Politics of Grand Strategy*, p. 52.

[121] Masson: *Histoire de la Marine*, pp. 224–225; Motte: *Une éducation géostratégique*, pp. 363–365, Ropp: *The Development of a Modern Navy*, pp. 325–326.

Predictably Pelletan slowed down the construction of battleships. He resumed the construction of the old *jeune école* favourite, *torpilleurs numérotés*, small torpedo boats with a displacement of a little less than 100 tons. 88 of these torpedo boats were ordered. A Parliamentary select committee of inquiry stated in 1909 that the torpedo boats were too small, and the commander of the *défenses mobiles* argued that the 100-ton torpedo boats had poor seagoing qualities and were unable to fulfil their mission, not only in bad weather, but also during conditions that one should expect the boats to manage.[122] The *jeune école* had left the idea that small torpedo boats were perfect for an offensive strategy years before Pelletan's programme was conceived. The *jeune école* had realized in the mid-1890s that the boats' alleged seagoing quality, autonomy and invisibility were not as good as the most optimistic had hoped, and they concluded that the *torpilleurs numérotés* were best suited for defensive operations in coastal waters. It was cruisers and submarines that from the mid-1890s were the offensive weapon in *jeune école*'s strategy.

The progress in submarine construction led to a revival of the ideas of the *jeune école* simultaneously with Pelletan's period in office. Although Pelletan had expressed that he "believed in nothing but submarines",[123] his policy represented a veritable setback for French submarine construction. When Pelletan arrived in office, the French submarine fleet was the most numerous in the world. The French Navy had 14 submarines in service while 25 were under construction. The Royal Navy had nine and the US Navy had eight in service or under construction. No other navies had submarines in service yet.[124] Lanessan had in May 1902 ordered the construction of 13 submarines of the *Aigrette* class. A few months later, in September 1902, Pelletan annulled Lanessan's decision and only the two that were under construction were to be finished. Instead Pelletan ordered the construction of an experimental submarine. In late autumn 1903 Pelletan ordered six submarines of the *Emeraude-class*, which was of a more standard type. The Programme of 1904 planned the construction of two submarines of the *Circé-class*, ten submarines of the *Guêpe-class*, two modified *Émeraude-class* and another submarine with a displacement of only 21 tons that should be carried on board a battleship. The main effort in submarine construction was

---

[122] Masson: *Histoire de la Marine*, p. 195.
[123] Quoted in Motte: *Une éducation géostratégique*, p. 367.
[124] *Ibid.*, p. 367.

thus to be the ten *Guêpe-class* submarines. These miniscule submarines were only 20.50 meters long and had a displacement of 45 tons.[125]

Pelletan was Minister of Marine for two-and-a-half years. Lanessan was the only Minister of Marine who had occupied the post for a longer period than Pelletan during the Third Republic. Pelletan should thus have had time to start a reform of the French Navy and a construction programme in accordance with the *jeune école*'s naval theory. The construction programme under Pelletan was not characterised by any overall plan, nor did it seem to be in accordance with any naval theory. The French Navy in 1905 had thirty-nine submarines representing no less than 16 different classes. Pelletan was definitely not the only Minister of Marine responsible for this diversity, but his construction programmes did nothing to improve the situation.

Pelletan's construction programme did not reflect the offensive thinking that had been the most important characteristic of the *jeune école* theory ever since it was developed and elaborated by Aube and Charmes. It was the offensive capabilities that Fontin and Fournier, among others, underlined as the main characteristic of the submarine. The offensive capability and the relatively low costs made the submarine a natural heir to Aube's and Charmes's autonomous torpedo boats and Fournier's homogenous cruiser fleet, and explain why the *jeune école* embraced the submarine as a new weapon that would wrest its command of the seas from the Royal Navy. Pelletan's main project in terms of numbers of submarines was the small submarines of the *Guêpe-class*, which could hardly be said to have an offensive potential.[126] Pelletan's lack of interest in offensive warfare was underlined by his cancellation of 11 out of the 13 submarines that Lanessan had ordered of the *Aigrette-class*. The *Aigrette-class* had been conceived in order to operate from Toulon and be able to cruise off Taranto, the most southerly and most distant of the major Italian naval bases. Laubeuf, the constructor of the *Aigrette-class*, succeeded in installing a diesel engine on board the submarine, and thus increased the operational radius significantly in comparison with the steam engines that had been the alternative for

---

[125] Only a few of the submarines from the Programme of 1904 were actually built. Le Masson: *Du Nautilus (1800) au Redoutable*, pp. 169, 171–172, 395–397.

[126] Not more than two of the ten ordered submarines of the *Guêpe-class* submarines were put under construction. The whole project was cancelled as soon as Pelletan was out of office, and none of them were ever launched. *Ibid.*, pp. 396–397.

surfaced navigation up till then.[127] Whereas the steam engine-propelled submarines could have an operational radius when surfaced of up to 450 nautical miles, the *Aigrette-class* had an operational radius of 1300 nautical miles at eight knots. The *Aigrette-class* also proved to have good seakeeping qualities.[128]

Pelletan's submarine policy was far from that envisaged by Fontin and Fournier. Fournier characterised the cancelling of the *Aigrette-class* programme as a disastrous mistake.[129] The disappointment over Pelletan's policy was also straightforwardly expressed in the *jeune école* magazine, *La Marine Française*. The author, in order to emphasise the frustration with Pelletan's ministry, chose to underline that *jeune école* officers would enthusiastically welcome Pelletan's successor:

> One would have been very surprised if someone had told us some years ago that the day would come when the appointment of Mr. Gaston Thomson as minister would be viewed with satisfaction by the most faithful disciples of Admiral Aube. Some years ago, in fact, our friends put all their efforts in hoisting into power the hirsute rhetorician whose bohemian style seemed a proof of independence and whose prestigious eloquence gave such an illusion of a strong and conscious will to serve the purest patriotism [...].
>
> Yes, we were all there around 1901. It was what one in a familiar way would put as sticking one's finger in the eye all the way up to the elbow.
>
> Hardly had he occupied Colbert's seat than, Mr. Camille Pelletan, under several different equally unacknowledged pretexts, broke abruptly with the school of Admiral Aube [...].[130]

The *jeune école* supporters criticised the fact that Pelletan postponed the construction of the torpedo boats he had proclaimed to be of such importance to the French Navy, but there were decisions by Pelletan that were perceived to be worse:

> This [the postponement of the construction of the torpedo boats] was not all: He soon made a decision even more disastrous. By an astounding

---

[127] Diesel engines are still in use in modern conventional submarines.

[128] Le Masson: *Du Nautilus (1800) au Redoutable*, pp. 168–169, 174.

[129] This very blunt criticism of Pelletan's decision was addressed after Pelletan had resigned. It is not known whether Fournier presented his view to the Ministry of Marine while Pelletan still was in office. SHM, BB4-2437: Vice Admiral Fournier to the Minister of Marine: *Mesures préparatoires à prendre d'urgence dans la flotte française en prévision d'une brusque agression de l'Allemagne*, 18 January 1906.

[130] Charles Duffour: "Le ministère Pelletan" in *La Marine Française*, No. 161, 3ème série, (February 1905), pp. 57–58.

ignorance, he gave M. Thibaudier, the *directeur du materiel* at the Ministry of Marine, the order to stop the construction of the submarines that had just proved their capabilities in a series of exercises at sea, conscientiously supervised by Vice Admiral Fournier, Inspector General of the torpedo boat and the submarine flotillas.

The success of these practical exercises represented no less than the dawn of the revolution that could, and consequently, should be implemented for the greater profit and glory of France.[131]

The lack of an overall strategy that characterised the construction programmes during Pelletan's period as Minister of Marine was also reflected in Pelletan's view on training and military readiness. Pelletan, shortly after he was appointed minister, withdrew more than a third of all the complements from the Mediterranean Squadron in November for the winter season, thus rendering the ships ineffective for action. He argued that the Squadron did not need 8,000 men to stay "at anchor at Toulon or for cruising off the Riviera" which it allegedly had done for thirty years.[132] In December the Parliament unanimously resolved to make no reductions in the Mediterranean Squadron and the fleet was placed on a war footing as it had been in recent years.

Pelletan suppressed the annual fleet manoeuvres in the summer of 1903 due to financial constraints. It was Aube who first inaugurated major manoeuvres for the French Navy. While the *jeune école* had been eager to experiment and train to maintain professional standards, Pelletan revealed by his decisions a disinterest in the military value of training and of keeping a certain level of readiness. Pelletan's initiatives were characterised by a will to reduce costs and not by military objectives. As Ray Walser has noted, "Pelletan as naval minister minimized the role of the minister as a shaper of naval strategy" and "[he] quickly became involved in the minutiae of naval affairs, allowing naval policy to disintegrate into a series of ad hoc decisions."[133]

It is possible to identify at least three different reasons why the Pelletan ministry was labelled as a *jeune école* ministry, despite the fact that few, if any, of Pelletan's decisions found their rationale in the *jeune école*'s naval theory and that several of his initiatives were contrary to the ideas of

---

[131] Duffour: "Le ministère Pelletan", p. 59. The trials and the exercises that Dufour is referring to were conducted with the submarines of the *Sirène-class*. It was, however, the construction of the *Aigrette-class* that Pelletan stopped. See Henri Le Masson: *Du Nautilus (1800) au Redoutable*, pp. 173–174.
[132] Quoted in Marder: *The Anatomy of British Sea Power*, p. 470.
[133] Walser: *France's Search for a Battle Fleet*, p. 113.

the *jeune école*. First, the tendency to label Pelletan as a *jeune école* minister was due to some of the initiatives he took as Member of Parliament and the lip service he paid to the *jeune école*. This label stuck to him through his period as Minister of Marine despite the policy he led.

Secondly, there was a tendency during the Third Republic to politicise most decisions in the French Navy, including decisions within the administrative domain. Personnel administration was often politicised, and increasingly so after the Dreyfus affair. The *jeune école* was known to be in opposition to what was viewed as the naval establishment, and a system where elderly officers blocked the younger officers' possibilities for promotion and their prospects of having a command at what the younger officers saw as a reasonable age. French naval officers were among the oldest in Europe, mostly due to a higher age limit for mandatory retirement than in most other navies. The average age to obtain ranks was also significantly higher than in navies such as the British, German, Italian and Japanese. The problem was accentuated by the relatively late age when an officer reached the position of command and authority in the French Navy. In the Royal Navy, for example, an officer could command a major warship by his mid-thirties, while a French officer might not experience the same responsibility and challenges until his middle or late forties. The system also cemented a conservatism that blocked the influence of *jeune école* ideas. Ray Walser has shown how connections and conformity to the traditional patterns of the Navy were important for an officer who wished to retire in the senior ranks. Both Lockroy and Lanessan initiated administrative reforms of the promotion system.[134] Pelletan managed to express these questions in ideological terms, primarily by describing the personnel administration system as undemocratic.[135] Since these questions were given a high political profile, they have been perceived as an important part of *jeune école* theory, although these questions can hardly be said to have any significant relevance for the *jeune école* as a naval theory as such.

Thirdly, for Pelletan, the *jeune école* was a useful platform for attacks on political enemies. It created an impression that almost any proposal or decision was based on a coherent naval strategy and that the

---

[134] *Ibid.*, pp. 103–107.

[135] Philippe Masson has described how Pelletan introduced changes to the practices of personnel management in order to republicanise and democratise the French Navy. Masson: *Histoire de la Marine, Tome II*, p. 224.

adherents of the *jeune école* in the French Navy supported the proposals and decisions. The association with the *jeune école* thus added a certain legitimacy to Pelletan's politics.

Summary

The progress in submarine construction led to a revitalisation of the *jeune école* by the turn of the century. The leading *jeune école* officers and politicians had all the way from Aube's period as Minister of Marine encouraged and supported the development and construction of the torpedo-carrying submarine. Both Aube and Charmes had described the submarine as small vessels with the same potential as cruisers. Yet, even the most optimistic adherents of the *jeune école* viewed the submarine as a boat for defensive operations near home ports well into the 1890s. As the quality of the submarine, especially its operational range, rapidly improved, a trend could be seen developing among an increasing number of officers, not only in the French Navy, to appreciate the progress in submarine construction and their operational potential. The optimism was predictably more prevalent among the *jeune école* supporters than other officers. The *jeune école*'s arguments for a large-scale construction programme of submarines and a radical reduction in numbers of battleships resembled arguments from the heyday of the *jeune école* with its view on the potential of the torpedo boats. It was evident that the *jeune école* saw the submarine as the new, revolutionary weapon that would allow the French Navy to wrest the command of the seas from the Royal Navy at low cost. The proposed tactical and strategic use of the submarine was more or less a copy of Aube's and Charmes's visions for the use of the torpedo boat. The submarine had just replaced the torpedo boat as the most important asset needed to carry out the strategy of the *jeune école*.

While the progress of the operational performance of the submarine gave new life to the *jeune école*, the development in European security politics with changing alliances was the essential factor undermining the relevance of the *jeune école*'s strategy for the French Navy. The *jeune école* strategy was tailor-made for fighting Great Britain with its dependence on seaborne trade. The Fashoda crisis had for a time resolved the question of which enemy was the most probable, but the Entente Cordiale, signed in 1904, gradually removed the foreign policy conflict scenario that was a prerequisite for the *jeune école*'s strategic solutions. The Entente

Cordiale, which at the outset was limited to settling colonial disputes, also proved the *jeune école*'s fundamental assumption wrong, that rivalry in Africa and Asia would inevitably lead to a conflict between the two colonial powers, and that a *rapprochement* between them was unthinkable. In the first year or two after the Entente Cordiale was signed, a certain scepticism among French naval officers, and especially among the *jeune école* officers, was noticeable as to whether the agreement really represented an end to the rivalry and military tension between the two nations. Great Britain was by many French naval officers seen as France's hereditary enemy, and the Entente Cordiale was regarded as just another temporary truce between two nations with permanent conflicting interests that could re-emerge at any time. The French Navy should thus continue to plan with the Royal Navy as a possible enemy. The rapid expansion of the German Navy and the ambitious foreign policy of Germany gradually convinced also French naval officers that Great Britain was more likely to be an ally than an enemy in the foreseeable future. Even the supporters of the *jeune école* began to accept the realities of French foreign politics, and the *jeune école* as an alternative naval strategy for fighting a superior power soon lost ground. It was hard to sell a strategy for an inferior power as long as the relationship between France and the world's dominant naval power improved. Attacks on the enemy's sea lines of communication, which had been a cornerstone in the *jeune école*'s naval theory, lost much of its relevance as a strategy when Germany appeared as the most probable enemy.

The influence on the *jeune école* of these two fundamental developments, the progress of the operational performances of the submarine and the shifting alliances in European politics, have undeservedly been overshadowed in historical research by the focus on the ministry of Camille Pelletan as more or less the only manifestation of the *jeune école* in the post-Fashoda period. The focus on Pelletan's period as Minister of Marine as a kind of comeback for the *jeune école* in French naval politics is somewhat surprising since most historians have emphasised the more bizarre decisions made by Pelletan in their presentation of his contribution to French naval politics. One should expect that the very fact that Pelletan's politics were inconsistent, demagogic and somewhat out of the ordinary would have raised questions as to whether one should take his word for it and accept that his politics were in accordance with any naval theory. A closer look at Pelletan's politics reveals that his decisions in important areas were contrary to the *jeune école*'s strategic thinking.

Two of Pelletan's decisions regarding the construction program could be interpreted as being in accordance with the *jeune école*'s strategy. He resumed the construction of torpedo boats and slowed down the construction programme for battleships. Torpedoes carried aboard torpedo boats had indeed in the 1880s and early 1890s been viewed by the *jeune école* as the most effective weapon to conduct offensive warfare against Great Britain. The *jeune école* had, however, by the mid-1890s realized that the torpedo boats of the size ordered by Pelletan did not have the seakeeping qualities and the necessary autonomy to conduct offensive operations. These torpedo boats were primarily suited for defensive operations. Cruisers and submarines carrying torpedoes had replaced the torpedo boats as the most valuable assets in the *jeune école*'s strategy. Pelletan chose to cancel the construction of the *Aigrette* class submarines ordered by Lanessan, except for the two that were under construction. These submarines were designed to operate in an offensive role. Pelletan chose to pursue a construction programme comprising smaller or even miniscule submarines with little or no offensive capacity.

Pelletan's reduction in the number of battleships could in itself be seen as part of the *jeune école*'s strategy, but he failed to replace the battleships' offensive capacity with other naval assets. Pelletan's initiatives were characterised by a will to reduce costs and not to follow or shape any naval strategy. Although the *jeune école* had great expectations towards Pelletan as Minister of Marine, they soon expressed their disappointment at his priorities. Their main complaint was that Pelletan ignored the importance of offensive capabilities, especially as it could be found in the submarine.

CONCLUSION

Anglo-American theoreticians have to a large degree dominated the forming and studies of modern naval strategy in Western countries. Geoffrey Till, in *Seapower—A Guide for the Twenty-First Century*, ascribes the modern dominance of Mahan (American) and Corbett (British) in maritime thinking to their conceptual insight, but he underlines that it is also a consequence of the maritime power their countries represented and the fact that they wrote in the most accessible of the world's languages.[1] The Anglo-American dominance has to a large extent resulted in a focus on how the superior power should exploit his superiority in order to reach his strategic aims. Naval power should be used to establish command of the seas, which in turn would secure own trade and open up for attacks on enemy trade and operations against enemy shores.

At first sight the *jeune école* differs from the dominant maritime strategies by being a strategy for the inferior power. The *jeune école* is not the only maritime strategy dealing with dilemmas of the weaker. Generally, one can divide the inferior powers' strategies into two broad categories. In the first category we find navies that choose a force structure reflecting that of the major sea power. The fleets are smaller than that of the competing power due to economic and political restraints.[2] Mahan, who is considered as the foremost advocate of the importance of command of the seas, did not view the smaller navies as powerless. He claimed that smaller navies could represent a threshold that could deter larger navies from aggressive actions:

> it is not necessary to have a navy equal to the greatest, in order to insure that sense of fear which deters a rival from war, or handicaps a rival from war [...]. A much smaller force, favourably placed, produces an effect far beyond its proportionate numbers [...].[3]

---

[1] Till: *Seapower*, p. 35.
[2] The inferior fleets can of course be superior to other potential enemies, like we have seen in the discussion in the French Navy concerning the potential enemies Great Britain or the Triple Alliance.
[3] Quoted in Till: *Seapower*, p. 41.

Tirpitz' naval plan and his "risk theory" is in many ways the foremost example of an inferior naval power copying the fleet structure of a superior rival, but accepting that it will not be able to outnumber it. Tirpitz had in the mid-1890s maintained, in accordance with Aube, that an inferior fleet could accomplish very little. A decade later he had changed his mind and declared that an inferior fleet at least two-thirds of the size of the British would be a "risk fleet" which could deter London from declaring war on Berlin, no matter how serious the conflict of interest between them might become.[4]

The second category is coastal defence theory.[5] Coastal defence has very often been the form of maritime operations given priority in weaker navies. The United States in the nineteenth century constructed a chain of fortifications along its eastern coast and combined these defensive measures with minefields and smaller vessels built for coastal operations. Both the Soviet and the Chinese navies have, depending on shifting strategic ambitions, vacillated between the two above-mentioned options for the weaker navy. The Norwegian and Swedish navies of the last half of the twentieth century are probably the European navies that best represent the ideal type of a pure coastal navy with an elaborate system of coastal artillery, minefields, fast torpedo boats[6] and small coastal submarines. The idea is to avoid challenging the superior navy where it is strongest, but to choose an approach favouring the defender where he can benefit from the topography of the coast and weapon systems suited for coastal warfare (e.g. minefields, shore based artillery and fast, small vessels).

The defensive measures proposed by the *jeune école* fit well into the coastal defence theory. The *jeune école* theory describes a sophisticated coastal defence where torpedo boats and gunboats operate from bases and havens guided by telegraph and semaphores in a coordinated war of concentration, dispersion and reconcentration. These defensive measures were to protect French territory, but as important, they were a prerequisite for the cornerstone of the *jeune école* theory: offensive operations against the enemy's trade. It is in the offensive use of naval forces that the *jeune école* differs from other strategies of the weak. While the traditionally composed "risk fleet" and the coastal defence theory

---

[4] Hobson: *Imperialism at Sea*, pp. 366–370.
[5] The concept "Coastal defence theory" is used by Tiller: *Seapower*, pp. 62–66.
[6] The torpedo boats were equipped with short- to medium-range surface-to-surface missiles from the 1970s.

have as their main objective to deter or eventually challenge the *naval forces* of the superior opposing power, the *jeune école* maintains that the war should be brought to the very heart of the enemy, not by attacking the enemy's navy, but by attacking the undefended foundations of its wealth.

The idea that the French Navy should attack the foundations of British prosperity instead of challenging a superior Royal Navy on its own terms was coupled with another idea that distinguishes the *jeune école* from most, if not all, other naval theories: their views on international law and what they perceived as the changing character of war. Aube had from as early as 1871 consistently argued that international law must be subordinated to the demands of war. The aim of war is to weaken the enemy by all means, Aube argued, and "everything is [...] not only permissible but legitimate against the enemy."[7] The *jeune école*'s reasoning on international law and the nature of future wars was influenced by the American Civil War and the Franco-Prussian War which both featured elements of total war. They were convinced that the nature of war was changing and that future wars would be existential wars with full economic and political mobilisation of the society. They were confident that future wars would have a character where the economic resources of the enemy and the popular support for the war rather than its armed forces alone would be targeted, and that this would blur the distinction between combatants and non-combatants. This view of the character of future wars allowed for the extreme form of commercial warfare that Charmes so succinctly summed up when he stated that "Commerce warfare has its rules that one should have the courage to express clearly: attack the weak without mercy and sail away at full speed from the stronger without shame, that is the formula."[8]

The openness and continuous search for technological innovations that could fit into the overall theory is another characteristic of the *jeune école*. The solutions searched for should help to balance Royal Navy's superiority and make offensive war against British trade more effective. The *jeune école* looked for naval vessels that could break enemy blockades and operate autonomously on the high seas destroying enemy trade. The preferred solutions varied during the 30–40 years when the *jeune école* represented a distinct alternative in French naval thought. The

---

[7] Aube: "Défense nationale—Défense des colonies", p. 11.
[8] Charmes: "La réforme maritime II", p. 141.

jeune école's embrace of technological inventions left an impression that its thinking was primarily a result or an adaptation to technological developments. Consequently, the *jeune école* has been characterised as a pronounced exponent of the materialist school within naval strategy. This school argued that strategy changed constantly as the weapons and other material conditions of warfare changed, while the historical school, exemplified by Mahan, claimed that strategic principles could be distilled from historic experience and that these principles were unchanging.[9]

The *jeune école* did indeed believe that technological developments had consequences, not only for tactics, but also for strategy. Aube maintained that the steamship had made blockade ineffective, and with the advent of the self-propelled torpedo he claimed that no naval power would dare to try to impose a close blockade. These developments made him reject the idea of the decisive battle: "the most decisive victory will only give the winning nation sterile glory and no other advantage than the more or less complete destruction of the defeated fleet."[10] It would not secure the command of the seas. Aube, Charmes and Fournier all made occasional statements in which they claimed that the advent of the steamship, the self-propelled torpedo, the autonomous torpedo boat or the submarine had revolutionised naval warfare and more or less changed it for the future. This sporadic euphoria, however, gradually faded away, giving way to a more general recognition that the principles of maritime warfare that could be deduced from a study of history were being qualified by the technological change of the late nineteenth century. It did not render strategic principles based on historic experience irrelevant.

Another characteristic of the *jeune école* was that most of its prominent representatives held influential positions in the French Navy. They were at the same time both theoreticians and practicians, and the organisation of the French Navy, tactical dispositions and technological possibilities were continuously evaluated and adapted as experience dictated in order to most effectively conduct maritime war according to the overall principles that the theory prescribed. The French Navy did not fight any war following the theory of the *jeune école*. The war at sea during

---

[9] Eugenia C. Kiesling: Introduction to Raoul Castex: "Strategic Theories" in John B. Hattendorf and Wayne P. Hughes, Jr. (eds.): *Classics of Sea Power* (Annapolis, Maryland, 1994), p. xiv; Coutau-Bégarie: *La puissance maritime*, pp. 62–65.

[10] Aube: "L'avenir de la Marine française", p. 190.

1914–1918, however, turned out to confirm some of the *jeune école*'s predictions. The inferior battle fleet's reluctance to go to sea to challenge the superior fleet's command of the sea, the torpedoes' and the mines' deterrent effect on battle fleets, and the inferior navy's resort to *guerre de course à outrance* represented by the German Navy's unlimited submarine warfare are significant examples of what the *jeune école* envisaged would be characteristics of future naval wars. Coteau-Bégarie has noted that "the fault of Aube was perhaps to be right too early [...]."[11]

---

[11] Coutau-Bégarie: *La puissance maritime*, p. 66.

APPENDIX

MINISTERS OF MARINE 1870–1914

4 September 1870:	Martin Fourichon, Vice Admiral
19 February 1871:	Louis-Pierre-Alexis Pothau, Vice Admiral
25 May 1873:	Charles-Marius-Albert de Dompierre d'Hornoy, Vice Admiral
22 May 1874:	Marquis Louis-Raymond de Montaignac de Chauvance, Rear Admiral
9 March 1876:	Martin Fourichon, Vice Admiral and also Senator from 16 May 1877
23 May 1877:	Albert-Auguste Gicquel des Touches, Vice Admiral
23 November 1877:	Albert-Edmond-Louis baron Roussin, Vice Admiral
13 December 1877:	Louis-Pierre-Alexis Pothau, Vice Admiral, and Senator
4 February 1879:	Jean-Bernard Jauréguiberry, Vice Admiral, and Senator
23 September 1880:	Georges-Charles Cloué, Vice Admiral
14 November 1881:	August Gougeard, Captain and *conseiller d'État*
30 January 1882:	Jean-Bernard Jauréguiberry, Vice Admiral and Senator
31 January 1883:	François-Césaire de Mahy, Minister of Agriculture functioning interim as Minister of Marine
21 February 1883:	Charles-Marie Brun, Senator
9 August 1883:	Alexandre-Louis-François Peyron, Vice Admiral
April 1885:	Charles-Eugène Galiber, Rear Admiral
January 1886:	Hyacinthe-Laurent-Théophile Aube, Rear Admiral, promoted to Vice Admiral
13 December 1886:	Hyacinthe-Laurent-Théophile Aube, Vice Admiral
13 May 1887:	Édouard Barbey, Senator
2 December 1887:	François-Césaire de Mahy, Member of Parliament
January 1888:	Jules-François-Émile Krantz, Vice Admiral
22 February 1889:	Constant-Louis-Benjamin Jaurés, Vice Admiral and Senator
9 March 1889:	Jules-François-Émile Krantz, Vice Admiral
10 November 1889:	Édouard Barbey, Senator
27 February 1892:	Godefroy Cavaignac, Member of Parliament
12 July 1892:	A. Burdeau, Member of Parliament
11 January 1893:	Ribot, Member of Parliament, Minister of Internal Affairs, and Prime Minister functioning interim as Minister of Marine
12 January 1893:	Adrien-Barthélemy-Louis Rieunier, Vice Admiral
3 December 1893:	August-Alfred Lefèvre, Vice Admiral
30 May 1894:	Felix Fauré, Member of Parliament

19 January 1895:	Ch. Dupuy, Member of Parliament, Minister of Internal Affairs Religion, and Prime Minister functioning interim as Minister of Marine
26 January 1895:	Trarieux, Senator and Minister of Justice functioning interim as Minister of Marine
28 January 1895:	Armand-Louis-Charles Gustave Besnard, Vice Admiral
1 November 1895:	Édouard Lockroy, Member of Parliament
29 April 1896:	Armand-Louis-Charles Gustave Besnard, Vice Admiral
28 June 1898:	Édouard Lockroy, Member of Parliament
22 June 1899:	De Lanessan, Member of Parliament
7 June 1902:	Camille Pelletan, Member of Parliament
24 January 1905:	Gaston Thomson, Member of Parliament
14 March 1906:	Gaston Thomson, Member of Parliament
25 October 1906:	Gaston Thomson, Member of Parliament
22 October 1908:	Alfred Picard, *Président de Section au Conseil d'État*
24 July 1909:	Augustin-Emmanuel-Hubert-Gaston-Marie Boué de Laperyrère, Vice Admiral
3 November 1910:	Augustin-Emmanuel-Hubert-Gaston-Marie Boué de Laperyrère, Vice Admiral
2 March 1911:	Théophile Delcassée, Member of Parliament
14 January 1912:	Théophile Delcassée, Member of Parliament
21 January 1913:	Pierre Baudin, Senator
9 December 1913:	Monis, Senator
10 June 1914:	Chautemps, Member of Parliament
13 June 1914:	Gauthier, Senator
26 August 1914:	Victor Augagneur, Member of Parliament

BIBLIOGRAPHY

Andrew, Christopher: *Théophile Delcassé and the Making of the Entente Cordiale* (London, 1968).
———: "The Entente Cordiale from its Origins to 1914" in Neville Waits (ed.): *Troubled Neighbours* (London, 1971).
Aube, Théophile. ("Un officier de marine"): "Les réformes de notre marine militaire" in *Revue des deux mondes* (Paris, April 1871).
———: "De la guerre maritime" in *Revue Maritime et Coloniale* (Paris, April 1873).
———: "L'avenir de la Marine française" in *Revue des deux mondes* (Paris, 1 July 1874).
———: "Un nouveau droit maritime international" in *Revue maritime et coloniale* (Paris, January–March 1875).
———: "La guerre maritime et les ports militaires de la France" in *Revue des deux mondes* (Paris, 1882).
———: "Italie et Levant" in *A terre et à bord. Notes d'un marin* (Paris, 1884).
———: "La pénétration dans l'Afrique centrale" in *A terre et à bord. Notes d'un marin* (1884).
———: *A terre et à bord. Notes d'un marin* (Paris, 1884).
———: "Défense nationale—Défense des colonies" in Henri Mager (ed.): *Atlas Colonial* (Paris, 1885).
Ausseur, Philippe: "La *jeune école*" in Service historique de la Marine: *Marine & Technique au XIXe siècle* (Paris, 1987).
Beeler, John F.: *British Naval Policy in the Gladstone—Disraeli Era 1866–1880* (Stanford, Ca., 1997).
Berg, Roald: *Profesjon-union-nasjon, 1814–1905*, Vol. II of *Norsk forsvarshistorie* (Bergen, 2001).
Boemeke, Manfred F., Chickering, Roger, and Förster, Stig (eds.): *Anticipating Total War. The German and American Experiences 1871–1914* (Cambridge, 1999).
Bourgois, Vice-amiral: *Les torpilleurs, la guerre navale et la défense des côtes* (Paris, 1888).
Brière, Paul: *Le Vice-Amiral Fournier. Marin, diplomate, savant* (Mayenne, 1931).
Broche, François: *La IIIe Rèpublique 1870–1895 de Thiers á Casimir-Perier* (Paris, 2001).
Bueb, Volkmar: *Die "Junge Schule" der französischen Marine. Strategie und Politik 1875–1900* (Boppard am Rhein, 1971).
Castex, Raoul: *Théories stratégiques, Tome premier* (Paris, 1929).
———: "Strategic Theories" in John B Hattendorf and Wayne P. Hughes, Jr. (eds.): *Classics of Sea Power* (Annapolis, Maryland, 1994).
Ceillier, Marie-Raymond (1928): "Les idées stratégiques en France de 1870 à 1914: La Jeune Ecole" in Coutau-Bégarie (ed.): *L'Evolution de la pensée navale* (Paris, 1990).
Charmes, Gabriel: "Préface" in Aube: *A terre et à bord. Notes d'un marin* (1884).
———: "La réforme de la Marine I. Torpilleurs et cannonières", in *Revue des deux mondes* (Paris, 15 December 1884).
———: "La réforme maritime II. La guerre maritime er l'organisation des forces navales" in *Revues des deux mondes* (Paris, 1 March 1885).
———: *Les torpilleurs autonomes et l'avenir de la marine* (Paris, 1885).
———: *La réforme de la Marine* (Paris, 1886).
Chassériaud, André-Henri: "Torpilleur et Torpilles" in *Nouvelle Revue* (Paris, 1 January 1885).
———: "La guerre navale par escadres cuirassées" in *Nouvelle Revue* (Paris, Vol. 33, 1885).

—— (*Un ancien officier de marine*): "La Torpille et le droit des gens. Réponse à M. le vice-amiral Bourgois" in *Nouvelle Revue* (Paris, Vol. 40, 1886).
Chickering, Roger: "Are We There Yet? World War II and the Theory of Total War." Paper presented at the International Conference at Hamburg, August 29–September 1, 2001: *A World at Total War. Global Conflict and the Politics of Destruction, 1937–1945.*
Clausewitz, Carl von (Michael Howard and Peter Paret eds.): *On War* (Princeton, N.J., 1976).
Colomb P.H.: "Naval Reform" in *Occasional papers. Journal of Royal United Service Institution* (1887).
Commandant Z and H. Montéchant: *Les guerres navales de demain* (Paris, 1891).
——: *Essai de stratégie navale* (Paris, 1893).
Coutau-Bégarie, Hervé: *La puissance maritime. Castex et la stratégie navale* (Paris, 1885).
Coutau-Bégarie, Hervé ed.: *L'évolution de la pensée navale* (Paris, 1990).
——: *L'évolution de la pensée navale*, II (Paris, 1992).
——: *L'évolution de la pensée navale*, IV (Paris, 1994).
Darrieus, Gabriel: *La guerre sur mer. Stratégie et Tactique. La doctrine* (Paris, 1907).
Duffour, Charles: "Le ministère Pelletan" in *La Marine Française*, No. 161, 3ème Série, (February 1905).
Epkenhans, Michael: "Technology, Shipbuilding and Future Combat in Germany, 1880–1914" in O'Brien (ed.): *Technology and Naval Combat in the Twentieth Century and Beyond* (London, 2001).
Feldbæk, Ole: "Denmark—Norway 1720–1807: Neutral Principles and Practice" in Hobson and Kristiansen (eds): *Navies in Northern Waters 1721–2000* (London, 2004).
Fontin, Paul: *Les sous-marins et l'Angleterre* (Paris, 1902).
Förster, Stig and Jörg Nagler (eds.): *On the Road to Total War. The American Civil War and the German Wars of Unification 1861–1871* (Washington, 1997).
Förster, Stig: "Dreams and Nightmares. German Military Leadership and the Images of Future Warfare, 1871–1914" in Boemeke, Chickering and Förster (eds.): *Anticipating Total War. The German and American Experiences 1871–1914* (Cambridge, 1999).
Fournier, F.E.: *La Flotte nécessaire. Ses avantages stratégiques, tactiques et économiques* (Paris, 1896).
Fournier, Vice-admiral: *La Politique Navale et la Flotte Française* (Paris, 1910).
Friedberg, Aaron L.: *The Weary Titan. Britain and the Experience of Relative Decline, 1895–1905* (Princeton, New Jersey, 1988).
Garelli, François: *Histoire des relations Franco-Italiennes* (Paris, 1999).
Garrigues, Jean: *Le général Boulanger* (Paris, 1999).
Gat, Azar: *The Development of Military Thought. The Nineteenth Century* (Oxford, 1992).
Gooch, John: *The Prospect of War. Studies in British Defence Policy 1847–1942* (London, 1981).
Greene, Jack and Alessandro Massignani: *Ironclads at War. The Origin and Development of the Armored Warship, 1854–1891* (Pennsylvania, 1998).
Grivel, Richild: *De la guerre maritime avant et depuis les nouvelles inventions. Attaque et défense des côtes et des ports. Guerre du large. Etude historique et stratégique* (Paris, 1869).
Guiomar, Jean-Yves: *L'Invention de la guerre totale* (Paris, 2004).
Hamilton, C.I.: "Anglo-French sea power and the Declaration of Paris" in *The international history review, IV* (Victoria, B.C., 2 May 1982).
——: *Anglo-French Naval Rivalry 1840–1870* (Oxford, 1993).
Hattendorf, John B.: "Maritime Conflict" in Howard, Andreopoulos, and Shulman (eds.): *The Laws of War. Constraints on Warfare in the Western World* (New Haven, 1994).
Hattendorf, John B. and Hughes Jr., Wayne P. (eds.): *Classics of Sea Power* (Annapolis, Maryland, 1994).
Hobsbawm, E.J.: *Industry and Empire. An Economic History of Britain since 1750* (London, 1968).

Hobson, Rolf: "Fra kabinettkrigen til den totale krigen. Clausewitz-tolkninger fra Moltke til Aron" in *Forsvarsstudier*, 6 (Oslo, 1996).
———: *Imperialism at Sea, Naval Strategic Thought, the Ideology of Sea Power and the Tirpitz Plan, 1875–1914* (Trondheim, 1999).
Hobson, Rolf and Kristiansen, Tom (eds.): *Navies in Northern Waters 1721–2000* (London, 2004).
Howard, Michael: *War in European History* (Oxford, 1976).
Howard, Michael, Andreopoulos, George J., and Shulman, Mark R. (eds.): *The Laws of War. Constraints on Warfare in the Western World* (New Haven, 1994).
Jessup, Philip C. and Deák, Francis: *Neutrality. Its History, Economics and Law*. Volume I: "The origins" (1935, New York, 1976).
Johnson, James Turner: *Just War Traditions and the Restraint of War. A Moral and Historical Inquiry* (Princeton, N.J., 1981).
Keiger, John F.V.: *France and the Origins of The First World War* (Houndmills, 1983).
Kennedy, Paul: *The Rise and Fall of British Naval Mastery* (1976, London, 1983).
———: *The Rise of the Anglo-German Antagonism 1860–1914* (London, 1980).
Kiesling, Eugenia C.: Introduction to Raoul Castex: "Strategic Theories" in John B. Hattendorf and Wayne P. Hughes, Jr. (eds.): *Classics of Sea Power* (Annapolis, Maryland, 1994).
Kulsrud, Carl J.: *Maritime Neutrality to 1780. A History of the Main Principles Governing Neutrality and Belligerency to 1780* (Boston, 1936).
Lambert, Andrew: *The Crimean War. British Grand Strategy, 1853–1856* (Manchester, 1990).
Lambert, Nicholas A.: *Sir John Fisher's Naval Revolution* (Columbia, South Carolina, 1999).
Lambi, Ivo Nikolai: *The Navy and German Power Politics, 1862–1914* (Boston, 1984).
Lanessan, J.-L. de: *Histoire de l'entente cordiale franco-anglaise* (Paris, 1916).
Lecalve, Franck and Roche, Jean-Michel: *Liste des bâtiments de la flotte de guerre française, de 1700 à nos jours* (La Société Française d'Histoire Maritime, October 2001).
Le Masson, Henri: *Histoire du torpilleur en France* (Paris, 1968).
———: *Du Nautilus (1800) au Redoutable (Histoire critique du sous-marin dans la marine française)* (Paris, 1969).
Le Roy, Antoine-Auguste: "Rapport de mer du torpilleur 61. Le lieutenant de vaisseau Le Roy commandant le torpilleur 61 à M. le vice-amiral, Préfet maritime à Toulon", in *Revue maritime et coloniale* (Paris, 1886).
Lieutenant X: Introduction to Commandant Z and H. Montéchant: *Essai de stratégie navale* (Paris, 1893).
Lockroy, Edouard: *La marine de guerre. Six mois rue Royale* (Paris, 1897).
———: *La défense navale* (Paris, 1900).
Luntinen, Pertti: *French Information on the Russian War Plans 1880–1914* (Jyväskylässä, 1984).
Luttwak, Edward and Stuart L. Koehl: *The Dictionary of Modern War* (New York, 1991).
Mager, Henri ed.: *Atlas Colonial* (Paris, 1885).
Marder, Arthur J.: *The Anatomy of British Sea Power. A History of British Naval Policy in the Pre-Dreadnought Era, 1880–1905* (New York, 1940).
Masson, Philippe: *Histoire de la Marine, Tome II. De la vapeur à l'atome* (Paris, 1992).
———: "La Marine Française de 1871 à 1914" in Pedroncini, Guy (ed.): *Histoire militaire de la France, Vol. 3, De 1871 à 1940* (Paris, 1992).
Masson, Renée: *La Marine Française lors de la crise de Fachoda (1898–1899). D.E.S. d'histoire, Université de Paris, Faculté des Lettres* (Paris, 1955).
Mathias, Peter: *The First Industrial Nation. An Economic History of Britain, 1700–1914* (London, 1969).

May, Ernest R. (ed.): *Knowing One's Enemies. Intelligence Assessment before the Two World Wars* (Princeton, New Jersey, 1984).
McPherson, James M.: *Battle Cry of Freedom, The Civil War Era* (New York, 1988).
——: "From Limited War to Total War in America", in Förster and Nagler (eds.): *On the Road to Total War. The American Civil War and the German Wars of Unification 1861–1871* (Washington, 1997).
Miquel, Pierre: *La Troisième république* (Paris, 1989).
Modelski, George and Thompson, William R.: *Seapower in Global Politics, 1494–1993* (London, 1988).
Monaque, Remi: "L'amiral Aube, ses idées, son action" in Coutau-Bégarie (ed.): *L'évolution de la pensée navale*, IV (Paris, 1994).
Morris, A.J.A.: *The Scaremongers. The Advocacy of War and Rearmament 1896–1914* (London, 1984).
Motte, Martin: *Une éducation géostratégique. La pensée navale française, de la jeune école à l'entre-deux guerres. Thèse d'Histoire pour obtenir le grade de docteur de l'Université Paris IV* (Paris, 2001).
Neely Jr., Mark E.: "Was the Civil War a Total War?" in Förster and Jörg (eds.): *On the Road to Total War. The American Civil War and the German Wars of Unification 1861–1871* (Washington, 1997).
Neton, Albéric: *Delcassé (1852–1923)* (Paris, 1952).
O'Brien, Phillips Payson (ed.): *Technology and Naval Combat in the Twentieth Century and Beyond* (London, 2001).
Offer, Avner: *The First World War: An Agrarian Interpretation* (Oxford, 1991).
Phillips, W. Allison and Reede, Arthur H.: *Neutrality. Its History, Economics and Law. Volume II. The Napoleonic Period* (1936, New York, 1976).
Réveillère, Contre-amiral: Introduction to Commandant Z and H. Montéchant: *Les guerres navales de demain* (Paris, 1891).
Roberts, Stephen Shepard: *Warships and Politicians. The Effect on Politics on French Naval Preparedness, 1886–1900.* Thesis for the degree Bachelor of Art submitted to the Department of History (Harvard University, 1965).
Ropp, Theodore: *The Development of a Modern Navy. French Naval Policy 1871–1904* (Annapolis, Maryland, 1987).
Rothenberg, Gunther: "The Age of Napoleon" in Howard, Andreopoulos, and Shulman, (eds.): *The Laws of War. Constraints on Warfare in the Western World* (New Haven, 1994).
Røksund, Arne: "The Jeune École: The Strategy of the Weak" in Hobson and Kristiansen (eds.): *Navies in Northern Waters* (London, 2004).
Pedroncini, Guy (ed.): *Histoire militiare de la France, Vol. 3, De 1871 à 1940* (Paris, 1992).
Service historique de la Marine: *Marine & Technique au XIXe siècle* (Paris, 1987).
Saint-André, Ernest du Pin de: "La question des torpilleurs (II). Torpilleurs et batimens (sic) de guerre et de commerce" in *Revue des deux mondes* (Paris, 15 July 1886).
Sondhaus, Lawrence: *Naval Warfare 1815–1914* (London, 2001).
Steiner, Zara S. and Neilson, Keith: *Britain and the Origins of the First World War* (Houndmills, 2003).
Sowerwine, Charles: *France since 1870. Culture, Politics and Society* (Houndmills, 2001).
Symcox, Geoffrey: *The Crisis of French Sea Power 1688–1697. From the Guerre d'escadre to the Guerre de course* (The Hague, 1974).
Taillemite, Etienne: "L'opinion française et la *jeune école*" in Service historique de la Marine: *Marine & Technique au XIXe siècle* (Paris, 1987).
—— (1992): "Un théoricien méconnu de la guerre maritime: L'amiral Richild Grivel", in Coutau-Bégarie (ed.): *L'évolution de la pensée navale*, II (Paris, 1992).

Tanenbaum, Jan Karl: "French Estimates of Germany's Operational War Plans" in Ernest R. May (ed.): *Knowing One's Enemies. Intelligence Assessment before the Two World Wars* (Princeton, New Jersey, 1984).
Teyssier, Arnaud: *La IIIe Rèpublique 1895–1919 de Félix Faure à Clemenceau* (Paris, 2001).
Till, Geoffrey *Seapower. A Guide for the Twenty-First Century* (London, 2004).
Tombs, Robert: "The Wars against Paris", in Förster and Nagler (eds.): *On the Road to Total War. The American Civil War and the German Wars of Unification 1861–1871* (Washington, 1997).
——: *France 1814–1914* (Harlow, England, 1996).
Waits, Neville (ed.): *Troubled Neighbours* (London, 1971).
Walser, Ray: *France's Search for a Battle Fleet. Naval Policy and Naval Power, 1898–1914* (New York and London, 1992).
Williamson, Jr., Samuel R.: *The Politics of Grand Strategy. Britain and France Prepare for War, 1904–1914* (1969, London—Atlantic Highlands, NJ, 1990).
Zorgbibe, Charles: *Théophile Delcassé. Le grand Ministre des Affaires étrangères de la IIIe République* (Paris, 2001).

INDEX

Agadir Crisis 188
Aigrette-class 217–18
Ajaccio 68, 71, 74, 169, 192
Alabama 19, 60
Algeria 62, 68, 72, 75, 104, 133, 169, 187, 211
Alquier, Admiral 90
American Civil War 9, 12, 18–19, 26–27, 38, 45–47, 51, 99, 227
André, General 214
Archibald, Douglas 204
Aubry, Commander 197, 198
Augusta 19–20, 60
Austria 2, 23, 55, 212

Bacon, Reginald 205
Ballard, George Alexander 126
Barbey, Edouard 116
Barbier, Edouard 77
Barréra, Admiral 91, 180
Bart, Jean 15, 16
Besnard, Admiral Armand-Louis-Charles-Gustave 111–12, 136, 146–47
Bismarck, Otto von 46, 54, 93, 130
Bizerte 168–69
Boer war 177–78, 183, 185
Bouet-Willaumez, Admiral Louis-Edouard 129
Boulanger, General Georges 54, 61, 82
Bourgeois, Léon xiii, 85, 111, 133
Bourgois, Admiral 25–27, 31–32, 34, 49, 121, 127, 130, 140
Brandenburg 92
Brest 14–15, 20, 61–63, 67, 76–78, 83, 86, 89–90, 122–23, 146, 152, 153, 167–68, 170–71, 180, 192–93, 210
Brière, Sous-commisaire 127–29
Burgoyne, General 181, 182

Caprivi, Leo 93–95, 102
Carnot, Lazare 40
Castex, Admiral Raoul xiii–xv, xvii
Ceillier, Marie-Raymond xv

Charmes, Gabriel xii, xvi, 1, 7, 11, 64, 79, 85, 105, 107, 119
Chassériaud, André-Henri 31–34, 70, 72
Cherbourg 63, 83, 123, 168, 193, 199
Chickering, Robert 37
Circé-class 216
Clausewitz, Carl von 44–45, 47, 98
Colomb, P.H. 1
Colston, Admiral Brown de 71–73, 76
Combes, Emilie 214
Commandant Z 97–108, 110, 125, 137–39, 195–96, 198, 207
Corbett, Julian 225
Council of Admiralty 51, 53, 55–58, 63, 77, 79–84, 87
Coutau-Bégarie, Hervé xv
Crimean War 2, 26, 59, 129
Crispi, Francesco 159
Cuverville, Admiral Cavalier de 180

Darrieus, Captain Gabriel 181, 191, 202–203
Davin, Captain 179, 197
Declaration of Brussels 128
Declaration of Paris 24–29, 45, 51, 100, 118, 125, 198
Degouy, Commander 121–27, 154, 159
Delcassé, Théophile 144
Démocratie 215
Denmark 43, 89
D'Entrecasteaux 136
Douhet, Giulio 36
Dunkirk 15, 90, 123, 169, 181
Dupleix 215
Dupuy de Lôme 116, 135, 146, 215

Edgar-Quinet 215
Egypt 144, 168, 172, 187–88, 201, 209
Emeraude-class 216
Entente Cordiale xiii, 177, 181, 183, 187–88, 202, 204–205, 209–10, 221–22
Ernest-Renan 215

Fashoda Crisis xiii, 86–87, 91–92, 96, 109–10, 112, 118, 130, 143, 145, 147, 149, 151–55, 157, 159–61, 163, 165, 167, 169, 171–75, 177, 179, 211, 221
Ferry, Jules 143, 215
First World War xiii, 143
Fisher, Sir John 205, 210
Fontin, Paul 97, 198–99, 217–18
Fournier, Admiral Francois-Ernest 85, 111, 113–18, 121, 125, 130–33, 135–36, 138, 140, 143, 147, 151–55, 165, 167, 179–80, 194–95, 199–203, 205–208, 210–11, 217–19, 228
Franco-Chinese war 126
Franco-Prussian War 2, 19, 25, 39, 46–48, 50–51, 54–55, 59–60, 95, 99, 129, 179, 227
Fredrick the Great 39
Freycinet, Charles Louis de Saulces de 53, 144
Friant 146
Friedberg, Aaron L. 185
Förster, Stig 46

Galiber, Charles-Eugéne 194
Gambetta, Léon 143, 215
German Wars of Unification 38
Gervais, Admiral Alfred-Albert 89, 194
Goblet, René xiii, 53, 85
Goltz, Colmar von der 48–49, 98–99, 130
Gooch, John 181–82
Goschen, George 136
Grey, Sir Edward 144, 188
Grivel, Captain Richild 1, 81, 143, 173
Guêpe-class 216
Gustave Zédé 191–92, 194, 196
Gymnote xii, 190–91, 193–94

Hamilton, C.I. ix
Hobson, Rolf 42
Hoche xii, 53, 81
Houette, Commander 95, 118–21
Howard, Michael 39, 44
Humann, Admiral 69, 155

India 8–9, 134, 144, 172, 201
Italy xi, 7, 36, 45, 55, 58, 60–62, 72, 74–76, 81–82, 86–89, 92–93, 96, 100–102, 104, 109, 116, 131–32, 138, 140, 143, 145–46, 150, 156–62, 174–75, 187, 209, 217, 220

Jaurés, Constant-Louis-Jean-Benjamin 54
Jeanne d'Arc 136
Johnson, James Turner 37
Jules-Ferry 215
Jules-Michelet 215
Justice 215

Kennedy, Paul 15, 183–85
Kitchner, Lord 144–45
Kulsrud, Carl J. 41

La France 21, 193
Lacantinerie, Baudry de 191
Lafont, Admiral 69–72
Lambert, Nicholas 172
Lamornaix, Admiral Sallandrouze de 180
Lanessan, Jean-Louis de 86, 110, 143, 161–71, 175, 177, 214, 216–17, 220, 223
Laubeuf, Maxime 192, 194, 197, 217
Le Roy, Lieutenant Commander 65–68, 78
Léon-Gambetta 215
Lézardrieux 169
Liberté 215
Lieutenant X 97–100, 102–103, 105, 110, 137–40, 195
Lockroy, Edouard xiii, 85, 110–13, 125, 130–31, 133–35, 137–38, 149–51, 155, 159, 174, 191, 194–97, 220
Lôme, Dupuy de 190, 193
Lorient 63, 83, 168
Louis XIV 15, 50
Ludendorff, Erich 36

Magenta xii, 53, 82, 192, 196
Mahan, Alfred Thayer 179, 225, 228
Maigret, Admiral de 180
Marchand, Captain Jean-Baptiste 144–45
Marocco 70, 183, 187–88
Marsi, Lieutenant Commander 64–68
Martel, Charles 192
Masson, Henri Le xiv, 212
Masson, Philippe xvi, 214
McPherson, James 45

Mediterranean Fleet   20, 53, 60–61, 63, 68, 70, 77, 87–89, 92, 123, 146–47, 149, 151, 155, 157, 168, 170, 178, 210
Mediterranean Squadron   122–23, 137, 146, 219
Moltke, Helmuth von   48
Monaque, Remi   xvi, 35
Montcalm   136
Montéchant, H.   97–108, 110, 125, 137–40, 195–96, 198, 207
Morse   191
Motte, Martin   vii, xvii, 104, 214

Nagler, Jörg   46
Napoleon I   3–4, 15, 42–43, 50, 182
Napoleonic wars   10, 15–16, 38, 41–44, 47, 51
Narval   192–94, 197
Nine Years War   14–15
No. 27 (Torpedo boats)   67–68
No. 61   64–65, 67, 78
No. 63   20, 107
No. 64   20, 107
No. 66   65
No. 69   78
No. 70   65
No. 71   65
Northern Fleet   89–92, 94, 123, 145–46, 170, 178, 180, 210–11
Northern Squadron   122–23
Norway   43, 226

Offer, Avnar   11
Oran   68, 72, 74, 169

Parrayon, Admiral   90–91, 94, 180
Patrie   215
Pelletan, Camille   171, 213–20, 222–23
Peyron, Admiral Alexandre-Louis-Francois   74–75, 77, 194
Phillips, W. Allison   43
Plongeur   25, 189
Pothuau   146
Prussia   ix, 19, 39, 45, 48, 130, 179,

Reede, Arthur H.   43
République   215
Réveillére, Admiral   98, 103
Rieunier, Admiral Adrien-Barchélemy-Louis   111
Rochefort   19, 21, 23, 164, 168

Ropp, Theodore   xii, xvii, 63–66, 79, 110, 145, 169, 171, 175, 193–94, 202, 214
Rouyer, Captain   203
Russia   2, 26, 93, 95–96, 102–103, 110, 124, 137, 147–49, 172, 178–79, 185–86, 190, 209, 227

Saint-André, Admiral Ernest du Pin de   25
Seven Years War   15
South Africa   177, 183–84
Spain   15, 24, 30, 41–42, 187–88
Squadron of Evolutions   59–60, 68–69, 71–74, 76–77
Sudan   140, 144–45
Suffren   215
Superior Council   86–87, 111, 113, 118, 130–33, 139, 149–52, 155–56, 164–65, 169–71, 174, 179–80, 209
Surcouf, Robert   15, 16
Sweden   226
Symcox, Geoffrey   14

Till, Geoffrey   225
Tirpitz Plan   92, 183, 210
Tomb, Robert   46, 143, 213–14
Toulon   15, 20, 25, 64–65, 67–68, 71, 73–74, 76, 78–79, 83, 86–89, 96, 122, 146–47, 152, 156, 160, 167–68, 170, 199, 217, 219
Triple Alliance   55, 61–62, 81–82, 86–87, 89–90, 92, 94–96, 100–101, 109–10, 119, 121, 124, 131–32, 143, 146, 150, 156, 158–62, 166, 168, 174, 189, 211
Tunisia   72, 104, 133, 160, 168, 187
Turkey   6, 149

United States   xviii, 9, 19, 24, 26, 42–43, 45, 192, 225

Vauban, Maréchal   14–15, 104, 207
Vérite   215
Victor-Hugo   215
Vignot, Lieutenant Mathieu-Jean-Marie   97

Waldeck-Rousseau, Pierre   214
Waldeck-Rousseau   215
Walser, Ray   214, 219–20
War of 1812   43
War of American Independence   4

War of the Austrian Succession 15
War of the Spanish Succession 15
Wars of the French Revolution 15–16, 38–44, 51
Weber, Max 38

Williamson, Samuel R. 189, 215
Wilson, Sir Arthur 204

Zédé, Gustav 190, 193–94